FIXED INCOME SOLUTIONS
NEW TECHNIQUES FOR MANAGING MARKET RISKS

CONTRIBUTORS

Chapter 1
Martha J. Langer and Gerd W. Stabbert
Metropolitan Life Insurance Company

Chapter 2
Robert R. Reitano
John Hancock Mutual Life Insurance Company

Chapter 3
Jonathan H. Nye
Alliance Capital Management L.P.

Chapter 4
Thomas S. Y. Ho
Global Advanced Technology Corporation

Chapter 5
Duen-Li Kao
General Motors Investment Management Corp.

Chapter 6
Si Chen
Fischer, Francis Trees & Watts

Chapter 7
Laurie S. Goodman, Linda L. Lowell, and Jeffrey Ho
PaineWebber Mortgage Strategy

Chapter 8
Patrick J. Corcoran
Nomura Securities International

Chapter 9
Raymond J. Iwanowski
Salomon Brothers, Inc

Chapter 10
Scott Y. Peng and Ravi E. Dattatreya
Sumitoma Bank Capital Markets, Inc.

Chapter 11
Robert M. Lally
AEGIS Insurance Services

Chapter 12
Thomas S. Y. Ho and Michael Z. H. Chen
Global Advanced Technology Corporation

FIXED INCOME SOLUTIONS
NEW TECHNIQUES FOR MANAGING MARKET RISKS

THOMAS S. Y. HO

Professional Publishing®
Chicago • London • Singapore

© Richard D. Irwin, a Times Mirror Higher Education Group, Inc. company, 1996

All rights reserved. No part of this publication may be reproduced, stored in a retrieval system, or transmitted, in any form or by any means, electronic, mechanical, photocopying, recording, or otherwise, without the prior written permission of the publisher.

This publication is designed to provide accurate and authoritative information in regard to the subject matter covered. It is sold with the understanding that neither the author or the publisher is engaged in rendering legal, accounting, or other professional service. If legal advice or other expert assistance is required, the services of a competent professional person should be sought.

From a Declaration of Principles jointly adopted by a Committee of the American Bar Association and a Committee of Publishers.

**Times Mirror
Higher Education Group**

Library of Congress Cataloging-in-Publication Data

Ho, Thomas S. Y.
    Fixed income solutions: new techniques for managing market risks
  Thomas S. Y. Ho.
      p. cm.
    Includes bibliographical references and index.
    ISBN 0-7863-0846-X
    1. Fixed-income securities. 2. Portfolio management. 3. Asset allocation. I. Title.
    HG4650, HG 1996
    332.63 2044—dc20   96–6376

Printed in the United States of America
1 2 3 4 5 6 7 8 9 0 BS 3 2 1 0 9 8 7 6

Introduction

Thomas A. McAvity, Jr.

1. FIXED INCOME SUBSECTOR ALLOCATION
MARTHA J. LANGER AND GERD W. STABBERT

Martha Langer and Gerd Stabbert present a case study on implementing fixed income subsector allocation in a life insurance company. Asset and subsector allocation are a major building block of a structured investment process and infrastructure. At MetLife they are separated organizationally from trading and security selection. MetLife has been implementing a total return paradigm with respect to a major part of their general account for about four years, using customized liability indices as the benchmarks for these portfolios, which are segmented by product line.

The authors propose an *asset cell matrix* that represents the end product of the allocation. The three primary dimensions are product line, sector, and duration ranges; additional dimensions include liquidity requirements and key rate durations. As the number of cells increases, the cell contents become more homogeneous, but the process becomes more complicated and harder to administer.

The asset class and sector weights are driven by the liability characteristics—key-rate durations, embedded options, average life, withdrawal provisions, and other liquidity requirements. For example, liabilities like pension buyouts and structured settlements, which have very long cash flows without withdrawal risk, are viewed as appropriate for equities, since equities outperform bonds and cash over long periods of time with a high degree of confidence.

Given that an insurance company gets most of its money from bond-like obligations to policyholders and cares about earnings and book value as well as total return, the traditional mean-variance approach to asset allocation is not sufficiently robust, even when extended to return and risk at the levered surplus level. Scenario analysis is necessary to adequately probe and control downside risk.

Other things being equal, the company would prefer overweighting cheap assets and underweighting rich assets in both the sector allocation and security selection phases of the investment process. The authors lament the difficulty of assessing rich/cheap relationships at the sector level, given the limitations of Wall Street research and finance theory.

2. MULTIVARIATE STOCHASTIC IMMUNIZATION: AN OVERVIEW
ROBERT R. REITANO

Bob Reitano proposes *stochastic immunization* as a technique to manage risk to surplus (assets minus liabilities) over time in a situation in which practical constraints mitigate against simply matching cash flows. This technique addresses nonparallel as well as parallel yield curve movements and can be applied to interest-sensitive as well as fixed cash flows. It is stochastic in the sense of formulating the problem as risk minimization subject to constraints, where the measure of risk can be variance of return to surplus or a more complex measure that incorporates worst-case downside risk.

Like Ho's key rate durations, Reitano's partial durations measure the sensitivity of price to a change in the yield of a particular maturity. Risk to surplus is approximated by taking the inner product of the vector of the partial durations times the vector of perturbations in the yields.

Stochastic immunization can be formulated as minimizing the residual risk in matching an investment portfolio to a desired cash flow payout schedule. Bob uses matrix algebra to express the risk and constraints, sets it up as a minimization problem, and derives a solution.

He uses an example of a five-year compound guaranteed interest contract (GIC) backed by a ten-year, 12 percent coupon bond and six-month commercial paper to illustrate the methodology.

3. CURRENT APPLICATION OF PERFORMANCE MEASUREMENT
JONATHAN H. NYE

Jonathan Nye explores how to set standards for performance measurement that are consistent with the risks of the strategy. Had such an approach been used before the fact as an integral part of the decision process, some major losses might have been averted or diminished.

Considering the purposes of performance measurement in the context of the overall decision and management process, he proposes criteria that a performance measurement system should have: measurement should be objective; results should be comparable across funds; the measure should be communicable and understandable; implementation should be within the capabilities of the organization; and the system should incent decision makers to seek results that are consistent with the goals of the fund.

It is difficult to meet all of these criteria in practice and to measure risk in a consistent manner. For example, we can easily implement a control for risk by specifying nominal constraints like duration and average credit quality, but this approach is not sufficiently discriminating in the sense of assuring that two conforming funds have the same risk. The value-at-risk approach is structurally appealing but hard to implement effectively and consistently;

semi-variance might be preferable to variance as the index of downside risk. Potential drawdown and pathwise valuation are even more comprehensive but more difficult to implement with more model-dependent results.

4. EVOLUTION OF INTEREST RATE MODELS: A COMPARISON
THOMAS S. Y. HO

Tom Ho reviews the evolution of interest rate models and assesses how the conceptual differences between them affect their suitability for different tasks. He begins by reviewing how the axioms underlying the relative valuation, arbitrage-free world of Black-Scholes relate to market realities. He introduces the idea of replicating derivatives by systematically adjusting long and/or short positions in the underlying securities. Merton's extension of the Black-Scholes model to bonds breaks down because of two problems: (1) the assumption of a fixed interest rate is inconsistent with the stochastic interest rates that govern the price of the underlying bond and (2) bond price volatility changes with time as the bond approaches maturity. The Black 1976 model for yield options is more satisfactory because it avoids the latter problem.

Both problems can be addressed by modeling bond prices and derivatives as a function of an underlying interest rate process. The early models proposed by Vasicek, Dothan, and others require estimation of the market price of risk for each risk source. General equilibrium models like that of Cox-Ingersoll-Ross are rooted in underlying economic factors, permitting the model price to be interpreted as a fair price in the context of the assumed economy. Most models are normal or lognormal in yield.

Arbitrage-free models like that of Ho and Lee are relative pricing models in the same risk-neutral spirit as Black-Scholes. Taking the existing yield curve (i.e., the

Introduction

curve implied by the prices of benchmark securities) as a given, they develop a model of yield curve movement. Extension to fitting a term structure of volatilities introduces mean reversion of rates and allows pricing of options in relation to observed option prices.

Ho also explore the tradeoffs between one, two and multifactor models. Depending on what problem is being modeled and what decisions are being made, the extra difficulties of additional factors may or may not be warranted.

5. DEFAULT RISK-BASED PRICING IN A TWO-ASSET SETTING
DUEN-LI KAO

Tony Kao presents a two-asset binomial pricing model in a risk-neutral framework. One of the factors is the default process, which reduces the size of future promised cash flows, estimating default losses by combining the default probability with the size of the loss, given default. The other is the term structure of interest rates for default-free securities. Correlation between the two factors is specified by the user.

In testing the model empirically, Kao models the default and loss for corporate obligations applying a Zeta credit risk score methodology to fundamental data on the issuer and the issue. The resulting time series of intrinsic values tracks historical prices well for a AAA-rated bond and a BBB-rated bond, with larger price differentials in the case of the lower-rated bond.

Kao applies the two-factor binomial tree to evaluating commercial mortgage-backed securities (CMBS). Working backwards through the tree, the user adjusts cash flows for losses and discounts them. He probes the sensitivity of the net spread to assumptions about how default is triggered. The assumption of "ruthless default" is not supported by the limited available empirical data; those data suggest that defaults are triggered with greater restraint. The process triggering default is driven by the evolution of the property value, which determines the loan-to-value ratio at future dates; the loan balance is known from the amortization provisions of the transaction.

6. IMPLIED PREPAYMENTS: A NEW PERSPECTIVE ON MORTGAGE-BACKED SECURITIES ANALYSIS
SI CHEN

Si Chen introduces implied prepayment models. The OAS of mortgage-backed securities (MBS) are unstable over time as the yield curve shifts and twists. Chen proposes that a major determinant of price changes and returns would be changes in the market's view of prepayment behavior.

That view is influenced by prepayment information entering the market. After seeing unprecedented prepayment speeds as the bond rally culminated in 1993, the market priced MBS as if prepayments were extremely sensitive to further drops in interest rates; a current coupon MBS was priced as if it was 50 b.p. away from the cusp. When yields rose in 1994, prepayments slowed, and the market priced MBS as if prepayments were much less interest sensitive and bonds were distant from the cusp.

Chen looks at market-implied prepayment behavior the way option traders look at market-implied volatility. With options we might take the most liquid, frequently traded options of each expiration date as the building blocks or bellwethers. Once we have calibrated the term structure of volatility to correctly price these options at mid-market, we can use that model to price less liquid products.

In the same way, he fits a three-parameter prepayment model to observed pass-through prices and uses that model to price CMOs, IOs and POs. The model provides a metric for measuring the value and hedge ratios of those structured securities relative to the underlying pass-throughs using a consistent set of assumptions about prepayment behavior as well as term structure volatility. His approach differs from option traders in that Chen assumes that OAS should be the same for all coupons; option traders take implied volatilities as a given.

The same framework provides an additional dimension of risk management and a factor to use in performance attribution. For example, if the implied prepayment model changed from the beginning of the period to the end of the period, that factor would explain part of your MBS performance.

7. FINDING VALUE IN MORTGAGE DERIVATIVES: A VIEW FROM THE TRENCHES
LAURIE S. GOODMAN, LINDA L. LOWELL, AND JEFFREY HO

The authors present five different approaches to gauging relative value of inverse floaters and inverse IOs, ranging from the traditional yield and average life profile available on Bloomberg to more sophisticated concepts. Conclusions about the strengths and weaknesses of these techniques are of broader interest in analyzing other complex securities. The investor should combine all five measures in assessing relative value.

The *yield and average life profile* for inverse securities is a table combining assumed levels of the floating index with shifts in the yield curve; with each such shift is associated the average life, duration, and window of the security. While the table illustrates the variability of yield, it does not quantify the risk of the security or reveal whether the investor is sufficiently compensated for the risk at a given price.

Re-creation analysis relies on the arbitrage pricing principle, valuing an inverse floater as the difference between the values of the underlying fixed-rate security and the floater. This arbitrage can be sticky and costly, allowing inverse securities to trade persistently at cheap levels. Subject to considering bid-offer spreads, this method can offer insights when these securities are traded, but it is less helpful with more complex structures involving two-tier index bonds. Re-creation value may reveal the cheapness or richness of the inverse floater relative to the floater and the underlying security, but it does not reveal whether it is cheap in relation to the universe of MBS or other inverse floaters.

Option-adjusted spread (OAS) analysis provides a consistent framework for comparing value across the universe of MBS, but the results depend on the prepayment model used as well as the method of constructing the yield curve scenarios and their probabilities. For levered securities, OAS should be higher than for unlevered securities, but it is unclear how much higher.

Yield to forward LIBOR is the yield with future LIBOR rates fixed at their respective forward rates, as if the LIBOR obligation embedded in the inverse security were hedged or delevered with Eurodollar futures, or an amortizing swap in which the investor pays fixed and receives LIBOR. With this method, the investor has a fixed yield that can be compared with that on other MBS. Because of the simplifying assumption that the futures or swap has a scheduled amortization as opposed to following the path-dependent experience of the pool, this approach understates the negative convexity of the security induced by average life variability. On the other hand, this method tends to understate value in failing to account for its embedded LIBOR cap.

Unbundling the options in an inverse floater begins with separating the streams of coupon and principal payments. The stream of principal payments can be valued as a structured PO, and the stream of interest payments is equivalent to an inverse IO, which can be compared to a floor with an amortizing notional amount with amortization driven by the path-dependent experience of the underlying security. That floor is worth less than a floor with a simple amortization schedule and the same expected average life.

8. DEBT AND EQUITY IN THE NEW REAL ESTATE MARKETS
PATRICK J. CORCORAN

Pat Corcoran applies a scenario-based credit loss model to look at relative value across securitized and traditional real estate debt and equity markets. Relying in part on confidence that real estate will not go through another major down cycle in the next decade, he concludes that the subordinated tranches of commercial mortgage-backed securities (CMBS) offer a more attractive profile of risk and return than directly owned properties, whether levered or not. Pool-specific risks can and should be widely diversified.

Corcoran models the delinquency for the mortgages underlying commercial mortgage-backed securities (CMBS) using the loan-to-value ratio as the key variable, where the evolution of property value over time is governed by several deterministic growth rate scenarios. His model recognizes dispersion of loan-to-value ratios and default risk among the underlying loans, which increases pool defaults except in the case that all loans in the pool are cross-collateralized.

In using ACLI data on default experience and loan-to-value ratios in life insurance company portfolios, Pat made adjustments for certain sources of bias that may have affected underwriting and valuations. The conclusions about prospective results incorporate an explicit view about the likely range of future experience.

9. AN INVESTOR'S GUIDE TO FLOATING-RATE NOTES: CONVENTIONS, MATHEMATICS, AND RELATIVE VALUATION
RAYMOND J. IWANOWSKI

Ray Iwanowski presents a general model for valuing floating rate notes (FRNs). The trading convention in that market is the *discount margin,* which is analogous to the yield spread on a fixed-rate bond. For a new issue priced at par, it is generally equal to the *reset margin* for the floating coupon. When the issue subsequently trades above (below) par, the discount margin is less than (greater than) the reset margin. If the price is less than par, then the market value of the note has a levered sensitivity to changes in the index, like a super floater. Owning a discount FRN is equivalent to being long a par floater and being short an annuity that pays the discount margin minus the reset margin.

Iwanowski shows how certain arbitrage relationships are natural in looking at spreads and relative value, using the swap or Eurodollar futures market to link fixed and floating rate securities. Buying a LIBOR FRN is similar to buying a fixed-rate note and then paying fixed in a swap and receiving LIBOR. Alternatively, a fixed-rate note (with unequal coupons) could be built by buying a LIBOR floater and going long a Eurodollar strip that would lock in the forward rates. He demonstrates empirically that spreads on floaters are in line with spreads that can be created in a synthetic.

The relative value of floaters on different indices can be compared by projecting cash flows deterministically using forward rates or stochastically with scenario analysis. Iwanowski reports historical spreads and correlations for the different popular floating rate indices.

10. LIQUIDITY RISK: A FIRST LOOK
SCOTT Y. PENG AND RAVI E. DATTATREYA

Peng and Dattatreya illustrate and quantify the increased liquidity risks posed by a mismatch of asset and liability risk profiles and, in so doing, introduce an innovative model of liquidity risk that draws on an analogy to a physical model from fluid mechanics. Liquidity risk is defined as the risk of insufficient cash to satisfy investor or shareholder redemption behavior. The liability risk profile represents the amounts that would be due to constituents, while the asset risk profile represents the liquidation value of the assets.

The physical model is a river assumed to have a constant depth. Its width—and, hence, its volume and flow mass—change in response to inflows and outflows, which are analogous to deposits and redemptions. The flow mass is analogous to the dollar volume of liabilities.

The river's temperature (analogous to liquidation value per share) may change from point to point (location is analogous to time) as it passes over heat sources and sinks. The river's energy or *quality* at a given point equals flow mass times temperature. Quality is the physical analogue for the portfolio liquidation value, which equals number of shares times liquidation value per share.

The authors simulate results using the model to quantify the effects of feedback between investor behavior and portfolio performance and liquidity values. Feedback can occur in two directions: (1) investor withdrawals become increasingly sensitive to portfolio performance as performance deteriorates, culminating in herd redemption behavior, and (2) the portfolio performance itself suffers as withdrawals increase. When feedback occurs in both directions, creating a vicious circle, the system can break down in a cascade. To the extent that the withdrawal price is guaranteed, the results can include institutional failure and/or the need for a costly bailout by the parent institution.

The authors proceed to consider how to manage liquidity risk. Assets and liabilities should be marked realistically and conservatively, with assets marked at bid prices. Risk can be reduced by maintaining a liquid cash reserve as a buffer and by acquiring a suitable catastrophe hedge. Products without fixed guarantees are less risky.

11. EFFECTIVE DURATION AND CONVEXITY: BACK TO THE BASICS
ROBERT M. LALLY

Bob Lally returns to basics to look at effective duration and effective convexity from the perspective of a portfolio manager, who is accountable to clients not only for managing instantaneous risk but also for achieving desirable returns. That motivates the idea of looking at duration as the average price return for parallel shifts of +/− 100 b.p., which may occur instantaneously or over a period. Convexity measures the asymmetry of the returns in the two shifts.

In using spread products, the portfolio manager should try to maximize long-run outperformance vs. a Treasury portfolio with the same effective duration, i.e., to achieve maximum excess return as a result of taking credit and option risk. Short run, however, the manager should minimize the risk of underperforming that Treasury benchmark.

In considering whether a bond should be bought or sold, Lally would project its performance in an up-rate environment and a down-rate environment, not just using its current estimated duration but taking into account the fact that the spread at which it trades might be different in the up environment than the down environment, and both spreads might be different from today's spread. Spreads may be affected by technical factors as well as by predictable changes in the value of embedded options.

Break-even analysis is a convenient way to make a tradeoff between the extra yield of a corporate and its potential price underperformance in the event of a large move in the yield curve; in an example, Lally computes how long the yield advantage must be enjoyed to offset the price underperformance resulting from a 100 b.p. rally.

12. ARBITRAGE-FREE BOND CANONICAL DECOMPOSITION
THOMAS S. Y. HO AND MICHAEL Z. H. CHEN

Ho and Chen present a new methodology for canonical decomposition of bonds and fixed-income asset-liability strategies. For analyzing complex securities like CMOs and designing complex strategies like those for single premium deferred annuities, traditional tools like option adjusted spread, duration, and convexity don't capture all of the important complexities. There is a need for a more comprehensive framework.

Ho's development of the theory considers all paths through an arbitrage-free binomial lattice of the term structure of interest rates. For each bond (or asset-liability strategy), Ho identifies the pathwise cash flows and then uses the discount factors along each path to compute its pathwise values. These pathwise values represent a set of characteristic values that serve to define the bond. For a bond with fixed cash flows, these values uniquely determine the cash flows. For a bond with embedded options that are path independent, the pathwise values also uniquely determine the bond, and it can be represented by a portfolio of zeros, caps, and floors.

Ho decomposes a bond in two stages and analyzes the residuals. The primary decomposition fits zero-coupon

Treasury bonds to the cash flows in a zero volatility world in which forward rates are realized. The secondary decomposition uses caps and floors to capture the path-independent option behavior of the pathwise values; these are the caps and floors which replicate the differences between the pathwise values of the bond and its zero volatility Treasury equivalents. If the bond's cash flows are path-independent, these caps and floors replicate its embedded options.

In the general case in which bonds or strategies may be path dependent, there will be a residual vector of net pathwise values; the caps and floors derived in the secondary decomposition will be a best fit rather than an exact solution. The residual pathwise values result from path dependency, risk sources excluded from the model, and liquidity premiums. When all of these factors are taken into account, any remaining difference from the market price would represent an arbitrage profit or loss.

For practical applications, Ho draws on the linear path space (LPS), which provides a tractable structured sample of the space of all paths through the lattice. The number of required caps and floors is commensurately reduced by using the LPS. He illustrates the method by analyzing a CMO support tranche. The bond's pathwise values differ markedly from the Treasury Equivalent (TE) cashflows from the primary decomposition, but the combination of TEs, caps, and floors fits pretty well.

CONTENTS

Chapter One 1

Fixed-Income Subsector Asset Allocation

Martha J. Langer, Investment Manager, and Gerd W. Stabbert, Assistant Vice President, Metropolitan Life Insurance Company

The Standard Model, 2
 Problems with the Standard Model, 3
 Options, 4
The Investment Process: A Reality Check, 5
Asset Cell Matrix, 10
Asset/Liability Factors, 13
Scenario Testing, 16
Relative Value Analysis, 18
Conclusion, 21
References 23

Chapter Two 25

Nonparallel Yield Curve Shifts and Stochastic Immunization

Robert R. Reitano, Second Vice President, Investment Policy & Research, John Hancock Mutual Life Insurance Company

Setup of the General Problem: Risk, 27

Setup of the General Problem: Constraints, 30

Solution of the General Problem, 31

    Example, 33

Risk Minimization of Example, 34

Efficient Frontiers, 38

Summary and Conclusion, 40

References, 41

Chapter Three 43

Current Application of Performance Measurement

Jonathan Nye, CFA and Vice President, Alliance Capital Management L.P.

    Two Recent Failures, 43

    Common Threads, 45

Investment Performance, 45

Measuring Investment Returns, 48

Investment Risk and Performance Measurement, 48

    Constrained Management as an Implied Risk Metric, 50

    Maximum Drawdown as a Risk Metric, 52

    Value at Risk, 57

    The Sharpe Ratio, 61

    Downside Risk, 63

Conclusion, 66

References, 67

Chapter Four 69

Evolution of Interest Rate Models: A Comparison

Thomas S. Y. Ho, President, Global Advanced Technology Corporation

Basic Framework, 71

Modified Black-Scholes Model, 75
Interest Rate Models: One Factor, 78
Interest Rate Models: Two Factor, 81
Arbitrage-Free Models: Normal Form, 82
Arbitrage-Free Models: Lognormal Form, 86
Arbitrage-Free Models: N-Factor Model, 86
Relative Valuation and Hedge Ratios, 88
Conclusion, 89
References, 91

Chapter Five   97

Default Risk-Based Pricing in a Two-Asset Setting

Duen-Li Kao, Director of Investment Research, General Motors Investment Management Corporation

The Concept of a Default Risk-Based Pricing Method, 99
Empirical Examples of Default Risk-Based Pricing, 100
Applying the Default Risk-Based Pricing to CMBS, 103
Two-Asset Binomial Pricing Model, 105
Analyzing Credit Risk of Commercial Mortgage-Backed Securities, 109
Summary, 114
References, 114

Chapter Six   117

Implied Prepayments: A New Perspective on Mortgage-Backed Securities Analysis

Si Chen, Portfolio Manager, Fischer, Francis Trees & Watts

The State of the Art: OAS Analysis, 108
Beyond the State of the Art: Implied Prepayments, 119
Why Implied Prepayments? 121
Application: Implied Prepayments through Time, 122
Application: Analyzing the Relative Value of CMOs, 127

Application: Analyzing IO/PO Strips, 128
The Implied Prepayments Approach and Risk Management, 131
Conclusions, 131
References, 132

Chapter Seven 133

Finding Value in Mortgage Derivatives: A View from the Trenches

Laurie S. Goodman, Managing Director; Linda L. Lowell, First Vice President; and Jeffrey Ho, Vice President; PaineWebber Mortgage Strategy

Traditional Mortgage Cash-Flow Measures: The Yield and Average-Life Profile, 135
Re-Creation Analysis, 138
Option-Adjusted Spread Analysis, 143
Yield-to-Forward LIBOR, 150
Unbundling the Options, 155
Conclusion, 161

Chapter Eight 163

Debt and Equity in the New Real Estate Markets

Patrick J. Corcoran, Vice President, Nomura Securities International, Inc.

A Broader Range of Real Estate Investments, 164
    Credit Losses for Commercial Mortgages and CMBS, 165
    A CMBS Example, 169
The Real Estate Outlook and Choosing Real Estate Scenarios, 171
"Default-Adjusted" Yields and Credit Spreads, 172
Equity Real Estate versus Subordinate CMBS, 176
Qualifications and Loan Structure, 181
Conclusion, 184
References, 185

Chapter Nine   187
An Investor's Guide to Floating-Rate Notes: Conventions, Mathematics, and Relative Valuation

Raymond J. Iwanowski, Vice President, Fixed Income Research, Salomon Brothers

Introduction   187
Floating-Rate Note Pricing: Equations and Definitions,   188
Price Sensitivities,   195
   Effective Duration,   195
   Partial Durations,   198
   Spread Durations,   199
Relationship between Discount Margins on Floaters and Fixed Corporate Spreads,   200
   Three-Month LIBOR (LIB3)-Indexed Floating-Rate Notes,   201
   An Alternative Specification,   204
A Case Study: Eurodollar Perpetual Floaters,   207
Comparing Floating-Rate Notes of Different Indices: Basic Risk,   212
   Understanding the Current Coupon Differential between CMT2 and LIB3,   216
   The Use of Historical Data in Assessing Basic Risk,   219
   Prime-Treasury Spreads,   227
   Using the Statistics to Assess the Basic Risk,   228
Optionality,   231
   Floored Corporate FRNs,   232
   Mortgage FRNs,   235
Conclusion,   238

Chapter Ten   241
Liquidity Risk: A First Look

Scott Y. Peng, Vice President, BlackRock Financial Management, and Ravi E. Dattatreya, Senior Vice President Sumitomo Bank Capital Markets

The Risk Universe, 242
Liquidity Risk, 243
Modeling of Liquidity Risk, 245
    Physical Model: The River, 246
    Analogy: Physical Model to Portfolio 247
Definition of Liquidity Crisis 247
Liquidity Analysis 249
    Conservation Laws, 250
    Coupling Investor Behavior to Portfolio Performance, 251
    Sample Portfolio, 255
Liquidity Analysis Results, 255
    Flow Simulation: One Simulation Run, 256
    Quality Simulation: Liquidity Risk, 256
    Simulation Analysis Conclusions, 259
Management of Liquidity Risk, 260
    Correctly Marking Assets and Liabilities, 260
    Maintaining a Liquid Cash Reserve, 261
    Partial Hedging of the Asset/Liability Risk Gap: The Catastrophe Hedge, 264
    Returning Shares at Their Market Values, 265
    Bailout by a Rich Parent, 266
Conclusion, 266

Chapter Eleven 269

Effective Duration and Convexity: Back to the Basics

Robert M. Lally, Chief Investment Officer and Treasurer, AEGIS Insurance Services

Basic No. 1: Definitions, 270
Basic No. 2: Effective Duration, 270
Basic No. 3: Effective Convexity, 271
Basic No. 4: Model Error, 274
Basic No. 5: Breakeven Analysis, 276

Basic No. 6: Comparison to Municipal Bonds, 278
Basic No. 7: Managing "Spread" Fixed-Income Assets, 280
Conclusion, 281

Chapter Twelve 283
Arbitrage-Free Bond Canonical Decomposition

Thomas S. Y. Ho, President, and Michael Z. H. Chen, Global Advanced Technology Corporation

Basic Framework, 285
Decomposition Theorems, 287
Canonical Decomposition, 289
    Primary Decomposition, 290
    Secondary Decomposition, 290
    Tertiary Decomposition, 291
A Numerical Example, 292
    Linear Path Space, 293
    Canonical Basis of Caps and Floors, 293
    Decomposition of FH1747:Q, 294
    Analytical Results of the Decomposition, 296
Conclusion, 298
References, 301
Appendix A: Proof of Proposition 1, 301
Appendix B: Proof of Proposition 2, 302
Appendix C: LPS Lattice and the Canonical Basis of Caps and Floors, 304
Index, 309

CHAPTER 1

Fixed-Income Subsector Asset Allocation

Martha J. Langer
Investment Manager
Metropolitan Life Insurance Company

Gerd W. Stabbert
Assistant Vice President
Metropolitan Life Insurance Company

Our discussion of fixed-income subsector asset allocation is presented in the context of the investment process of a liability-oriented financial institution such as an insurance company. The emphasis is not on answers but on the questions that must be addressed in order for the subsector asset allocation process to be organizationally effective and to provide significant value added within the investment process.

The discussion covers:

1. An introduction to what we mean by fixed-income subsector asset allocation;

2. An overview of the investment process at our institution, including a discussion of our past efforts in terms of the customized-indexing approach, the present structure of our investment operations, and our expectation of where we go as an organization using this asset allocation framework;[1]

3. The analytical approaches that are available to deal with asset allocation issues;

---

[1]MetLife is not likely to provide the answer for other institutions, but the issues will largely be the same for others, so the example is useful.

4. Performance measurement—a topic which is now an integral part of the investment process and through which the entire process has now been structured as a feedback loop; and

5. Some of the challenges that confront any organization in the investment management business.

The key to managing the investment process at a life insurance company is to remember that we live in a liability world. The first issue to be addressed, then, is how to characterize the liabilities in terms of the cash flows, the duration, and convexity. In an insurance company, the actuaries generally take the major role in providing this information. Next, several levels of asset allocation must occur. After the broadest level of asset classes has been determined, then we determine the allocation among the fixed-income sectors, and finally we have to establish an asset portfolio. Fixed-income subsector asset allocation in this context is the process by which the investor decides what types and how much of fixed-income assets should be held.

THE STANDARD MODEL

The standard approach to high-level asset allocation is the mean/variance technique, which uses means, variances, and correlations among broad asset classes as inputs. Standard asset classes include cash, equities, fixed-income securities, and real estate, to name a few, but can also include gold, collectibles, fine art, i.e., anything that the investor might consider as an investment asset. Mean/variance space is where the decision as to allocation takes place—mean and variance of return are judged to be the only factors that are important in the allocation decision. Variance is taken to be the only measure of risk that counts.

Individual asset types are examined first for mean and variance characteristics, and mapped out in mean/

variance space. Next, efficient combinations are obtained using the correlations among asset classes. These are used to trace out an efficient frontier. The final step is to pick the right place along the efficient frontier. That decision depends on the organization's utility trade-off between risk and return.

PROBLEMS WITH THE STANDARD MODEL

Even in the broadest context of asset allocation, where the asset sectors are defined to provide the maximum differences among asset types, this model has various problems. The assumption of the normality of returns is not beyond reproach. Quite the contrary—there are many reasons to suppose that many assets have return patterns with "fat tails," statistically speaking. That is, there are more outliers, periods with very good and bad returns, than would be implied by a normal distribution. This raises problems with the use of variance. Ignoring statistical problems, variance may not be the best measure of risk—many people would say that variation on the upside is something that should not be avoided. One modification of the framework is to use semi-variance rather than variance to measure risk, but that also has its flaws.

The lack of stability among the inputs—means, variances, and correlations—represents a serious problem. The model is truly meant to have as inputs the expected means, variances, and correlations among asset classes, but in order to avoid problems of estimation that can bias the results, generally those inputs are estimated using historical data. Differences in the time period chosen or time series used can lead to very different results.

The liabilities tend to present a problem in this model. They're often added as negative assets, as if they themselves were assets with market values and variances, and certainly for institutions with complicated assets this is a problem in and of itself. The net result of this approach is that the risk/return frontier is represented by the risk/return position of the company's surplus. The whole curve is highly leveraged, being the net of assets and liabilities, which magnifies the effects of all of the assumptions used to generate the analysis.

For an insurance company, or for any institution where the value of the liabilities moves with the level of rates, the duration becomes the driving force behind the variance of the surplus. Both the assets and the liabilities respond predominantly to interest rate changes in proportion to their duration. This results in a significant correlation among the asset classes which distorts the analysis. Also, the variance doesn't really seem to capture the effects of the differences between the fixed-income asset classes. This problem is partially due to convexity, and may be partially caused by the outlier effects.

Options

These deficits mean that this paradigm is not appropriate for our purposes. An alternative theoretical framework that will provide reasonably robust results and will reflect the relevant factors must be found to guide the investment process.

In addition, on a more practical level, a usable asset allocation scheme must be developed, with or without a sound theoretical foundation, since, in the end, assets will end up being allocated in one manner or another.

One default option is to pattern asset allocation based upon an index. Many investors tend to measure investment performance through comparisons to indexes, so once an index is chosen, divergence from the index allocation means divergence from the index performance. However, this reverses the logical order of priority. For the investment process to work properly, the asset allocation decision should take precedence over, and in fact drive, the decision about what index to use.

THE INVESTMENT PROCESS: A REALITY CHECK

One crucial aspect of asset allocation is that for any type of investment strategy, whether tactical or strategic, it is necessary to have an investment process. This process will facilitate the implementation of the appropriate strategy. Organizationally, it is inefficient to randomly pick and choose a strategy on a case-by-case basis. In order to establish a track record as an investment manager, it becomes necessary to have a consistent process in place.

In an investment process, guidelines must be established within which your organization manages money. There must be a common language between the various participants, whether they are senior management, portfolio managers, or asset specialists. The investment process also provides the structure that will facilitate developing the systems necessary to implement any successful strategy. The investment world has become much too complicated to evaluate strategy on the back of an envelope, and if an investment process is clearly defined, it becomes much easier to explain to existing or potential clients exactly what was accomplished from a performance perspective and how this performance was attained.

Historically, MetLife approached the investment process as if it were entering a maze. The company began the process, found itself at a dead end from time to time, and had little control over the final outcome. This is not to say that we didn't become conditioned to the marketplace after a trial-and-error learning process. However, there was no methodology which could be readily transferred to establish the proper path. In the marketplace, the world keeps changing, so the dead ends keep changing as well.

Using a total rate of return approach to managing portfolios has been the innovation that has led to some major changes at MetLife. Although not new to money management, total rate of return is a quite radical concept for an insurance company, considering that you are managing money in a liability world that is tied to book value accounting. The approach that was used to address some of the outstanding issues regarding total rate of return for an insurance company was the development of a custom liability index. (Stabbert, 1995) This was a long-term project involving both investment and actuarial professionals which took about four years to implement. The result was a process that was used in managing four liability portfolios with approximately $12 billion assets under management.

Significantly, this process necessitated an organizational change. No longer was the general account managed on an aggregate basis, with a Portfolio Strategies Department acting as a pseudo-portfolio manager and a liaison to the business lines. A Portfolio Management Department was created that had specific responsibility for specific portfolios. Therefore, a shift in the paradigm occurred, facilitated by the benchmarking and custom liability efforts that were taking place.

Very simply, a customized liability index defines the fixed-income universe that a portfolio manager can access. At MetLife, portfolio managers cannot go out and buy whatever they want to buy. In order to establish a benchmark that is a valid representation of what is available to the portfolio manager, you want to customize an index that reflects the securities that can be purchased. At MetLife, this index incorporates the various investment guidelines that we have established over time.

The asset allocation process at MetLife has been incorporated into the customized liability indexing process.

The question arises as to whether or not this should be the driving force in asset allocation. Moreover, is this the correct methodology from a tactical as opposed to a strategic perspective?

Is the customized indexing process also the asset allocation process? The answer to that is no, not exactly. The index will tend to reflect many of the company's institutional quirks, but it will also provide a default asset allocation.

How are we currently using customized indexing? It is being used to select the assets that, under certain model assumptions, maximize the total rate of return in certain portfolios. The index is being used as a benchmark to measure performance. It is a process whereby the performance of any contributor—senior management, portfolio management, or asset allocators—can be measured. Performance measurement also provides the ability to measure the risk and reward for portfolio actions by means of performance attribution.

From a practical perspective, subsector allocation at MetLife is still largely driven by a grassroots approach. Traditionally, private placements have always been our strength and, consequently, we have a strong credit and asset specialist orientation. The total rate of return approach is just beginning to take hold. Total rate of return as an investment management philosophy has been evolving at MetLife over the last few years, but as a member of the insurance industry, we as an organization are still being driven by book value in addition to—and sometimes as opposed to—the market value approach of total rate of return. Market value is a great concept if both assets and liabilities are looked at from this perspective. It definitely helps manage a portfolio, but it doesn't provide all of the answers. In other words, it is relatively easy to put an investment process into place, but in order for it to succeed as an element of the broader organization, there are many pieces that have to fit and organizational issues that must be resolved.

The question therefore becomes: Where are we today? The answer is that we are at a crossroads. We're looking at the customized liability indexing process that has been in place for awhile and evaluating the value that is being added overall to MetLife. Organizationally, what was done was to create a Portfolio Management Department. However, creating a department of portfolio managers without the infrastructure necessary to support what essentially was a prototype investment process resulted in a painful realization that the necessary tools were not yet in place for success. Too much of portfolio management became a manual process that was overburdened with high expectations. The moral to our experience is: Don't let the infrastructure become an afterthought. Systems development and something as simple as clean data that portfolio managers can use in their decision-making process are critical success factors for any investment process. You may have the brightest portfolio managers, but if they do not have the necessary tools at their fingertips, the job will not get done. In order to be successful, it takes a lot of technology, different skill sets, and people to support this entire process.

Infrastructure is only one of the necessary components that an organization needs to successfully implement its investment strategies. Strategies will not succeed unless an organization is in place that is willing to move an investment process forward. Once again, the key to successful investment management is to be process-driven. This means using a structured approach to fixed-income management.

The structured approach that we are using is a systematic analysis of the various portfolio alignments. This

FIGURE 1-1

Allocation Process

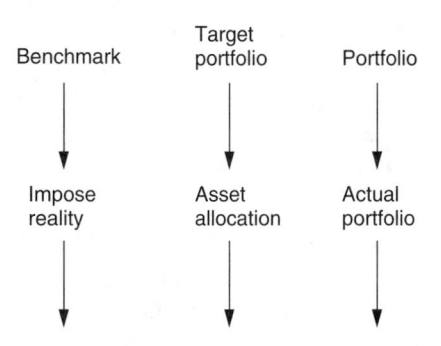

```
    Benchmark        Target            Portfolio
                     portfolio
        │                │                │
        ▼                ▼                ▼
     Impose            Asset            Actual
     reality         allocation        portfolio
        │                │                │
        ▼                ▼                ▼
```

analysis is accomplished by using various financial engineering tools such as GAT, Salomon's *Yield Book,* BARRA, or others that may be available. The methodology that is utilized identifies the various mismatches that may exist in any one portfolio, and then adjusts the portfolio to correct these mismatches. Figure 1–1 illustrates the basic components of this process. On the left side is the benchmark. This imposes the reality of the fixed income universe that is available to the portfolio manager. The underlying assumptions in this benchmark reflect all of the investment constraints.

The target portfolio is what senior management has been dictating in terms of asset allocation—how much we should have in mortgage-backed securities (MBS), Treasuries, corporates, etc. The final column reflects the existing composition of the portfolio. Historically, this last column is a given. The composition of this portfolio is not going to change overnight because of such factors as transaction costs. Moreover, some of the asset classes are beyond the control of the portfolio manager. The following section provides the framework to begin evaluating and adjusting these portfolios.

ASSET CELL MATRIX

A structure MetLife uses to construct the portfolios that will reflect the results of the fixed-income subsector asset allocation is the asset cell matrix. The shape of this matrix will have a major impact on how the theoretical work on asset allocation must be done. At its most general, Figure 1–2 illustrates the concept. For each portfolio, the amounts of each asset class are shown per the asset allocation. The sum of all the asset classes equals the total assets in the portfolio, and the sum of the cells of a certain asset class equals the company's total holdings of that asset class.

Clearly this will not be sufficient information for the traders to go out and start buying assets. There are other dimensions to this matrix, most notably duration ranges, which can correspond to key rate durations. An additional dimension might be liquidity, and another might be convexity. Once the asset classes are established with sufficient precision, and the duration ranges and other categories are set, this matrix should provide enough information so that the trading desk knows what it has to buy and sell at any point in time. The matrix will have an irregular shape, since some of the asset classes will not span the full range of durations.

Since our company has to some extent divorced the management of the portfolios from the asset specialists and traders, the objective of the asset cell matrix is to exercise control over the composition of the portfolios, while at the same time leaving some scope for relative value judgements within the cells to be exercised by the traders or asset specialists. Thus, there are two factors in contention with each other in setting up the dimensions of the matrix. The more cells there are, the more cumbersome it will be to administer the cells—to give orders to the trading desk and to have them keep track of acquisitions and dispositions. Room for tactical decisions on relative value will also be limited.

FIGURE 1-2
Target Allocation
Distribution/Duration

	Treasury	Public corporations	Mortgage backed securities	Collaterized mortgage obligations	Asset-backed securites	Private corporations	Commercial mortgages
Institutional pension							
Retail pension							
Personal insurance							
Group							
Total							

But the fewer cells there are, the less homogeneous each cell will be, and that has two effects. One is that it will make the asset allocation analysis more difficult. Second is that it will make the output less meaningful since the characteristics attributed to each of the cells will be more general and thus less specific as to the assets that the cell will actually contain. This will mean that the total portfolio's characteristics, and the performance of the actual portfolio, will be less predictable. As an organization, MetLife has not fully resolved this conflict. It may be that there is no one solution applicable to all organizations, but that the nature of the organization will determine the optimum balance between tightness of control and flexibility.

One additional question is whether the right asset classes are in the grid used for asset allocation. This is extremely important from a pragmatic point of view because in a large institution it's very hard for a new asset class to become part of the standard set of assets. Derivatives are a good example.

To digress for a moment, there are conceptual problems with fitting derivatives into this framework. Derivatives need not be assets per se, of course, but they are certainly investment instruments. One approach is to place synthetic assets, constructed with derivatives, within the matrix. The synthetic is treated as if it were a real asset in that particular cell. Credit exposures may need to be adjusted for the derivative position, and there may be differences in the behavior of the derivative from that of the underlying asset class.

In addition, hedging doesn't necessarily fit in this neat cell structure, since hedging is designed to reduce the risk of assets and/or liabilities. For many institutions, these questions are a moot point because of regulatory constraints. But for other institutions, these should be considered important issues.

ASSET/LIABILITY FACTORS

As a substitute for the standard mean/variance approach, an analysis of the factors that drive performance of assets and liabilities is used. Beginning with a liability perspective is extremely important, and for an insurance company it is the key to successful asset allocation. The first step is to characterize the liabilities in terms of factors that are of importance to them, and pick the asset mix that complements the characteristics of the liabilities. Therefore, the impact of the same factors on both assets and liabilities must be examined.

One implicit assumption being made here is that it is easier to alter assets in a short period of time than to alter liabilities. This is true for most insurance companies and for most insurance products. In Chapter 10, Scott Peng discusses ways for an insurance company to customize its SPDAs, and certainly there is no technical impediment to doing so. For many products, the difficulty is largely organizational, and lies primarily in the rigidity of the distribution channels for these products. Thus, while it is perfectly possible to alter the mix of liabilities, often it cannot be accomplished quickly, and if a successful mixture has been attained from a marketing point of view, the organization will be understandably reluctant to alter it for a short-term advantage if corresponding alterations can be made instead on the asset side. The assumption is therefore that the assets generally will be picked to conform to the liabilities.

The factors or characteristics that generally appear to be important in this process include duration, time horizon, liquidity, credit exposure, and optionality, including negative convexity.

Duration, as used here, is shorthand for general responsiveness to interest rate movements, and usually includes key rate durations. In order to eliminate or control the impact of the general level of rates on the value of surplus, the duration of assets must be brought into alignment with that of liabilities. The duration of some of the liabilities is very hard to analyze, including ordinary life insurance and a whole raft of rate reset products. Options are embedded in the products, some of which can be economically exercised, including withdrawal options and options to add funds to certain investment products. Information on customer responsiveness to options is considerably scarcer on the liability side than for assets of similar complexity, so there is less certainty about the durations of liabilities than about assets with such features, although that is not to suggest that there is great certainty about duration for asset classes such as mortgage-backed securities.

Time horizon has an impact on asset choices that is independent of duration, though long liabilities may generally permit the use of a long time horizon. However, liabilities with rate reset mechanisms, but with very limited withdrawal options, may also permit the use of long time horizons. Certainly, liabilities with long time horizons provide more asset allocation flexibility. For example, a common assumption is that equities will outperform fixed-income securities in the long run. So a long time horizon tends to allow a larger allocation to equities. This may also be the case with other risky assets, since the long horizon lowers the chances of being forced out of an asset at the wrong time in the asset cycle. A long time horizon will also make liquidity less important. Some of our long or intermediate products also have other features that will give the effect of a long time horizon. A portfolio rate mechanism, accepted by the customer, represents a rate-averaging feature that will allow some risks to be absorbed by the customer.

Liquidity is another factor that may be of importance. Liquidity here is defined as the ability to sell an asset quickly at a price approaching fair value. As mentioned above, the time horizon of the liability has some effect on whether liquidity is important. Withdrawal provisions also have an impact on the importance of liquidity. If there can be a run on the bank or the insurance company, liquidity may be more of a concern. Limiting withdrawal provisions can mitigate this factor. Some institutions have more funds with a propensity to move for economic reasons because of their market niche. Liquidity of existing assets becomes much less important if a portfolio is expected to grow. The new money will provide a margin for error. Thus, liquidity has a strategic role rooted in liability characteristics, but it also has a tactical role because it facilitates portfolio adjustments.

The basic credit question on the asset side is whether investors are paid enough at any point in time to take additional credit risks. This is a relative value question. There are also other issues. Most insurance companies have a segmented asset portfolio, with different assets backing different liabilities, and the specific business units bear the credit risk of specific assets. In this sort of arrangement, even a large institution may find itself exposed to diversification effects. In some cases, credit exposures also exist on the liability side. These customer exposures are not fully integrated into our analysis. Also, there is the problem of which asset sector should acquire credit risk. Salomon has done a good deal of work on that question, distributed through its relative value publication, and has also worked extensively on the issue of which duration range is the best one in which to take credit risk.

The issue in optionality is generally the negative convexity to which the assets and liabilities are exposed. Insurance companies' liabilities are more convex than their assets, so surplus tends to be exposed to large swings in interest rates. Finance professionals have certainly studied the options in the assets extensively, but the analysis needs to start with the liabilities to gain insight into the sort of asset options the portfolio can take. There has also been significant analytical work on liabilities such as SPDAs. Certain liabilities have options embedded in them. Generally, these are in favor of the customer, but some of them are held by the company. There are withdrawal options and minimum-rate guarantees against us. Offsetting factors include our option to reset rates in certain rate reset products. In general, insurance companies do not expect the options held by their customers to be exercised efficiently. Inertia is an extremely powerful force.

Only by examining assets and liabilities within a consistent framework can the answers be determined to such fundamental asset allocation questions as: What is the best place for equities? Where are mortgage-backs really dangerous? Which portfolios need significant amounts of Treasuries, either for liquidity reasons or for duration management?

In the face of existing portfolios, the easiest decisions to make are to change asset targets at the margin, that is, to raise or lower the target for each asset category. Such changes are likely to be the result of long-term considerations, and thus are strategic rather than tactical. In many cases, it is possible to tell the direction of a desired movement even when the exact magnitude of the change is unclear.

SCENARIO TESTING

It is essential to develop a framework for a more systematic consideration of these factors for both sides of the balance sheet. The most fundamental building block of such a framework is the ability to value assets and liabilities for different states of the world, that is, over different time horizons and different interest rate scenarios. To accomplish this, sophisticated asset/liability modeling is essential.

One of the problems with the mean/variance approach is that it accepts the average result as a reflection of the meaningful result, and the standard deviation as a reflection of troublesome deviation. In fact, most organizations have death scenarios—situations in which things may fall apart to such an extent that the institution cares about avoidance more than would be indicated by probability weightings. These scenarios may vary by product. For liabilities with minimum rate guarantees, the death scenario may be a long period of very low interest rates. That scenario was certainly preying on a lot of minds a few years ago. For other liabilities, where customers are rate-sensitive and withdrawal options exist, it may be long-term rates staying at or above the 12 percent level for a significant amount of time. Scenario analysis can allow the organization to examine such situations in considerable detail, in addition to spanning a probability space.

Running an extensive set of scenarios will shed light on the interaction between the assets and the liabilities. The relevant time horizons are likely to be different for different portfolios and products. Moreover, just running the interest rate scenarios so beloved by the regulators is unlikely to be sufficient. A whole series of scenario runs must be used to examine the sensitivity of assets and liabilities to other factors, including credit and liquidity.

After scenarios are run, what steps are necessary to decide on the asset allocations? After attributing values to each of the factors, target budgets must be established for factors, or factor combinations, for each of the portfolios.

Then, of course, the factors have to be attributed to the cells. Here is where a degree of homogeneity within a cell becomes important. It must be possible to assume that assets within a given cell are going to have a certain amount of liquidity, convexity, and credit risk in order to figure out the final characteristics of the portfolio.

Finally, there must be an analysis of which cells are rich and cheap *relative to the factors within the cell* in order to decide on the allocation. However, the rich/cheap analysis is where the transition occurs from strategic decisions rooted in the factor mix to the tactical ones of exactly what assets to buy, since analysis to determine whether cells are rich or cheap can also discover whether assets are rich or cheap.

One difficulty in implementing this sort of analysis is that factors will have different rankings for different liabilities. The key to asset allocation among the sectors will be relative value analysis, and that is going to be very hard unless all the assets and liabilities are on the same platform, i.e., analyzed using the same assumptions. Undoubtedly, it will not be possible to use exactly the same model for all levels of analysis. Different models will handle some assets and liabilities better, but it is important for the assumptions and methodologies to be consistent in order to place any sort of reliance on the results.

The subjectiveness of much of the analysis means that it will not be possible to arrive at a black box, turnkey system of asset allocation that will produce model portfolios without any sort of human intervention. The process will be less scientific, and will involve a good deal of judgement.

RELATIVE VALUE ANALYSIS

Since relative value among sectors is a key to asset allocation, it is worth taking a look at the nature of the relative value publications produced by the investment banks and distributed to customers. Some are organized by sector and others cut across sectors. They are designed to help the customer decide which assets should be bought and sold, and what the current asset allocation should be. A wide variety of approaches are used, but most reflect complex analytic techniques.

Many of these publications contain valuable insights, but some dangers arise in using them. One is that the inventory position of the investment bank may influence the analysis provided. Lack of integration represents another problem. In some cases, the publications appear to be put together with a page from each of the desks that the publication covers, and virtually no effort is made to integrate the different analyses.

There is generally too little discussion of transaction costs, especially since an implicit assumption seems to be that investors have a very short time horizon. Frequently, a recommendation is made to reverse the trade that was first suggested a very short time previously. This is not a fruitful approach for many institutions, even those moving to more active management, in that it implies a very high turnover rate. MetLife, like many other institutions, has residual elements of buy and hold in its psyche, both out of conservatism and out of a belief that transaction costs often outweigh market misalignments. In addition, many investment decisions are strategic in order to take advantage of a long time horizon. For those, one would not expect to be trading in and out of positions.

So what does a relative-value institutional investor really want to know? First and foremost, what is rich or cheap. A useful analysis might run like this: Last year was a good time to give up liquidity in return for higher yield because, at that time, the economic trade-off was favorable. But now the market has changed and, to take advantage of the situation, one should trade convexity for yield. This type of analysis suggests that the analysts are trying to relate the different factors, and are thinking in terms of how the market is valuing the factors.

In addition, it is extremely important to know how the Street is deciding on fair value for a sector or a security. Sometimes this is difficult and requires a clear explanation of very complicated factors. Laurie Goodman does this sort of analysis very well, and her chapter illustrates the complexities involved. She gives five different methodologies for determining cheap-rich which clearly illustrate the different ways to dissect a trade. In the example given, all of the methodologies point in the same direction, thus confirming the set of strategies that were tested.

The need for the use of a number of different methodologies makes the black box approach impossible, since different techniques will be necessary and will carry different weights in different situations. This kind of analysis must be done outside the asset allocation framework, but in tandem with it. The situation will certainly arise when the methods of analysis point to different answers, and in some cases action must still be taken. This type of situation makes assessing the respective reliability of each method of analysis quite important.

Another frustration with the Street's research is that it is very difficult to tell whether the analysis across sectors is comparable. The most suspect class is mortgage-backed securities. It is very important to know how they are modeled. One major investment bank announced with some fanfare that it would now base the interest rate movements in its mortgage model on those of its Treasury model. It is not clear what they were doing before, or how much difference the change made.

The difference of opinion about the term structure of credit spreads also becomes apparent in relative-value publications. They illustrate that a lack of rigorous review may make results unreliable. Furthermore, some of the comparisons are not with the general universe, but among the bonds of individual issuers. For a single issuer, the conclusions that can be reached will be useful from a tactical point of view, but perhaps not from a strategic one.

Often historical relationships provide the foundation for relative-value judgements, at least short-run ones. If the assertion is made that spreads are very high or very low relative to what they have been, the period of comparison needs to be clear, as well as why that period was chosen. More carefully considered reasoning should be supplied with the analysis, with enough specificity so that the analysis can be replicated. There is nothing that adds as much comfort for an institutional investor as the statement that the analysis can be replicated on a given software. This permits tests of the effect of changing assumptions. In addition, it provides an acid test of understanding of the analysis.

CONCLUSION

We have discussed the steps involved in the asset allocation process from the point of view of a large investor with a variety of liabilities. In an effort to close the loop, it is necessary to tie asset allocation back to performance measurement. It is this step that permits an evaluation of the investment process, whether it's on a benchmarking basis or an asset allocation basis.

From a performance measurement perspective, MetLife is implementing a total rate of return approach—a change from the traditional book-value basis. Customized indices are being developed as the benchmarks for the portfolios. The level of customization varies with the portfolio and the liability type.

Putting the customized indexing process and the asset allocation process into a single framework adds a significant level of organizational complexity. It's not as simple as just managing a portfolio against the Lehman or Salomon Index, because there are so many factors to evaluate. Indexes must be designed for all the liabilities segments, some of which are very difficult to model, such as Whole Life, or Universal Life, or even the SPDAs.

In addition to the indexes developed for portfolios, it may be desirable to examine indexes for specific asset categories, particularly in a situation where asset acquisition is divorced from portfolio management. This will serve two purposes. It will permit some assessment of how effective asset allocation decisions have been in terms of picking high-performance sectors, and it will permit an evaluation of the performance of asset sector specialists.

MetLife is in the process of developing the infrastructure and the technology to implement this ambitious plan. In addition to the hurdles to the plan already mentioned, other complicating factors include risk-based capital charges, taxes, and regulatory issues. To reiterate the issues of infrastructure and technology, the big question is: Can analysis be used effectively? Can it be brought into a usable framework for the trader and the portfolio manager? It is not an easy task.

One of the practical issues confronting large institutions is the availability of specific securities. While economists expect increased demand to result in greater supply, every trader believes that there are not enough corporate securities available to satisfy institutional needs.

Another practical issue is pipeline capacity of assets acquired in specialized transactions, including private placements and commercial mortgages. Large organizations have been established to acquire these assets. For these asset classes, there are difficulties in implementing the allocation shifts at a reasonable cost. Also, there are more general trading issues. How is portfolio rebalancing accomplished, and how often? If very active trading begins, there are also organizational difficulties, and weighing transaction costs becomes extremely important.

One final question is whether the specific portfolio approach being described here is not too constraining. Obviously, the constraints of 20 portfolios summing to the whole company are greater than would be found for a single portfolio, even ignoring the possibility of offsetting risks. This raises the question: Can the company as a whole take more risk than the sum of the desired individual portfolios would imply? If so, how can a structure be put in place that will retain as much local control as possible while capturing the gains from combining all assets and liabilities? The current approach has been to seek lower-level control and to work out procedures for asset allocation at that level before working on issues of combination. This is an area where delving into specific issues raises significant questions. It is imperative, therefore, to establish a consistent analytical framework right from the start.

REFERENCES

Stabbert, Gerd W. 1995. "An Analytical Approach to Asset/Liability Performance Measurement," In *Fixed Income Investment: Recent Research*. T. S. Y. Ho, ed. Burr Ridge, IL: Irwin Professional Publishing.

CHAPTER 2

Nonparallel Yield Curve Shifts and Stochastic Immunization

Robert R. Reitano
Vice President, Investment Policy & Research
John Hancock Mutual Life Insurance Company

Over the last several years, general price function models reflecting multivariate yield curve specifications have been introduced. They make it possible to define a variety of duration and convexity measures which greatly improve the understanding of yield curve shift risk (Reitano 1989, 1990a, 1991a,b, 1992b; Ho 1990, 1992). Traditional immunization theories also generalize to these yield curve models (Reitano 1990b, 1991c, 1992a). In general, we can conclude that the larger the class of yield curve shifts against which we seek immunization, the more restrictive the necessary immunization conditions become. Conversely, the smaller the class, the more likely the strategy will fail.

For example, immunization against parallel shifts requires a constraint on the modified durations of assets and liabilities, and also a constraint on convexities, although this latter restriction is generally far less important in practice. Analogously, against any other one parameter

---

The author acknowledges the technical assistance of C. Dec Mullarkey and the support of the John Hancock Company in the development of the examples in this chapter. This chapter has been previously published in the Journal of Portfolio Management, Winter 1996, pp. 71–78.

model for yield curve shifts, we need identical restrictions on so-called "directional" durations and "directional" convexities, where the direction vector reflects the "shape" of the shift assumed. These strategies are easy to implement, yet are likely to fail when an unanticipated shift occurs.

Choosing several yield curve shifts to immunize against, for example based on a principal component analysis (Theil 1971; Wilks 1962) as in Litterman and Scheinkman (1991), we now need a like number of directional duration and directional convexity constraints, where the direction vectors reflect the "shape" of the principal components. Finally, in seeking to immunize against all yield curve shifts allowable within a given yield curve model, the immunizing conditions put restrictions on the asset and liability partial durations and partial convexities. As the yield curve model is refined further, these partial-duration constraints simply push the portfolios closer and closer toward cash matching in a fixed cash flow application. When embedded options exist, generalized cash matching occurs in the sense that both portfolios will have identical behaviors with respect to arbitrary 'infinitesimal' yield curve shifts.

Of course, besides the practical shortcomings of implementing such severe restrictions, there is also the problem that one might be inadvertently immunizing against even infeasible yield curve shifts, and shifts too unlikely to worry about.

A new framework has been developed for full yield curve immunization. Rather than seek immunization in the classical sense of eliminating downside risk, we seek immunization in the stochastic sense of risk minimization. The risk measure used is a weighted average of the portfolio variance, as used in Markowitz (1959), and a measure of worst-case yield curve risk. We provide explicit formulas for the solution of the risk minimization problem, where the solution can be made to satisfy various constraints on one or several directional durations and the expected yield curve return, as well as other constraints reflecting the specific assets available for trading. Here, the theory is presented through the detailed analysis of an example introduced in Reitano (1990a, 1991a, 1992b). For more mathematical rigor and details on the theory, as well as additional considerations in its application, see Reitano (1993). For a review of other stochastic approaches to duration matching and dedication, see Hiller and Schaak (1990).

SETUP OF THE GENERAL PROBLEM: RISK

We denote by $P(\bar{i})$ a price function defined on a yield curve vector, $\bar{i} = (i_1, \ldots, i_m)$, which describes the term structure through the identification of m yield points, referred to as "yield curve drivers" in the above Reitano references, or "key rates" in Ho. Yields at other maturities are assumed to depend on these m identified yields in a formulaic way, such as via interpolation. The current yield curve vector is denoted $\bar{i}_o$, and the yield curve shift model is denoted:

$$\bar{i}_o \to \bar{i}_o + \overline{\Delta i}, \tag{1}$$

where $\overline{\Delta i} = (\Delta i_1, \ldots, \Delta i_m)$ denotes the vector of quantities by which each yield point shifts during a given and fixed time period. During this period, $\overline{\Delta i}$ is interpreted as a random vector.

In practice, $P(\bar{i})$ may denote any price function, but for immunization applications, it will usually denote the surplus price function, $S(\bar{i})$, or forward surplus price function at time t, $S_t(\bar{i})$ (see Reitano 1992a, 1993). For yield curve shift analyses over shorter periods, the distribution of $\overline{\Delta i}$ may reflect an historical analysis of actual yield curve shifts or a theoretical model based on such an analysis, with the theory below then applied to $S(\bar{i})$. For longer time periods, for which simple yield curve differences distort the true evolution of yields due to time drift, it is better to base the analysis of historical shifts on a "predictor yield curve" interpretation, and apply the results below to $S_t(\bar{i})$. As developed in greater detail in Reitano (1995), the yield curve shift, $\overline{\Delta i}$, is then defined as the shift from the initial yield curve, $\bar{i}_o$, to the predictor yield curve of the end of period curve, $\bar{i}^P$. Predictor yield curves are denominated in beginning-of-period time units, thereby allowing a simple yet meaningful subtraction: $\overline{\Delta i} = \bar{i}^P - \bar{i}_o$.

As detailed in Reitano (1993), the ratio function, $P(\bar{i}_o + \overline{\Delta i})/P(\bar{i}_o)$, can be linearly approximated by $R(\overline{\Delta i})$:

$$R(\overline{\Delta i}) = 1 - \sum D_j(\bar{i}_o)\Delta i_j \qquad (2)$$
$$= 1 - \overline{D}(\bar{i}_o) \cdot \overline{\Delta i},$$

where the $D_j(\bar{i}_o)$ are the partial durations of $P(\bar{i})$ evaluated on $\bar{i}_o$. The second expression in (**2**) reflects the dot or inner product notation for the vector product of $\overline{D}(\bar{i}_o) = (D_1(\bar{i}_o), \ldots, D_m(\bar{i}_o))$, called the total duration vector, and $\overline{\Delta i}$, the vector shift. We formally assume $P(\bar{i}_o) \neq 0$, although the theory can readily be adapted to circumvent this restriction.

We now define a general risk measure for the price function $P(\bar{i})$. First, following Markowitz (1959), it is natural to consider the variance of $R(\overline{\Delta i})$, since this approximates the total return risk as measured by $P(\bar{i}_o + \overline{\Delta i})/P(\bar{i}_o)$. In addition, one may wish to limit outlier risk from the random vector, $\overline{\Delta i}$ which may not be adequately reflected in the variance measure because of a low implied weighing. To do this, we note that the absolute difference between $R(\overline{\Delta i})$ and its expected value is bounded by the product of the length of the total duration vector, denoted $|\overline{D}(\bar{i}_o)|$, and the length of the vector shift less its expected value, $|\overline{\Delta i} - E(\overline{\Delta i})|$. Consequently, if the length of $\overline{D}(\bar{i}_o)$ is made small, outlier risk to $R(\overline{\Delta i})$ is made small, so $|\overline{D}(\bar{i}_o)|$ can be interpreted as a worst-case risk measure.

In light of these comments, we define a risk measure, $RM(w)$, with weighting parameter w, as the weighted average of these two risk measures:

$$RM(w) = w \, \text{Var}[R(\overline{\Delta i})] + (1-w)|\overline{D}(\overline{i_o})|^2, \quad (3)$$

where the weighting parameter is chosen: $0 \le w \le 1$. Note that in (3), the length of $\overline{D}(\overline{i_o})$ is reflected to the square so that it is of second order, as is the variance function.

This risk measure can be compactly expressed as a matrix product:

$$RM(w) = \overline{D} \, \overline{K}_w \overline{D}^T \quad (4)$$

where $\overline{D}$ denotes the total duration vector which is by convention identified with a row matrix, $\overline{D}^T$ is its column matrix transpose, and $\overline{K}_w$ is the weighted average of $\overline{K}$, the covariance matrix of $\overline{\Delta i}$, and the identity matrix, $\overline{I}$:

$$\overline{K}_w = w\overline{K} + (1-w)\overline{I}. \quad (5)$$

Of course, when $w = 1$ in (5), the risk measure in (4) reduces to $\text{Var}[R(\overline{\Delta i})]$ by (3). Also, while in theory we only require $0 \le w \le 1$, in practice we must chose w very close to 1 or else the worst-case risk term will dominate due to the difference in scale between the units of $\overline{K}$ and those of $\overline{I}$ (see the Example on page 33).

For our purposes, $\overline{K}_w$ has the mathematically convenient property of positive semi definiteness, which we can assume to be in fact positive definiteness by a change in the yield basis. By positive definiteness is meant that $RM(w)$ in (4) can be 0 only if $\overline{D}$ is the zero vector, otherwise, it is strictly positive. Geometrically, this means that for any fixed value of $c > 0$, the set of total-duration vectors defined by $RM(w) = c$ form an ellipsoid in m-dimensional space.

SETUP OF THE GENERAL PROBLEM: CONSTRAINTS

Our goal is to minimize the risk measure, $RM(w)$. Of course, this is a trivial problem without further restriction on $\overline{D}(\bar{i}_o)$, since, as noted above, the minimum of $RM(w)$ is 0, and this is achieved exactly when $\overline{D}(\bar{i}_o) = \overline{0}$, the zero vector. If $P(\bar{i})$ reflects a surplus portfolio, this condition implies that assets and liabilities are "dollar partial duration" matched. Consequently, the only question remaining is how to trade within the given asset portfolio to achieve this target total-duration vector (see Equation 11).

As it turns out, restrictions of interest on $\overline{D}(\bar{i}_o)$ involve restrictions on the dot product $\overline{D} \cdot \overline{N}$ for various values of the vector $\overline{N}$. For example:

1. *Directional durations, $D_N(\bar{i}_o)$*, may be restricted in one or several directions, because $D_N(\bar{i}_o) = \overline{D} \cdot \overline{N}$. For example, $\overline{N} = (1,1,\ldots,1)$ can be used to restrict traditional duration.

2. *Expected period yield curve return, r'*, also provides a restriction of this type since:

$$E[R(\overline{\Delta i})] = 1 + r' = 1 - \overline{D} \cdot \overline{N} \qquad (6)$$

where $\overline{N} = E[\overline{\Delta i}]$ is the expected yield curve shift.

3. *Asset trading set limitations* can also be reflected this way with a little thought. Assume that we have a specified collection of assets from which we wish to trade, with the logical constraint of cash neutrality: that total sales equal total purchases. This collection may or may not place a restriction on the total duration vectors that are achievable by trading in the given portfolio. To find out, we form the matrix, $\overline{A}$, with column vectors equal to the total-duration vectors: $\overline{D}_j - \overline{D}_n$, for $j = 1,\ldots, n-1$. Here, we assume that there are n assets, with $\overline{D}_j$ denoting the corresponding total duration vectors. We can choose any

asset for $\overline{D}_n$; the purpose of the subtraction is to assure a cash neutral trade.

We then solve the system of equations:

$$\overline{A}^T \overline{N} = \overline{0}, \tag{7}$$

and, in particular, look for the maximum number of linearly independent solutions. That is, we seek a basis for the null space of $\overline{A}^T$. Of course, (7) may have no nontrivial solutions (i.e., solutions other than $\overline{N} = \overline{0}$).

The given trading set of n assets then introduces the following constraints on feasible total duration vectors, $\overline{D}$:

$$\overline{D} \cdot \overline{N}_j = \overline{D}(\bar{i}_o) \cdot \overline{N}_j \tag{8}$$

where $\overline{N}_j$ are the independent solutions to (7), and $\overline{D}(\bar{i}_o)$ is the initial total duration vector. That is, (8) states that, given these n assets and the requirement of a cash-neutral trade, one cannot change the directional durations of the original portfolio in the $\overline{N}_j$ directions.

Of course, if (7) has no nonzero solutions, which will happen when there are sufficiently many assets, no restrictions are introduced in (8).

SOLUTION OF THE GENERAL PROBLEM

We now present an explicit solution to the following constrained minimization problem, assuming only that the constraint vectors, $\overline{N}_j$, are consistent, i.e., linearly independent (see Reitano [1993], or Martin et al [1988] for a derivation):

$$\text{Minimize: } \overline{DK}_w \overline{D}^T \tag{9}$$
$$\text{Subject to: } \overline{D} \cdot \overline{N}_j = r_j, \quad j = 1, \ldots, p$$

To express the solution compactly, we denote by $\overline{B}$ the matrix with the $\overline{N}_j$ vectors as columns, and by $\bar{r}$ the column vector of $\bar{r}_j$ values. Consequently, the p constraints in

(9) can be expressed, $\overline{D}\,\overline{B} = \bar{r}^T$, where we recall that total duration vectors are identified with row matrices. Denoting by $\overline{D}_o$ the solution to (9), we then have:

$$\overline{D}_o^T = \overline{K}_w^{-1}\,\overline{B}\,(\overline{B}^T\overline{K}_w^{-1}\,\overline{B})^{-1}\,\bar{r}, \qquad (10\text{a})$$

and the value of the risk measure $RM_o(w)$ is given in (4) by:

$$RM_o(w) = \bar{r}^K(\overline{B}^T\overline{K}_w^{-1}\overline{B})^{-1}\bar{r}. \qquad (10\text{b})$$

While equations (10a) and (10b) may look imposing, these matrix calculations are easily performed in a variety of computer software from spreadsheets to APL.

Of course, equation (10a) provides the risk-minimizing total duration vector for the portfolio which satisfies the various constraints of interest, while (10b) gives the corresponding value for the risk measure defined in (3). One interesting consequence of expression (10b) is that one can only achieve zero risk if $\bar{r} = \bar{0}$, the zero vector. This is due to the fact that $\overline{B}^T\overline{K}_w^{-1}\overline{B}$, and hence its inverse, are also positive definite.

To calculate the necessary cash-neutral trade from the given asset set is now easy. Let $\bar{a}' = (a_1, \ldots, a_{n-1})$ denote the amounts traded of each of the first $n-1$ assets, where $a_j > 0$ denotes a purchase, $a_j < 0$ a sale, and where $a_n = -\sum_{1}^{n-1} a_j$ for cash neutrality. Then this trading vector is given as the solution to:

$$\overline{A}\bar{a}' = P(\bar{i}_o)[\overline{D}_o - \overline{D}]^T, \qquad (11)$$

where $\overline{A}$ is given as in (7). Equation (11) may be readily solved for $\bar{a}'$ where $\overline{D}_o$ denotes the target total duration vector from (10a), and $P(\bar{i}_o)$ and $\overline{D}$ denote the price and total duration vector of the original portfolio. A transpose symbol appears on the right hand side of (11) to make the total duration vector into a column matrix.

Because of the constraints in (8), equation (11) will always be solvable within the asset trading set. However, with sufficiently many assets, the solution need not be unique, so one will have significant latitude in choosing a trading solution based on other considerations.

Example

As in Reitano [1990a, 1991a, 1992b], we let $\bar{i}_o$ = (.075,.090,.100) represent semiannual equivalent yields at 6 months and 5 and 10 years, respectively. The asset portfolio consists of $50 million par of a 10-year, 12 percent coupon bond with market value of $56.40 million and duration of 6.16, and $17.48 million par of 6-month commercial paper with a market value of $16.85 million and duration of .48. Together, assets total $73.25 million with a duration of 4.86. The single liability is a $100 million GIC payment in year 5, with a market value of $63.97 and duration of 4.86. Consequently, surplus equals $9.28 million, and the duration-matching strategy was chosen to immunize the surplus ratio of 12.67 percent against parallel yield curve shifts. The total duration vector for surplus is given by:

$$\overline{D}(\bar{i}_o) = (4.20, -35.23, 35.88). \tag{12}$$

We use monthly treasury data from the period January 1987 to April 1994, from which is estimated the following mean vector $\overline{E} = E(\overline{\Delta i})$ and covariance matrix $\overline{K}$;

$$\overline{E} = (-28.24, -62.23, -43.03) \times 10^{-5} \tag{13}$$

$$\overline{K} = \begin{pmatrix} .63 & .71 & .58 \\ .71 & 1.21 & 1.05 \\ .58 & 1.05 & .97 \end{pmatrix} \times 10^{-5}$$

In practice, because of the strong dependency of $\overline{E}$ on the economic cycle, it may be prudent to either set $\overline{E}$ equal to a forecast shift in which one wants to take a position, or in the absence of such a forecast, implicitly set $\overline{E} = \overline{0}$ and ignore it as a problem constraint. Below we develop returns using the above $\overline{E}$ for illustrative purposes only.

From equation (4) with $w = 1$ and equation (6), we easily calculate the monthly expected value and variance of $R(\overline{\Delta i})$:

$$E[R(\overline{\Delta i})] = .9947 \qquad (14)$$
$$\text{Var}[R(\overline{\Delta i})] = .000773$$

Consequently, the current portfolio has an expected monthly return of −.53 percent, and a monthly standard deviation of about 2.78 percent, based on data from this historical period.

RISK MINIMIZATION OF EXAMPLE

For the illustrations below, we consider two risk measures for minimization, $RM(1)$ or the variance, and $RM(.99999)$, which puts about-equal weight on the minimization of variance and worst-case risk, due to the difference of scale between the units of $\overline{K}$ in (13), and those of the identity matrix $\overline{I}$. For convenience below, we refer to the corresponding minimization problems as Case 1 and Case 2. While $RM(1)$ is given in (14), we note for comparisons below that $RM(.99999) = .026239$ for the original portfolio, and $|\overline{D}| = 50.5$.

As a first application, we ignore asset trading sets and simply minimize risk in the portfolio subject to the one constraint of maintaining the current surplus duration of 4.85. That is, in (9) we have the one constraint $\overline{D} \cdot \overline{N} = 4.85$, where $\overline{N} = (1,1,1)$. We then obtain from (10), the following:

Case 1: $\overline{D}_0 = (5.20, -7.84, 7.48)$, $RM = .000099$ (15)
Case 2: $\overline{D}_0 = (2.35, .95, 1.55)$, $RM = .000262$

In Case 1, the implied standard deviation was reduced 64 percent, from 2.78 percent to .99 percent per month, compared to the original portfolio. For Case 2, the variance reduction was 53 percent to 1.32 percent per month, even though a reduction in standard deviation was not the primary objective of the problem. On a risk measure basis, the Case 1 reduction was 87 percent, while for Case 2 the risk-measure was reduced 99 percent from its original value of .026239. The implied monthly returns on these risk-minimized portfolios are −.02 percent and +.19 percent, respectively, while the $|\overline{D}|$ values are 12.0 and 3.0 respectively.

We next abandon the modified-duration constraint in favor of a constraint on tradable assets. We consider three assets: 6-month commercial paper; a 5-year, 9 1/2 percent coupon note; and the original 10-year, 12 percent coupon bond. Their relevant features (market values are per 100 par) are:

	Commerical Paper	5-Year Note	10-Year Bond	
MV	96.39	102.00	112.80	(16)
D_1	.48	.02	.04	
D_2	0	3.95	.22	
D_3	0	0	5.90	
D	.48	3.97	6.16	

First, we assume only trading between the 5- and 10-year securities. The matrix $\overline{A} = [\overline{D}_1(\bar{i}_o) - \overline{D}_2(\bar{i}_o)]^T$ in (7) is given by:

$$\overline{A} = (.02, -3.73, 5.90)^T, \qquad (17)$$

where here, $\overline{D}_1$ corresponds to the 10-year bond and $\overline{D}_2$ the 5-year. Because the matrix and $\overline{A}$ its transpose clearly have rank equal to one, we expect two linearly independent solutions of (**7**), and a calculation produces the following as one such pair:

$$\overline{N}_1 = (0, 1.5818, 1), \overline{N}_2 = (-295, 0, 1). \quad (18)$$

Using these values and the original portfolio's total duration vector in (**12**), we obtain the constraint values from (**8**):

$$\overline{D} \cdot \overline{N}_1 = -19.8468$$
$$\overline{D} \cdot \overline{N}_2 = -1203.12$$

which when used in (**10**) produces the following solutions:

Case 1: $\overline{D}_o = (4.16, -27.40, 23.50)$, $RM = .000575$ **(19)**
Case 2: $\overline{D}_o = (4.07, -10.51, -3.23)$, $RM = .002866$

For this problem, we observe respective reductions in risk of 26 percent and 89 percent from the original portfolio, with corresponding changes in implied standard deviations of −14 percent and +39 percent. Respective expected monthly returns on the portfolio using (**6**) are −.58 percent and −.68 percent, while the respective duration values for these surplus portfolios have moved from 4.85 to .25 for Case 1, and −9.67 for Case 2. Finally, respective values for $|\overline{D}|$ are 36.3 and 11.7.

To determine the necessary trades, we now solve (**11**), where here $\overline{a}' = (a_1)$ denotes the trade of the 10-year bond, and $a_2 = -a_1$ equals the corresponding 5-year bond trade. A calculation produces $a_1 = -9.48$ million in Case 1, and $a_1 = -61.52$ million in Case 2, both requiring a sale of 10-year assets and a purchase of the 5-year.

As the last example, we solve the minimization problem with all three trading assets in (**16**), both with and without a duration constraint. In both cases, we must solve (**7**), with:

$$\overline{A} = \begin{pmatrix} \overline{D}_1(\bar{i}_o) - \overline{D}_3(\bar{i}_o) \\ \overline{D}_2(\bar{i}_o) - \overline{D}_3(\bar{i}_o) \end{pmatrix}^T = \begin{pmatrix} -.44 & -.46 \\ .22 & 3.95 \\ 5.90 & 0 \end{pmatrix} \quad (20)$$

where $\overline{D}_i(\bar{i}_o)$, $i = 1,2,3$ denotes the total duration vectors of the 10-year bond, 5-year note, and 6-month commercial paper, respectively.

As $\overline{A}$ is easily seen to have rank equal to 2, there will be only one linearly independent solution to (**7**), for example:

$$\overline{N}_1 = (1, .1165, .0702), \quad (21)$$

which has the corresponding constraint value from (**8**):

$$\overline{D} \cdot \overline{N}_1 = 2.6173.$$

We first solve the minimization problem in (**9**) with only the above asset trading set constraint, and obtain:

Case 1: $\overline{D}_o = (2.84, -2.80, 1.38)$, $RM = .000016$ \quad (22)

Case 2: $\overline{D}_o = (2.70, -.47, -.40)$, $RM = .000100$

for respective risk reductions of 98 percent and 99.6 percent, respectively, corresponding reductions in implied monthly standard deviations of 86 percent and 83 percent, and expected monthly returns of $-.04$ percent and $+.03$ percent. Note that, in this case, the durations of both resulting portfolios again differ from the original value of 4.85, equaling 1.42 and 1.82, respectively. In addition, respective values of $|\overline{D}|$ are 4.2 and 2.8.

To fix the duration of the resulting surplus portfolio to equal 4.85, we add to the above asset trading set constraint the constraint $\overline{D} \cdot \overline{N} = 4.85$, with $\overline{N} = (1,1,1)$. This is not a problem in this case because $\overline{N}$ here is linearly independent from $\overline{N}_1$ in (**21**) above.

Again solving (**9**), only with two constraints, we obtain:

Case 1: $\overline{D}_o = (2.79 - 6.91, 8.97)$, $RM = .000123$ (**23**)
Case 2: $\overline{D}_o = (2.40, .93, 1.52)$, $RM = .000262$

for respective risk reductions of 84 percent and 99 percent. These results are logically inferior to the risk reductions observed in (22) due to the presence of the additional constraint on the portfolio duration.

For these last two problems, we summarize trading results below, obtained by solving (**11**) for $\overline{a}' = (a_1, a_2)$, and setting $a_3 = -a_1 - a_2$.

| | No Duration Constraint || Duration = 4.85 ||
	Case 1	Case 2	Case 1	Case 2
10-year (a_1)	−54.07	−57.07	−42.33	−54.04
5-year (a_2)	79.20	84.83	68.89	87.96
6-month (a_3)	−24.94	−27.76	−26.56	−33.92

EFFICIENT FRONTIERS

Equation (**10b**) defines the risk, $RM_o(w)$, of the risk-minimizing portfolio as a function of $\bar{r}$, which quantifies the limitations on the constraints in (**9**), and of $\overline{B}$, which contains the direction vectors with respect to which these constraints are defined. Fixing these direction vectors, therefore, equation (**10b**) can be thought of as describing an efficient frontier in (Risk, $\bar{r}$) space. It is efficient in the sense that for any given $\bar{r}$ value, and any portfolio that satisfies the constraints $\overline{D} \cdot \overline{N}_j = r_j$, or, more compactly, $\overline{D}\,\overline{B} = r^T$, the corresponding risk $RM(w)$ must satisfy:

$$RM(w) \geq RM_o(w). \qquad (24)$$

For $w = 1$, the risk measure reduces to variance, so for the single-direction vector $\overline{N}_1 = \overline{E}$, the expected yield curve shift, equation (**10b**), describes the risk-return efficient frontier of Markowitz, with a transformed return measure. This measure is transformed because, by (**6**), the actual yield curve shift return for the portfolio is $r' = -r$.

In this simple two-dimensional model, we can rewrite (**10b**) to reflect an efficient frontier in true risk-return space, (RM, r'):

$$RM_o(1) = c(r')^2 \qquad (25)$$

where c is the positive constant produced by the matrix product in (**10b**), with $\overline{B} = \overline{E}$. Clearly, this efficient frontier is a parabola in (RM, r') space or (Variance, Return) space.

For the above example, it is easy to solve the variance minimization problem for an arbitrary yield curve shift return specification r'. To do this, we use (**10**) with $\overline{B} = \overline{E}$, as given in (**13**), to obtain:

$$\overline{D}_0 = (-1232.74, 4595.32, -3512.81)r' \qquad (26)$$
$$\overline{D}_o = 150.22 r'$$
$$RM_o(1) = 16.307(r')^2$$

For the given portfolio, $r' = -.0053$, $D = 4.85$, and Variance $= .000773$. From (**26**), we see that the variance minimizing portfolio with this return has $D_o = -.80$ and Variance $= .000458$, for a 41 percent reduction.

As another simple application, we can also investigate the efficient frontier in (Variance, Duration) space, or more generally, risk-duration space. Again using (**10b**), we obtain:

$$RM_o(1) = b\, D_N^2, \qquad (27)$$

where b is the positive constant produced by the matrix product in (**10b**) with $\overline{B} = \overline{N}$, the direction vector of interest, and D_N denotes the targeted value for this directional duration. For the above example, with $\overline{N} = (1,1,1)$ for traditional duration, we obtain:

$$\overline{D}_o = (1.07, -1.62, 1.54)D_o \qquad (28)$$
$$RM_o(1) = 4.193\, D_o^2 \times 10^{-6}$$

Again, the efficient frontier in (**27**) and (**28**) is a parabola in (RM,D) space.

More generally, it can be shown that the efficient frontier in (**10b**) is always a paraboloid in $(RM,\bar{r})$ space. This is because the matrix $(\bar{B}^\mathrm{T}\bar{K}_w^{-1}\bar{B})^{-1}$ is positive definite, as has been noted above.

In summary, by (**10b**) we have a general way of defining the efficient frontiers which result as a function of both portfolio returns and/or portfolio directional duration values. These directional durations may be explicitly desired, or implicitly required by (**8**) due to limitations imposed by the asset trading set. Of course, this frontier is also dependent on $\bar{B}$ which identifies the direction vectors used.

SUMMARY AND CONCLUSIONS

While traditional immunization is simple to implement, it often fails due to the failure of the underlying assumption of parallel yield curve shifts to be realized. While formally generalizable to other models of yield curve movements, and even to a completely general model for these shifts, portfolio restrictions increase as more protection is sought. In the limit, only a cash-matching strategy, over yield curve regions, or more generally a dollar partial duration matching strategy, will provide protection in the most general case.

To avoid the consequences of this conclusion, which may be unnecessarily restrictive because the theory may require protection even where it is not needed in practice, a new paradigm for immunization is required. The notion of stochastic immunization replaces the classical immunization paradigm of no downside risk, with the more flexible paradigm of risk minimization.

Explicit solutions to the risk-minimization problem show that risk can be defined to reflect a flexible balance of two important individual risk measures: variance and worst-case risk. In addition, these problems can be solved with restrictions reflecting a desired portfolio yield curve return, desired portfolio directional durations, and/or restrictions on the assets available for trading. All that is required is that the implied restrictions be consistent.

REFERENCES

Hiller, Randall S., and Christian Schaak. 1990. "A Classification of Structured Bond Portfolio Modeling Modeling Techniques." *The Journal of Portfolio Management* (Fall): 37–48.

Ho, T. S. Y. 1990. *Strategic Fixed Income Management.* Homewood, IL: Dow Jones–Irwin.

_____. 1992. "Key Rate Durations: Measures of Interest Rate Risks." *The Journal of Fixed Income* (September): 29–44.

Litterman, Robert, and Jose Scheinkman. 1991. "Common Factors Affecting Bond Returns."*The Journal of Fixed Income* (June): 54–61.

Markowitz, Harry. 1959. *Portfolio Selection: Efficient Diversification of Investments.* New York: John Wiley & Sons.

Martin, John D., Samuel H. Cox, and Richard D. MacMinn. 1988. *The Theory of Finance: Evidence and Applications.* New York: The Dryden Press.

Reitano, Robert R. 1989. "A Multivariate Approach to Duration Analysis." *Actuarial Research Clearing House* 2: 97–181.

_____. 1990a. "Nonparallel Yield Curve Shifts and Durational Leverage." *The Journal of Portfolio Management* (Summer): 62–67.

_____. 1990b. "A Multivariate Approach to Immunization Theory." *Actuarial Research Clearing House* 2: 261–312.

_____. 1991a. "Nonparallel Yield Curve Shifts and Spread Leverage." *The Journal of Portfolio Management* (Spring): 82–87.

_____. 1991b. "Multivariate Duration Analysis." *Transactions of the Society of Actuaries* XLIII: 335–91.

_____. 1991c. "Multivariate Immunization Theory." *Transactions of the Society of Actuaries* XLIII: 392–438.

_____. 1992a. "Nonparallel Yield Curve Shifts and Immunization." *The Journal of Portfolio Management* (Spring): 36–43.

_____. 1992b. "Non-Parallel Yield Curve Shifts and Convexity." *Transactions of the Society of Actuaries* XLIV: 479–507.

_____. 1993. "Multivariate Stochastic Immunization Theory." *Transactions of the Society of Actuaries* XLV: 425–84.

_____. 1995. "Predictor Yield Curves and the Analysis of Period Yield Curve Shifts on Price." Working paper.

Theil, Henri. 1971. *Principles of Econometrics*. New York: John Wiley & Sons.

Wilks, Samuel S. 1962. *Mathematical Statistics*. New York: John Wiley & Sons.

CHAPTER 3

Current Application of Performance Measurement

Jonathan Nye
CFA and Vice President
Alliance Capital Management L.P.

Over the course of the early to mid-1990s, a number of large financial losses and outright failures caused investors and regulators to revisit the issue of what constitutes investment performance. The question arose: Is the typical representation of investment performance as useful as it could be? Is there information to be gleaned from a more properly formulated performance analysis which could help improve the investment process? And finally: Would such failures have been as likely to occur if our notion of performance was different? This chapter is intended to help form the basis for answering these questions.

Two Recent Failures

The Orange County, California, Investment Fund (OCIF) was established as a short-duration alternative in which statewide public entities could jointly invest. For several years, the fund earned consistently strong results and, as a consequence, attracted significant amounts of new money.

The OCIF achieved relatively high returns through two strategies:

1. Borrow short and invest long. Through much of the early 1990s, the OCIF employed considerable leverage by borrowing funds secured by portfolio assets. By late 1993, the fund had reverse repurchase agreements in place totalling approximately $13 billion, the proceeds of which were invested in long-dated securities. At that time, the fund's book value totalled $7.4 billion while the assets had a market value of nearly $20 billion.

2. Invest in high-yielding leveraged market-sensitive securities. A substantial portion of the fund was invested in mortgage derivatives. Roughly $8 billion was invested in inverse floaters—securities whose value can increase dramatically when rates fall but suffer when rates rise.

For several years, the OCIF benefited from this strategy as rates stayed within a tolerable band and the yield curve remained steeply sloped. With the economy gaining momentum in 1994 and the Federal Reserve Board tightening monetary policy, interest rates rose and the curve flattened. As a result of the market's movement, the OCIF posted losses estimated at around $1.7 billion, or nearly 25 percent of book value. One consequence of this loss was the nation's largest municipal bankruptcy.

In hindsight, the fund's apparently strong results were due to either an unknowing or explicit bet on stable or falling interest rates. Given that this strategy embodied significant risk, one has to wonder whether the apparently good results prior to the rate backup in 1994 truly constituted quality performance.

In Singapore, the head of the local office for Barings PLC, who by most accounts had a solid track record of controlled arbitrage trading, changed strategy and placed significant bets on the direction of Japanese markets. When these bets went against the trader, over $1 billion of the firm's capital was lost, forcing the firm into receivership.

If, hypothetically, the markets had moved in the trader's favor, he and the bank would have realized huge gains. In all likelihood, had this been the case, the trader personally and the bank in general would have been credited with having produced outstanding performance.

Yet, like the Orange County case, we are left wondering whether in this hypothetical case the results would have truly constituted financial accomplishment. When gains are realized through a course of action which includes a reasonable possibility of significant distress, has performance actually been realized?

Common Threads

In these two situations the performance measurement scheme and reward structure did little if anything to (a) discourage position-taking which embodied excessive risk, or (b) discourage doubling-up of risk positions after markets had started to move against them. From this perspective, it is clear that we need a way of accounting for performance which reflects the fund's exposure to risk.

INVESTMENT PERFORMANCE

From these two examples derives the idea that the investment performance is not analogous to investment return. Instead, investment performance should be considered in terms of the cost. Instead, investment performance should be considered in terms of the cost of constructing a particular portfolio with cost being the fund's exposure to risk. With reasonably efficient markets, higher returns cannot be achieved without undertaking commensurately higher risk. Therefore, performance should be measured in terms of return per unit of risk. This is analogous to the concept of value-added investment management. If the manager produces incremental returns beyond what could be achieved simply through additional risk-taking, value-added performance has resulted. While this distinction is noncontroversial, moving from this concept to the actual implementation of a performance measurement structure has often proved difficult.

Assuming we can agree on what we actually mean by investment return and risk (to be discussed later), the ideal performance measurement scheme should have three additional elements: *quantification, attribution,* and *significance.*

The term *quantification* refers to the numerical representation of risk and reward, *attribution* alludes to the decomposition and identification of those underlying causes which produce the actual return and risk profiles, and *significance* relates to the ability we have to make statistically sound inferences from the data. This chapter is focused on quantification issues and provides a survey of measures which attempt to capture return and risk and show how they can be combined to represent performance.

Before tackling some definitional issues and proceeding with a more formal presentation, it is would be useful to clarify several additional points.

Investment performance is most useful when thought about in relative terms. Though it is possible to think about performance in absolute terms, more generally we gain insight when thinking about performance in terms relative to a benchmark or some measure of our liabilities or cost of funds.

Second, it is vitally important that we account for risk on the basis of our exposure to risk as opposed to realization of risk. Perhaps with enough observations and assuming a consistent management style and objectives, we can infer that ex post risk accurately represents the fund's exposure to risk. Failing this, risk as measured ex post becomes critically period-dependent. For example: An investor whose strategy is to constantly write covered call options could, for long periods of time, show extraordinary performance using an ex post measure of risk. Yet as soon as the underlying markets rallied, returns and performance would suffer. Correctly applied, the performance analytic must assess the manager a risk penalty consistent with the option's ever-present hidden risk.

Third, having asserted that return and performance are not perfectly synonymous, it must be recognized that the process of describing how the fund did or what was the manager's contribution becomes much more difficult to represent. It would therefore be useful to review what desirable qualities any representation of performance should have:

Objective
The performance measure should be independent of any bias. Independent efforts to calculate performance should produce the same results and lead to the same conclusions.

Comparable
The performance of different funds should be comparable regardless of strategy, style, market, or leverage.

Communicable
The performance measure must be communicable and its relevance easily understood.

Implementable
The process which produces the performance analytic should be attainable with reasonable computing and technical resources within a reasonable period of time.

Properly reinforces
The system must give decision makers the incentive to seek results which are consistent with the goals of the fund. Otherwise known as the agency problem, this situation crops up whenever the manager as agent for the owner of the managed funds is given incentives based on a performance structure which is potentially at odds with the client's objectives.

Is nonintrusive
Performance measurement systems should not be set up resulting in limitations which eliminate manager flexibility. While it may be appropriate from a risk control standpoint to impose restrictions, this should not be the role of the performance measurement system. Correctly applied, the performance measurement system should promote the rational and efficient pursuit of value-adding opportunities within any previously established guidelines.

These criteria are reviewed here because it must be acknowledged that different techniques for measuring risk and hence risk-adjusted return will fullfill these objectives to different degrees. Tradeoffs will inevitably have to be considered. At one extreme lie processes which measure performance in some theorectically correct way but are associated with a potentially severe loss of comparability, onerous computational requirements, and a significant loss of communicability. Alternatively, one could choose a process that represents a theoretical compromise but which, given current understanding and computational power, can be readily implemented in a way that still enhances the likelihood that the fund will meet its objectives.

MEASURING INVESTMENT RETURNS

The appropriate quantification of investment return is well appreciated and documented. For the purposes of this chapter it will be assumed that time-weighted rate of return is the correct way to gauge investment return. While arguments have been proposed, particularly in the financial services industry, that measures such as net spread or present value of distributable earnings do a better job of reflecting real-world conditions, convincing arguments can nonetheless be made that market value growth of net assets is the most-appropriate measure of value.

INVESTMENT RISK AND PERFORMANCE MEASUREMENT

Significantly more contentious is the issue of risk measurement. First, however, we must establish that risk be defined in terms consistent with reward. Therefore, if our rewards are defined as market-value returns, risk must be denominated accordingly. For example, it would be inappropriate to characterize reward as total return and risk as the possibility that cash flow will be insufficient to cover liability payments. To do so would produce conflicting objectives which would be difficult if not impossible to resolve. Therefore, given that we are using total return as our measure of reward, investment risk, in general terms, becomes the uncertainty associated with various levels of return.

The following material surveys five different risk schemes in terms of their suitability for use when risk-adjusting returns to calculate performance. This material draws primarily on the world of fixed income, though conceptually could be extended to equity, currency, and derivative markets. Examples of different performance calculations will be provided using monthly Salomon Brothers index data. The two series used are the 7–10-year Treasury Sector and the 30-Year FNMA Mortgage Passthrough Sector. For demonstrative purposes, it will be assumed that the Treasury index is our benchmark against which the FNMA's performance will be compared.

Throughout this chapter it will be assumed that however defined, risk is perfectly quantifiable. Yet for large numbers of security types, this is not the case. An ideal scheme should reflect the fact that models are imperfect. Securities which are particularly sensitive to model assumptions such as certain complex options or behavioral assumptions such as derivative mortgage-backed securities should be assessed a model error premium. This would be done not with the intention of punishing their use, but to reflect the fact that uncertainties exist as to how they will actually pay off with time and changing circumstances. This is not to say that using an assumption of perfect knowledge is without merit. Ultimately as systems get increasingly sophisticated, measures of model risk can be layered on. In the meantime, quantifying risk based on perfect knowledge represents a worthwhile step.

Constrained Management as an Implied Risk Metric

The first approach violates the tenet above that risk be denominated in terms consistent with reward. Due to its prevalence, however, a discussion of this approach is warranted.

The constrained management approach accounts for risk in the form of a series of nominal constraints, with the presumption that the resulting actual risk profile will mirror that of the benchmark and, by implication, the client's objectives. If the fund outreturns the benchmark, performance is said to have been realized.

For example, a portfolio manager might be given the following set of operating guidelines:

Duration	+/– 10%	of the benchmark
Sector limits	+/– 10%	of the benchmark
Quality	=	benchmark

The key shortcoming of this approach is that it enables users to avoid any discussion of risk. Instead, duration and, especially, sector and issuer limits are presumed to constrain risk (which has been left undefined). Typically, duration limits bound the set of possible interest-sensitive returns, but it is less clear how sector and issuer limits directly influence the set of possible returns. Furthermore, this approach gives no allowance for the possibility that more efficient portfolios can be created because risk has not been quantified.

Even as risk proxies, constraints often do not have the intended effect.

- Duration is an imperfect measure and while duration matching using key rate durations or other reshaping durations would improve the fund's interest sensitive match relative to the benchmark, enough instances have occurred where the security's empirical was not what was modelled to suggest that predictions of a bond's sensitivity to changes in interest rates are not completely reliable. Particularly when using non-default-free bonds in proportions different from the benchmark, returns as a function of changes in interest rates may vary significantly from what would be predicted by modified or effective durations and convexities.

- Sector limits in and of themselves do not directly account for risk for two reasons. First, various sector weights in combination with various durations can dramatically alter the portfolio's risk profile versus the benchmark. And while a solution to this would be to impose dollar-duration sector constraints, to do so potentially limits further the flexibility of the manager. Secondly, it is the implicit assumption that all securities within a sector share the same systematic exposure to fundamental factors. Yet there is often a degree of arbitrariness about how to classify a security suggesting that this may not always be the case. Also, how fine a sector scheme to use is open to question. Lastly, even if sector limits were appropriate by themselves, this would only be true when the benchmark is an asset portfolio having its own sector weights. What if the benchmark is a liability stream? In this case, sector constraints lose much of their relevance.

- Quality limits usually assume that any combination of securities resulting in the benchmark's average is equally risky. Yet intuitively this should not be the case; a portfolio of all single-A bonds is not as equally credit sensitive as a portfolio of two-thirds Aa and one-third Ba bonds. The process of averaging typically assigns a linearly increasing value to each rating category. This is despite the empirical evidence that the default rates and spread volatilities are not linearly related with rating levels.

In response to these concerns, it would be natural to continually fine-tune the constraints with the goal of crafting a risk profile identical to that of the benchmark. This, however, would most likely be argued as imposing too harsh a set of restrictions the result of which would be a quasi-indexation. Little opportunity would exist for portfolio managers to apply judgement through actively managing their portfolios.

A further concern when using nominal controls is the gap between what is used and the actual objectives underlying the need for constraints. If the goal is to limit the possibility of returning less than some amount while encouraging the manager to maximize relative return, we are left without a unified way of capturing the costs implied by each constraint. What, for instance, makes a sector limit of +/–10 percent appropriate? How does one evaluate the impact of making a duration constraint more binding while relaxing the issuer limitation? Clearly the answers to these questions can be deduced from modelling possible outcomes. However, the tendency may be to impose limits which appear appropriate but are without analytic rigor.

Lastly, such an approach makes it impossible to compare a portfolio's performance with that of another when the second portfolio has slightly different constraints. This will be a problem with any technique which proxies risk as opposed to attempting to actually measure and quantify it.

Maximum Drawdown as a Risk Metric

Drawdown risk is a concept that originated in the commodities markets as a measure of the maximum extent to

FIGURE 3-1

Alternative Drawdown Methodologies

A. Principal drawdown

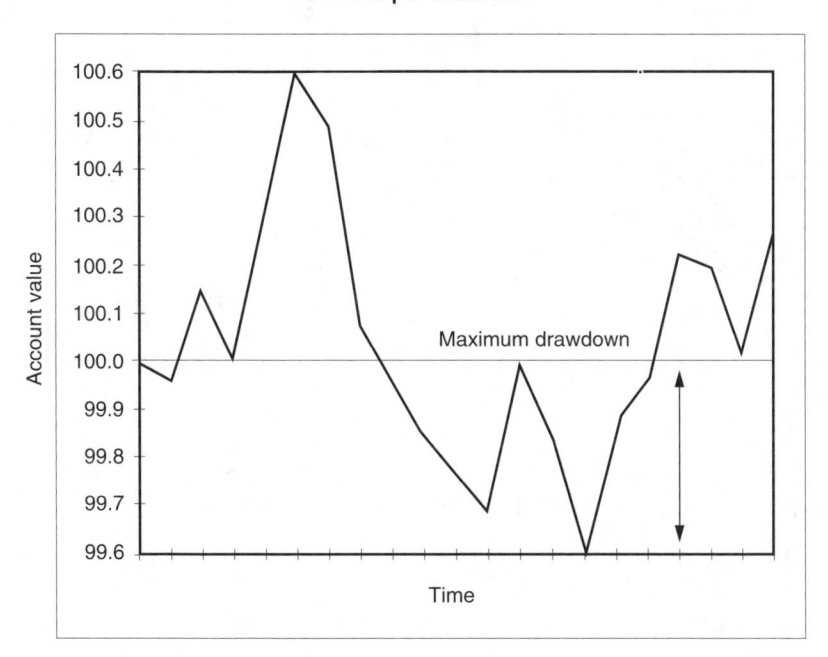

[Chart showing Account value vs Time, y-axis from 99.6 to 100.6, with "Maximum drawdown" labeled]

which returns can be expected to be, or if measured after the fact were, substandard. Maximum drawdown measures the worst string of performance over the measurement period.

There are different way of measuring drawdown, depending on what basis is chosen for defining the peak in a return series and the time horizon. The choices are shown in Figure 3–1.

Figure 3–1(a) assumes that our concern is with a loss of beginning principal, and hence our threshold is a zero rate of return. Figure 3–1(b) supposes that we are interested in the most we can lose relative to where we stood when returns turned negative. Figure 3–1(c) assumes

B. Peak to trough drawdown

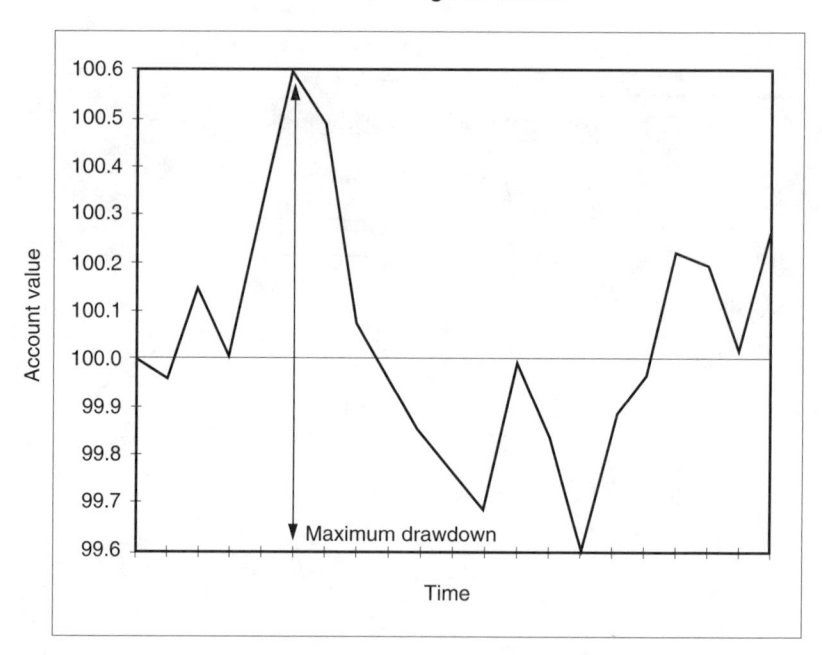

C. Required rate of return drawdown

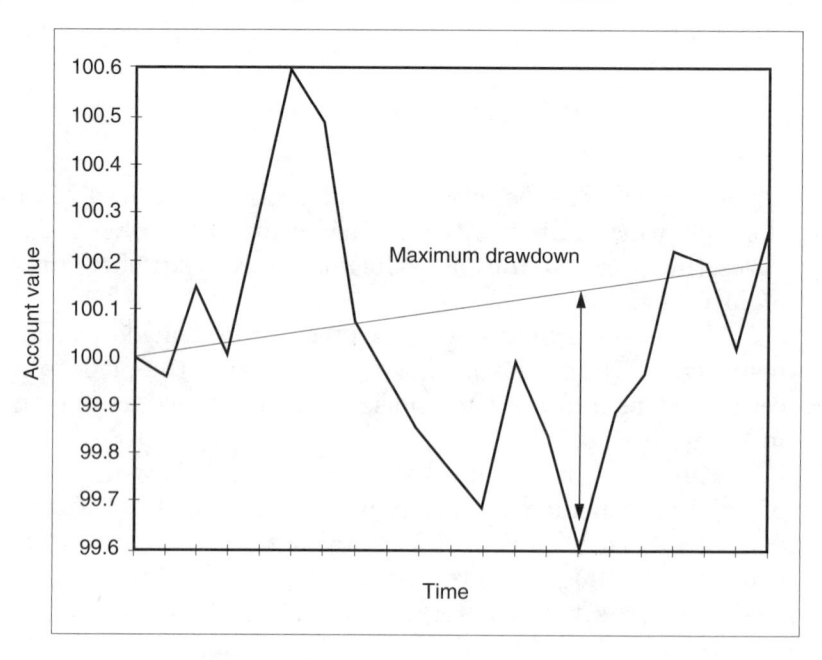

D. Relative drawdown

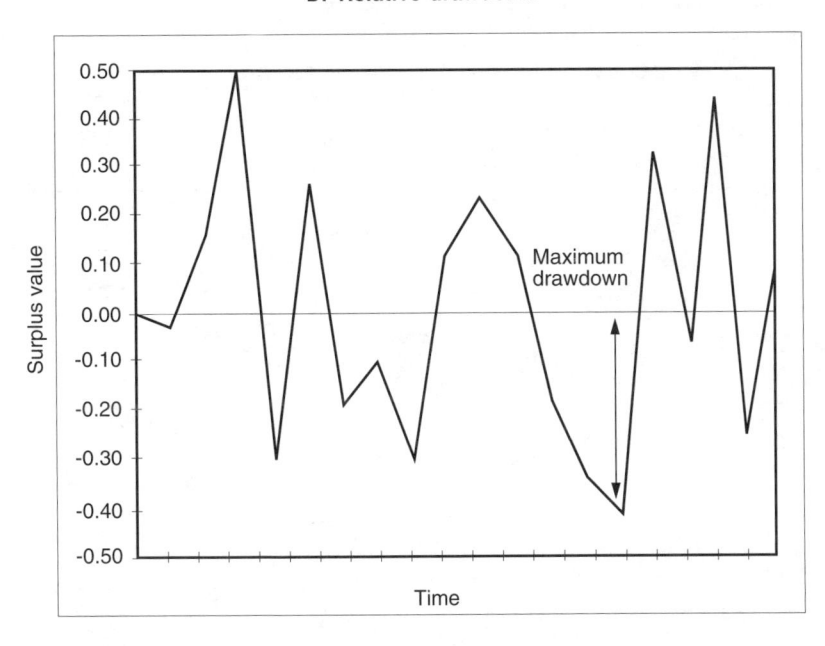

we have a required rate of return where our downside becomes the maximum sustained loss relative to the required return. Figure 3–1(d) is based on the notion that we care about the expected period of underperformance relative to our benchmark.

Calculating expected drawdown requires either a probability-based runs test or the sampling of a number of outcomes to determine the maximum likely drawdown for a given probability of occurrence. Given our calculation of maximum drawdown, performance becomes return per unit of drawdown, with drawdown expressed as a percent of beginning value.

Using the Salomon data described above, it is possible to calculate ex post maximum relative drawdown. Figure 3–2(a) plots the cumulative growth of $100 invested in each of the indices, while Figure 3–2(b) plots the cumula-

Chapter 3

FIGURE 3-2

Cumulative Value

$100 Invested in 30-Year FNMA vs. 7-10 Year Treasuries

Account value

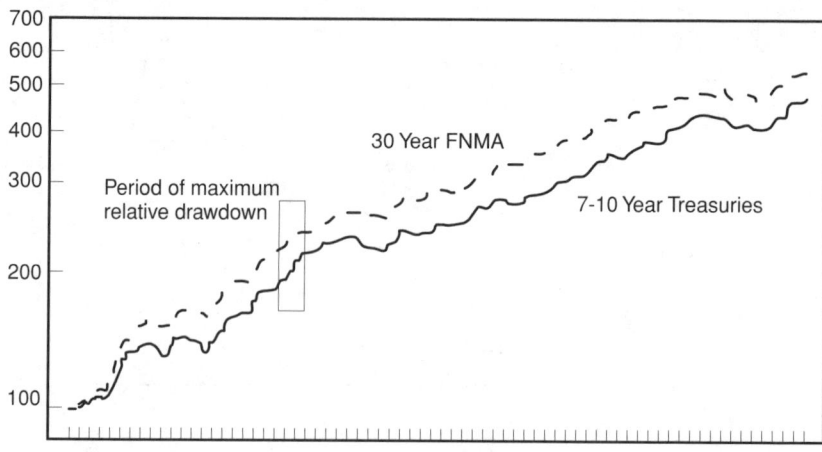

- 30 Year FNMA
- 7-10 Year Treasuries
- Period of maximum relative drawdown

Surplus value

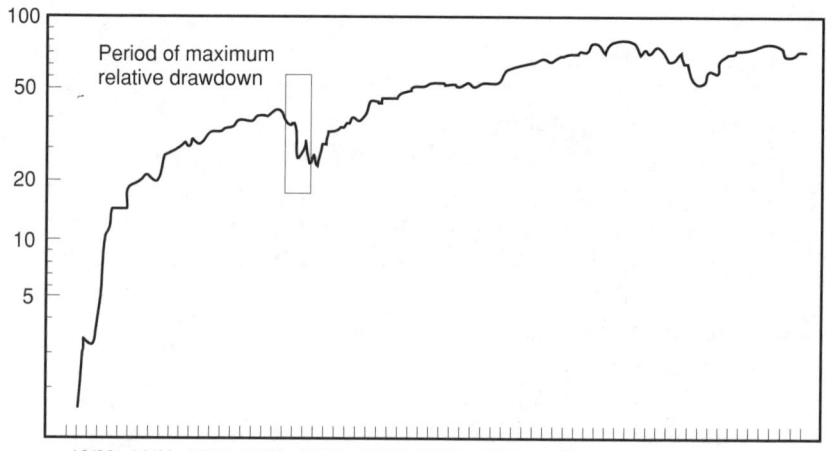

- Period of maximum relative drawdown

tive difference. Maximum drawdown occurred in July 1986 when the mortgage portfolio, having grown to $233.60 by December 1985, rose only 7.09 percent over the next seven months while treasuries rallied by 17.44 percent. The result is a relative drawdown of 44.25 percent of the accumulated gains.

	7–10-Year TSY	30-Year FNMA	Difference
Peak value	$194.39	$233.60	39.21%
Trough value	228.30	250.16	21.86
Drawdown	—	—	44.25

This assessment device captures the maximum drawdown over the 13.5-year measurement period. An alternative approach would be to rank all drawdowns and find the drawdown for a desired percentile.

Drawdown risk, while potentially useful in terms of a capital adequacy measure, has several shortcomings as a performance analytic. First, implicit in the use of maximum drawdown is the assumption that investors do not distinguish between sharp declines in value resulting in drawdowns which occur over short periods of time versus those which extend over longer periods. Second, drawdown fails to discriminate between a single drawdown of, say, $100 versus multiple drawdowns of $100 and subsequent recoveries. Intuitively, it would seem that investments which produced each of the series would be felt to have different risk.

Value at Risk

Value at risk (VAR) is similar to drawdown in that when calculated both measures estimate the amount of expected loss for a particular percent of the time. While drawdown risk evaluates the maximum cumulative loss at any point in time, VAR quantifies how much a portfolio or security can lose for a set horizon.

FIGURE 3-3

Return Distribution

Return distribution

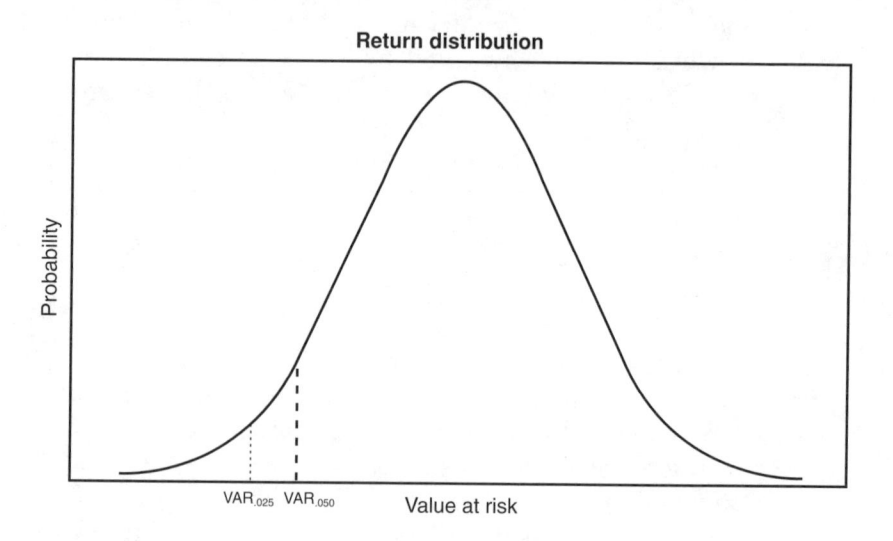

[Bell curve with VAR$_{.025}$ and VAR$_{.050}$ marked on the left tail; x-axis: Value at risk; y-axis: Probability]

Given a set of variances, correlations, and a confidence level, it is possible to calculate VARs for a range of possible outcomes. For example, we might have a distribution of probable returns as shown in Figure 3–3.

Risk is then characterized as follows: If we choose to concern ourselves with those occurrences which can be expected 5 percent of the time, we calculate VAR to be VAR$_{0.05}$ (a 90 percent confidence interval); if, however, we are less sensitive to relative low values, we could calculate VAR to be the level of expected loss 2.5 percent of the time, and hence the relevant VAR is VAR$_{0.025}$. As always, our risk measure, in this case VAR, can be cast in absolute terms, or relative to a benchmark portfolio or index in which case we can think of VAR as surplus at risk. Also, it is a simple matter to translate VAR from dollar terms to rate of return terms.

Used as part of a performance metric, various levels of return/VAR, with VAR expressed as a percent of loss

TABLE 3-1

Periods of Monthly Underperformance

	BIG Treasury 7–10 Year Sector	BIG 30-Year FNMA Sector	Difference
3/31/86	5.076	1.504	−3.572
6/30/86	4.609	1.122	−3.487
2/28/86	5.592	2.382	−3.210
12/31/91	4.646	1.869	−2.777
7/31/92	3.287	0.795	−2.492
12/31/85	4.390	2.132	−2.258
6/30/93	3.022	0.868	−2.154
8/31/93	2.497	0.470	−2.027

relative to beginning market value, become representative of performance.

Again using the Salomon data, we can rank from lowest to highest the months of negative relative returns. By finding values at various percentiles, we can calculate an empirical VAR. Table 3–1 shows the eight worst months (1/20 of the observations). If we are willing to assume that the data is representative of the future, we conclude that 5 percent of the time the mortgage index will underperform the Treasury index by 2.03 percent per month or more.

With the FNMA index producing a excess return of 0.08% annually over the measurement period, the performance metric becomes .08/2.03, or 4.05%. This value can then be compared to alternative strategies and other managers' values to determine whether performance was superior to the alternatives.

The advantages of using Return/VAR include:

- Given a set of parameter inputs (variances and correlations) for all eligible investment markets, value-at-risk calculations are computationally easy to derive and reasonably comparable across portfolio types and managers.

- Value-at-risk measures have the valuable advantage that portfolios can be constructed to minimize the risk of returning less than some critical amount.

Despite compelling reasons for using VAR as a risk and, ultimately, a performance metric, several issues need to be addressed.

- Using VAR for risk-adjusting purposes requires a common set of ex ante inputs (variances and correlations).
- Confidence intervals should be the same for different managers in order to compare their risk exposures (VARs).
- In its simplest form, VAR requires the assumption of normally distributed returns. The last point can be addressed by eliminating the assumption of normality and, instead of employing parametric-based calculations of risk, sample directly a sufficiently rich set of expected returns to calculate the floor rate of return at a targeted probability (or, alternatively, the probability of returning some minimum amount).

Also, if we recognize that returns are potentially non-normal or, in the extreme, distribution-free, the arbitrariness of a single floor return or probability target becomes apparent. When looking at a single point of reference, the two distributions shown in Figure 3–4, while greatly exaggerated for effect, would have the same value at risk. Both return distributions have the same expected return and have the same VARs for a 90 percent confidence interval. Distribution A, however, is not expected to return less than VAR' while Distribution B would be expected to return less than VAR' less than five percent but more than zero percent of the time.

FIGURE 3-4

Return Distribution

Return distribution

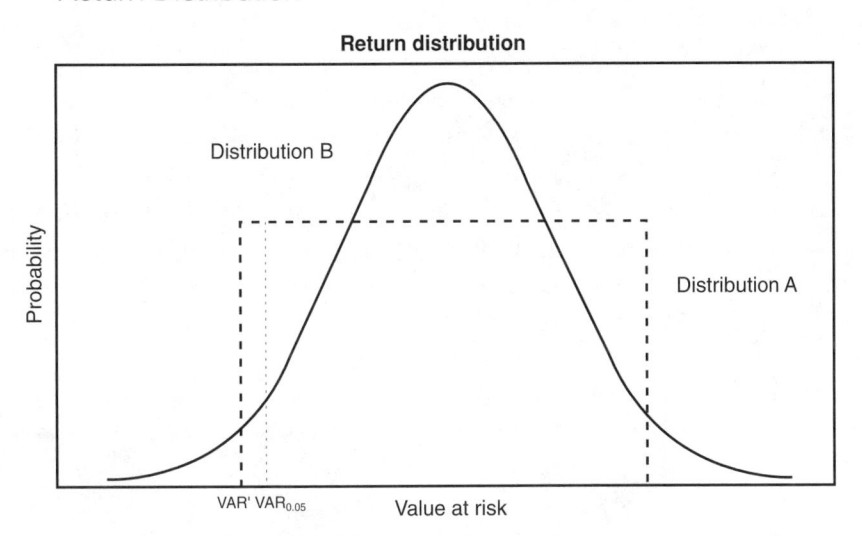

[Figure: A bell-shaped normal distribution curve labeled "Distribution B" with a superimposed rectangular "Distribution A". The x-axis is labeled "Value at risk" with markers VAR' and VAR$_{0.05}$. The y-axis is labeled "Probability".]

The Sharpe Ratio

Sharpe (1966) proposed the use of a reward-to-variability ratio to quantify ex ante and ex post performance. Subsequently called the Sharpe Ratio, the ex ante value is defined as:

$$\text{Sharpe Ratio} \quad \frac{R_p - R_b}{\sigma_{p-b}} \quad (1)$$

where R_p is the portfolio return, R_b is the benchmark return, and σ is the standard deviation of $R_p - R_b$. The ex post version of this equation modifies the numerator and denominator so that they are the average and standard deviation, respectively, of a series of excess returns. Whether analyzed ex ante or ex post, this gives us a measure of the excess return per unit of excess risk.

FIGURE 3-5

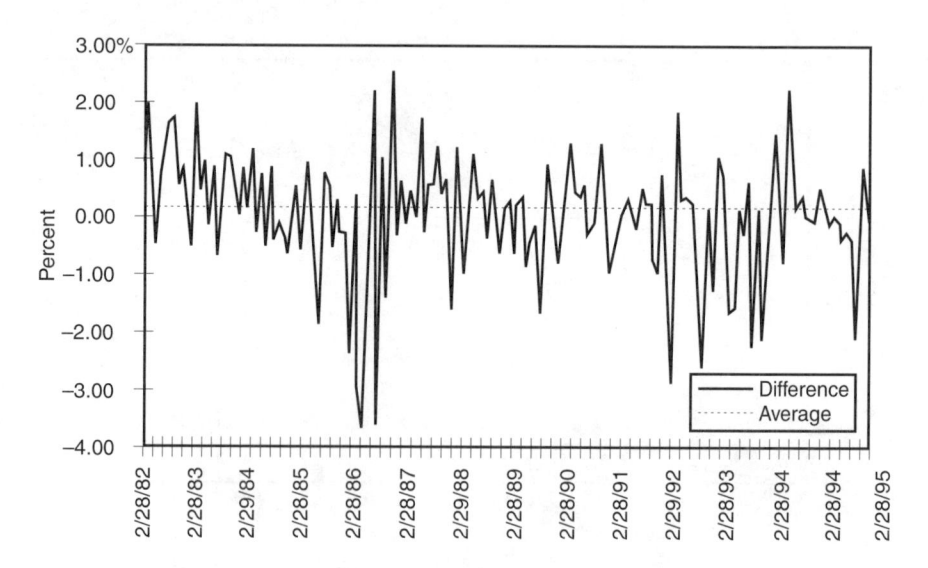

Figure 3–5 plots the excess monthly return of mortgages over Treasuries. From this series, the average excess return is calculated to be 0.08 percent, and the standard deviation of the excess return 1.03 percent, producing a Sharpe Ratio of 7.98 percent. This measure would then be compared to other portfolios to determine whether a better risk/return profile could have been achieved.

While generally accepted as a performance metric, questions have been raised with regard to the measure's suitability in light of increased utilization of non-normally distributed assets. Sharpe (1994) alludes to but chooses not to discuss the possibility that mean and standard deviation are insufficient measures to characterize risk and return. The implication is that additional moments about the distribution may be necessary when considering certain securities and/or portfolios. For a portfolio of securities such as mortgage-backed securities, collateralized mortgage obligations, structured notes, and derivatives whose payoff is expected to be nonnormal, the relevance of standard deviation as a measure of risk is called into question. In addition, it is reasonable to ask whether certain of these securities' return distributions can ever be sufficiently characterized using standard parametric analysis. Having said this, nonnormality of returns is often less of an issue than might be thought. If the benchmark has been properly constructed as an accurate representation of the style and objectives employed to manage the portfolio, the difference in returns is likely to more closely approximate normality than the actual portfolio and benchmark returns.

As always, we run into the issue of whether to use ex ante or ex post risk when calculating performance. If ex post σ_{p-b} incorporates a period of low realized volatility, relative to expected volatility, performance will appear better than it should.

Downside Risk

Downside risk is a generic term for describing the risk of returning less than some defined level. Hence drawdown and VAR are forms of downside risk, albeit ones which require prespecified confidence intervals. More generally measures of downside attempt to quantify the full range of possible return shortfalls.

One variant of downside risk, originally discussed by Markowitz (1959), is semivariance. Semivariance is the sum of deviations which fall below the mean of the distribution squared. Algebraically:

$$SV = \frac{\Sigma (R_1 - \overline{R}, 0)^2}{(n-1)} \qquad (2)$$

and n equals the number of observations of $R_1 - \overline{R} < 0$.

Markowitz points out that semivariance could be used advantageously to quantify risk and construct efficient portfolios. The concern was expressed that then-current computing capabilities and optimization techniques were insufficient to handle problems involving semivariance. This led to the early adoption of variance as a risk metric.

As a measure of risk, semivariance gains relevance when returns are not symmetrically distributed about their mean. When the distribution is symmetrical, semivariance equals 1/2 the variance. Also when returns are symmetrical, semivariance offers little advantage over duration and convexity in terms of capturing interest-sensitive risk.

Downside risk, in its more general form, employs negative deviations relative to a benchmark as opposed to the expected mean of the series.

$$Downside\ risk = \frac{\Sigma\ (R_i - R_{b_i}\ T)^x}{(n-1)} \qquad (3)$$

where T replaces the mean of the excess returns and is instead some predetermined threshold below which results are considered to be unsatisfactory.

The benchmark return can be an index, peer portfolios, liabilities, or an absolute level.

Like semivariance, measures of downside risk have value when the expected or realized distribution is nonsymmetric. When employed using securities whose payoff is expected to be nonsymmetric, downside risk has the following advantageous properties:

- Downside risk does not depend on the assumption of normality.
- Downside measures quantify the character of the entire distribution falling below T as opposed measures which result from having picked a specific confidence interval.
- Both sides of the distribution can be measured and compared.

FIGURE 3-6

Alternative Specification of x.

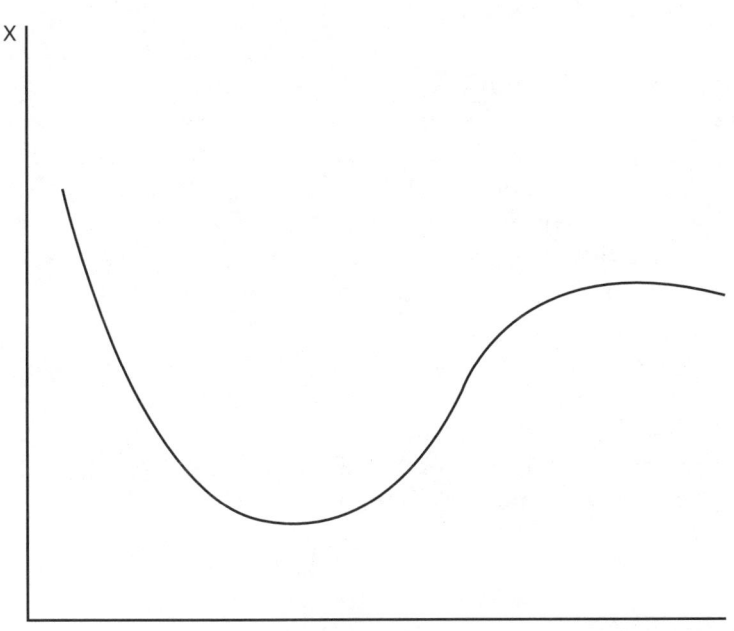

[Figure: curve showing x as a function of $R_p - R_b$, decreasing steeply then rising to a plateau with a small dip]

- Since we are only working with one side of the distribution at a time, we can embed a utility preference or aversion for extreme results by altering the power to which we raise the deviations. A higher power penalizes more heavily negative outliers and, if we choose to measure the upside semivariance, rewards the securities/strategies with large positive outliers. Raising the power from 2 to 3 is analogous to calculating a semiskewness, and from 3 to 4 a semikurtosis. Furthermore, we may find it useful to consider x as a function of $R_p - R_b$. An example of such a function is shown in Figure 3–6, where ever-increasing penalties are imposed for any negative relative returns while the benefit of large positive returns is capped at a fixed level.

Using the Salomon data, $T = 0$, and $x = 2$, we calculate the downside measure to equal .575. For comparison, the upside value is calculated to be .487. By ratioing the two, upside divided by downside, we get a representation of the skewedness of the distribution. Here, a value of .847 suggests that we are more likely to experience large negative relative returns than large positive relative returns. This upside/downside ratio is potentially superior to convexity as a measure of interest rate risk. By incorporating a wide range of possible outcomes, the upside/downside ratio captures a more complete range of interest rate scenarios than the parallel shifts of +/–50 basis points typically used to calculate convexity.

Again, alternative portfolios would have to be compared to see if a better risk/return tradeoff was possible.

CONCLUSION

Properly done, performance measurement is a vitally important part of the investment process. Whether as part of formulating strategy to create optimal portfolios or after the fact in evaluating whether strategy was efficient with respect to risk, performance measurement gives us both a yardstick and guidepost in the management of a fund. Performance management acts as a yardstick by (a) comparing ex ante strategies, thereby enabling us to make informed decisions as to the attractiveness of various choices, or (b) assessing the success of our strategic choices and any additional contribution coming from the managers. It acts as a guidepost by helping to steer the actions of the manager in a direction consistent with the goals and risk tolerances of a fund.

This has been a largely conceptual discussion of the broad considerations necessary to craft a performance measurement scheme and a brief description of a number of alternative risk-adjusted return measures. Whether any of these measures can ever achieve the desired qualities remains an open question. And while we are still far from having a robust, agreed-upon process for measuring performance across clients and managers, there is no reason not to begin the process on an individual client-manager basis, with the intention of promoting dialogue and more-efficient management. Such will be the natural benefits of any discussion of performance, once that discussion focuses on risk as well as return.

REFERENCES

Markowitz, Harry M. 1991. *Portfolio Selection,* 2nd ed. Oxford: Basil Blackwell.

Sharpe, William F. 1966. "Mutual Fund Performance." *Journal of Business* (January): 119–138.

———. 1994. "The Sharpe Ratio." *Journal of Portfolio Management* (Fall): 49–58.

CHAPTER 4
Evolution of Interest Rate Models: A Comparison

Thomas S. Y. Ho
President
Global Advanced Technology Corporation

Interest-sensitive securities are everywhere. The values of these securities are in large part determined by the yield curve and its stochastic movements. Publicly traded bonds are the obvious examples. These include Treasuries, corporate bonds, mortgage-backed securities, and collateralized mortgage obligations. Other important examples are interest rate derivatives: swaps, structured notes, bond futures, and options. Less obvious are the products created by financial institutions, such as loans, certificates of deposit, and retail deposits for banks, and auto insurance, worker's compensation, whole life, and term life for insurance companies.

Interest-rate models that simulate yield curve movements are an integral part of valuing these interest-sensitive securities. With the dramatic growth in the interest-sensitive securities market and an equally dramatic

---

The author thanks Vernon Budinger, Michael Chen, Pamela Hyder, Marcy Markowitz, David Pfeffer, and Serge Shuster for their comments and suggestions.

increase in interest rate risks, the past 20 years have seen tremendous progress in the development of interest-rate models. This progress has made important contributions to our financial markets in that these models are used in trading, portfolio management, risk control, asset/liability strategies, performance measurement, and many other applications.

In applying interest-rate models, financial engineers are typically confronted with the problem of determining which model to choose. Many issues are involved. Which is the "best" model? What are the limitations of the current models? Will these models be obsolete soon? This chapter provides an overview of the models from a historical perspective. I emphasize the conceptual differences between the models rather than the technical and implementational differences. This way, we can better understand the limitations of the various models and apply them appropriately.

There is prior literature that provides a review of interest-rate models. For example, Abken (1990) presents a clear exposition of arbitrage-free models, both the concepts and the implementations, and he contrasts this approach with the traditional hypotheses concerning the term structure of interest rates. Courtadon (1991) provides an excellent survey of bond option models, and derives mathematically the standard valuation models. Further, he also compares the performance of these models. Hull and White (1993) present the basic differences in the models' assumptions and show how these models can be used to value interest-sensitive securities. The exposition is self-contained and the coverage is extensive.

The choice of a model begins with deciding how the model will be used. Too often financial engineers focus on the technical aspects of the models without fully understanding their end usage. I compare the models from a theoretical point of view and then show how such differences affect their applicability. This way, users of models can understand their limitations and choose the appropriate model for their particular application.

BASIC FRAMEWORK

We begin the survey of models with the relative valuation methodology. Relative valuation was first proposed by Black-Scholes (1973) in pricing stock options. In order to understand the validity of the relative valuation approach, we have to begin with the underlying assumptions they made.

These are the basic Black-Scholes assumptions, but extended to interest-rate-sensitive securities:

1. The market is frictionless. There are no taxes and no transaction costs, and all securities are perfectly divisible.

2. The market clears continuously, and there is unlimited riskless borrowing and lending at the continuously compounded (short-term) rate.

3. We define a discount bond of maturity T, a real number (not necessarily an integer), to be a bond that pays $1 at the end of T years, with no other payments to its holder. The bond market is complete in that there exists a discount bond for each maturity.

4. We define a factor to be a source of risk. The risk is modeled by a lognormal diffusion process (geometric Brownian motion) or by the normal process (Gaussian or Brownian motion). A derivative is defined as a security, whose uncertain price movement (the price dynamics) is completely specified by a set of factors called the "underlying factors."

5. There is no riskless arbitrage opportunity at any time.

These assumptions enable us to adjust the basic valuation models to capture the important aspects of the real fixed-income markets. For this reason, financial modeling is often viewed as an art, where judgment is made in the validity of these adjustments, particularly in instances where empirical tests are difficult to perform (for example, designing new products).

The first assumption suggests that the relative valuation approach is less useful for valuing securities where taxes are an important input to the valuation—for example, tax-exempt securities. Nearly all bonds incur transaction costs in trading. For this reason, model prices are viewed as the benchmark prices, and the actual traded price is considered reasonable if the price is within the arbitrage band within which transaction costs are taken into account. On the other hand, the prices of Treasury bonds and their actively traded derivatives are set by arbitrage trading activities. This price formation process is not affected by taxes and transaction costs. For this reason, these securities are appropriate for relative valuation.

Alternative to the second assumption is a discrete time model where we assume that the market clears at regular intervals. Discrete time models often are more intuitive, and if we make the intervals arbitrarily small, the prices obtained by the model should converge to those obtained by the continuous time model. In this chapter, it is more convenient to use the continuous time model to present the basic ideas.

The value of bonds and their derivatives are based on the Treasury term structure. Therefore, the discount function for these securities depends on the discount values derived from actual Treasury prices. However, swap markets are often based on the LIBOR (swap) curve. In this case, we often use the LIBOR (swap) rates to derive the discount function. Assumption 3 above simply asserts the existence of these Treasury or LIBOR (swap) rates.

Factors may be prices of securities that can be bought or sold—for example, stock or bond prices. Or the factors may be the S&P 500 Index, inflation rates, or some other price or market-related index value. Assumption 4 defines derivatives to be securities dependent on a combination (usually a small number) of these factors. For example, in a modern portfolio theory context, stock is not a derivative because we cannot represent stock movement completely by a set of factors like inflation, earnings, and the like. However, if we think of the market value of the firm as the sum of equity value and total bond value, then the stock price is a derivative of the firm value (see Merton 1973).

The purpose of the fifth assumption is to establish the "fair value" of a security. If a security is traded at the model price, then there is no riskless arbitrage opportunity. If a security is traded at a price higher than the model price, we say that the security is "rich." If it is traded at a price lower than the model price, we say that it is "cheap."

The Black-Scholes model assumes that the price of a share of stock (S) follows a lognormal process:

$$dS = \mu S dt + \sigma S dz, \tag{1}$$

where μ is the drift or instantaneous stock return, σ is the volatility, and dz is standard Brownian motion.

The short-term interest rate (r) is a constant. A European call option, whose value is denoted C, is a derivative of S, that is,

$$C = C(S, t) \tag{2}$$

At expiration, the payoff is

$$C = \max(S - K, 0), \tag{3}$$

where K is the option's strike price.

Under these assumptions, the Black-Scholes model shows that, at each instant in time, we can hedge the option position by buying stock on margin. As a result, we can replicate the option by continually adjusting the stock position and the borrowing position. Hence, we can derive the Black-Scholes model:

$$C = SN(d_1) - Xe^{-r(T-t)}N(d_2) \tag{4}$$

$$d_1 = \frac{ln(S/X) + (r + \sigma^2/2)(T-t)}{\sigma(T-t)^{.5}}$$

$$d_2 = d_1 - \sigma(T-t)^{.5}$$

where

C is the value of an European Call Option to buy one share.
S is the current Stock Price.
$N(x)$ is the cumulative probability distribution function for a standardized normal variable (i.e., the probability that such a variable will be less than x).
X is the strike Price of Option.
T is the time of expiration of option.
t is the current time.
σ is the volatility of stock price.
r is the risk-free rate of interest for an investment maturing at time T.

The hedge ratio is H. That is, we hold H shares of stock for each option, and we adjust H continuously to perfect. Note that the hedge ratio is the dynamic hedge.

$$H = N(d_1). \tag{5}$$

The two most important insights provided by this relative valuation are:

1. The derivative instrument is priced relative to the price of the underlying share of stock. The model does not state whether the stock itself is correctly priced.

2. The pricing of the derivative instrument depends on a dynamic hedging argument.

Therefore, in our discussion of interest-rate-sensitive securities, we need to identify, first, the underlying factors of the securities, and second, the dynamic hedging strategy the model requires in order to value the derivative instrument. We will follow this theme throughout the rest of the chapter.

MODIFIED BLACK-SCHOLES MODEL

The Black-Scholes option pricing model is used to price options on common stocks. But, more generally, the model can be used to price any risky asset. In particular, the risky asset can be a long bond, say, for simplicity, a zero coupon bond.

Merton (1974) first proposed the modified Black-Scholes model for bond option valuation. We can treat long-term bond prices as following a stochastic process much like the one that common stock prices follow. Let B denote the bond price and C denote the call option on the bond. We can then assert:

$$dB = \mu B dt + \sigma B dz \tag{6}$$

where

μ is the growth rate in the bond price,
σ is the volatility of B, which is assumed to be a known function of time,
dz is the Wiener process, and

$$C = C(B,t) \tag{7}$$

with $C = \max(B - K, 0)$ at expiration.

Now we can price the option on the long bond by applying the Black-Scholes dynamic hedging arguments.

That is, we can always continuously hedge the bond option by buying the long bond, with a portion of the investment borrowed at the prevailing short-term interest rate. This investment amount and the amount borrowed will change as the bond price rises and falls.

More precisely, the Merton model takes the following form:

$$C = BN(d_1) - Xe^{-r(T-t)}N(d_2) \tag{8}$$

$$d_1 = \frac{ln(B/X) + (r + \sigma^2/2)(T-t)}{\sigma(T-t)^{.5}}$$

$$d_2 = d_1 - \sigma(T-t)^{.5}$$

where the variables are as previously defined. Note that since the option pricing model uses a continuous hedging argument, the instantaneous drift (the instantaneous return) of the bond need not be specified because the bond return does not affect the option price. Whether the bond is over- or undervalued does not affect the option price because the option price is determined relative to the bond price. We can view the drift of the bond return as the short-term rate (r). This approach is generally referred to as the "risk neutral" valuation.

The problem with this approach is the specification of the borrowing rate and the volatility. According to the Black-Scholes model, the short-term rate is fixed (constant). Clearly, the short-term interest rate cannot be assumed constant while the long bond price is uncertain. However, if we try to price an option on a long bond and the expiration of the option is short (for example, three months), then the model is approximately correct.

The specification of the volatility is generally more problematic. The reason is that the option value is much more sensitive to the volatility than to the short-term interest rate. Also, the volatility is not a constant number. Starting from the issue date, the variance of the distribution of bond prices must increase with time (as with stock prices). With the passage of time, the range of possible bond prices must increase. But, as we approach maturity, the bond price must converge to the principal value (assuming no risk of default). Therefore, the range of possible bond prices must eventually decrease with the passage of time. This behavior necessarily violates the assumption often made for stocks, specifically, that the variance of the stock price distribution is linearly related to time.

Ball and Torous (1983) propose a bridge process to explain bond price movement. That is, the initial bond price and the final bond price are fixed, much like a bridge fixed by the bases at the two ends. This bridge process can then capture the following behavior of the options. A short-dated option on a long-term bond would have high option value, while an option expiring near the underlying bond's maturity date would have a low value.

But the bridge process still requires that some assumptions be made regarding how the bond price distribution changes over time. Suppose we assume that the yield curve moves somewhat parallel up and down. And suppose we also assume that the yield curve volatility is constant into the future. Now consider a Treasury bond whose duration is approximated by the weighted average life. Its price volatility is approximated by the duration times a constant.

Schaefer and Schwartz (1984) make use of this result to model bond price movement assuming a bridge process. Therefore, having fewer unknown parameters, or "moving parts," gives more structure to the model. As long as the assumptions are appropriate, the model would be more accurate.

The modified Black-Scholes model has many applications. For a long bond, we can measure the bond price volatility. Therefore, it is subject to little model error (error resulting from using incorrect model input). Modified

Black-Scholes models can be useful for trading certain types of options, such as options on long Treasury bonds. Since the model is simple, it is also used as a pricing benchmark. For example, the implied volatilities of caplets and floorlets are often quoted in terms of the modified Black-Scholes model. This version of the model is referred to as the Black model. (See Black 1976.)

However, there are many disadvantages to the modified Black-Scholes model for other applications. It is difficult to do portfolio analysis because we need to know the appropriate volatility for each type of option. Also, it is difficult to price options on more complicated securities, for example, options on GNMAs. How do we extend the Black-Scholes model to value these other interest-rate-contingent claims?

INTEREST RATE MODELS: ONE FACTOR

In valuing a bond option, it is not necessary to model bond price movements directly. Instead we can first model the underlying interest rate process, and then relate the bond price movements to the underlying interest rate process.

Vasicek (1977) and Dothan (1978) propose a one-factor interest rate movement model. All bond prices are perfectly correlated. The model assumes that all bond prices are driven by the short-term interest rate. This short-term interest rate seeks to converge to a fixed long-term rate. If the long-term rate goes too high, it will tend to revert back to the constant long-run short-term rate. The model may be normal in that the distribution of interest rates obeys a Gaussian process:

$$dr = a(b - r)dt + \sigma dz \qquad (9)$$

where a, b, and σ are constants, b is the long-term rate, and r is the instantaneous short-term rate.

Letting $B(T)$ denote the bond price for maturity T, we assume that

$$B(T) = B(r,t;T) \qquad (10)$$

Courtadon (1982) and Cox, Ingersoll, and Ross (1981) propose the lognormal model, where the interest rate process is of the form:

$$dr = a(l - r)dt + \sigma r^b \, dz \qquad (11)$$

with the variable a defined as the mean-reversion speed. The higher the mean-reversion speed, the faster the short-term rate will converge to the constant long-term rate (l).

That is, we assume that all bond prices depend on the movement of rate (r) and that all bond prices move in tandem depending on one factor. At first, this may seem somewhat counterintuitive. The yield curve seems to have many degrees of freedom in its movement, so how can we assume that there is only one factor involved? In a somewhat surprising discovery, Litterman and Scheinkman (1991) show that, historically, the yield curve has tended to move up and down in tandem, making a "parallel shift." This parallel movement explains over 80 percent of the yield curve movements historically. Dybvig (1989) extends this discovery to explain why the one-factor model offers an appropriate first-order approximation to modeling the yield curve movement. In other words, a one-factor model may be acceptable from an empirical standpoint.

But on a theoretical basis, the one-factor model just discussed is not a direct extension of the Black-Scholes model. The model cannot assure that all bonds can be priced on a risk-neutral basis, that is, by discounting the cash flows by the (stochastic) risk-free rate, as in the Black-Scholes model. This is so because the risk-free rate (r) is not a security that can be bought and sold in implementing a dynamic hedging strategy. However, the arbitrage-free condition does impose a condition on the drift (μ) and the risk (σ) for all bonds. This condition is:

$$(\mu - r)/\sigma = \lambda \tag{12}$$

Lambda depends on the factor (r) and time, but it is independent of the nature of the derivatives, which in this case are the interest-rate-sensitive securities. Lambda is called the market price of risk for the factor (r).

This analysis shows that there is a risk premium ($\mu - r$) in the returns on bonds, and that this risk premium is proportional to the standard deviation of bond returns. This premium is called the term premium. Cox, Ingersoll, and Ross (1981) and Abken (1990) clearly explain the concept of term premium and compare it with the traditional hypotheses of liquidity premium and preferred habitat. In essence, the arbitrage-free argument cannot provide additional economic insights into the specification of the term premium with respect to economic variables. When we assume that there is no term premium, we are positing that the "local expectations hypothesis" holds.

Cox, Ingersoll, and Ross (1985) propose a general equilibrium model. In their model, the underlying factors are production processes, investment, and the consumption behavior of individuals. The yield curve becomes the derivative of these factors. In this general equilibrium model, we can analyze the behavior of the yield curve as a function of the underlying economic activities. Since the market price of risk for each of the risk sources (for example, production risk) is unobservable, we have to make some assumptions about the market price of risk in each case in order to gain insight into the yield curve's behavior.

For these models, we cannot use the factors as hedging instruments. We first have to make certain assumptions about the market price of risk. Then we can derive the price movement relationship between two derivatives (for example, a bond and a bond option) based on these factors. From this relationship, we can then calculate the hedge ratios.

INTEREST RATE MODELS: TWO FACTOR

One-factor models do not allow for the yield curve becoming positively sloped or negatively sloped as a source of risk. If such a risk affects the value of a security, then a one-factor model would be inappropriate. Brennan and Schwartz (1979), Richard (1978), and Longstaff and Schwartz (1992) propose a two-factor model where the two factors are the short-term interest rate and the long-term interest rate (the consol rate).

The model is specified as follows:

$$dr = a(l - r)dt + s_1 r\, dz \qquad (13)$$

$$dl = s_2\, l\, dw \qquad (14)$$

where $dw dz = \rho$

and where r denotes the short-term rate, l denotes the long-term rate, s_1 and s_2 are the standard deviations of the short rate and long rate, respectively, and ρ is the correlation between the two rates. Now, we assert that for any bond with maturity T, $B(T)$ is determined by both the short-term rate and long-term rate. Since the long-term rate is for a consol bond that we can buy and sell, only the short-term rate requires a market price of risk. Hence the price of a bond, B, of maturity T varies with the short-term and long-term rates and the market price of risk:

$$B = B(r, l, \lambda;\, T) \qquad (15)$$

ARBITRAGE-FREE MODELS: NORMAL FORM

Interest rate models assert that the shape of the yield curve depends on the short-term rate (one-factor model) or the short-term and long-term rates (two-factor model) and the market price of risk for the short rate. Therefore, these models may be used to determine the fair values of Treasury bonds, according to theory.

The general equilibrium model takes this approach further. The general equilibrium model incorporates economic information on production, the inflation rate, and other factors to explain the behavior of the yield curve. The usefulness of this approach is that it enables investors to decide on the fair values of bonds relative to economic activities.

On the other hand, if we want to price an option relative to the underlying bond without questioning whether the bond is fairly priced or not, the equilibrium model would not be able to provide an accurate value. In this case, we should take the observed yield curve as given, and develop a one-factor model of yield curve movement. This approach is the same as the Black-Scholes model, which takes the stock price as given and develops an option price relative to the stock price. These models are called arbitrage-free rate movement models. Ho and Lee (1986), Hull and White (1990), Pedersen et al (1990), and Jamshidian (1989) are some examples of models of this type.

For example, Ho and Lee propose the following model:

$$dr = \theta(t)dt + \sigma dz \qquad (16)$$

where $\theta(t)$ is a function of time such that the values of the Treasury zero coupon (i.e., the term structure of interest rates) bonds fit the Treasury yield curve exactly. σ is assumed to be constant, although Ho and Lee suggest that the model could be extended to allow σ to be time dependent.

By fitting the Treasury spot curve to the Treasury observed bond prices, and not basing the relative valuation on a short-term interest rate, we do not need to estimate or assume a value for the market price of risk of the short-term rate. The interest rate process is the implied (or "risk neutral") process, and the resulting distribution of interest rates cannot be interpreted as the rates forecasted by the debt market. This result is similar to the Black-Scholes model: The stock return process should not be interpreted as that forecasted by the stock market.

Pedersen, Shiu, and Thorlacius (1990) and Ritchken and Boenawan (1990) extend the Ho and Lee model to incorporate the time dependent behavior of interest rate volatility. This time dependency is called the term structure of volatility. That is, equation **(16)** is modified:

$$dr = \theta(t)dt + \sigma(t)dz \qquad (17)$$

When there is a term structure of volatility, we can determine both the short-term rate volatility and the long-term rate volatility for the next instant. If the short-term rate volatility is higher than the long-term rate volatility, the yield curve would exhibit a mean reverting behavior. If interest rates continue to rise, the yield curve would continue to be inverted. In that case, interest rates would be more likely to fall than rise in the future. Conversely, if interest rates continue to fall, the yield curve would continue to steepen. In this case, interest rates are more likely to rise in the future.

This mean-reverting process differs from the Cox-Ingersoll-Ross model in that the arbitrage-free model does not assert that there is a constant long-term rate to which the short-term rate will always seek to converge. Instead, in the arbitrage-free model, the analogous long-term rate changes continuously, as defined by the shape of the yield curve.

Clearly, the term structure of volatility is very important to pure interest rate options like caps and floors. However, it does not affect the value of pure cash flows in an arbitrage-free model. In a recent paper, Ritchken and Sankarasubramanian (1994) study the dependencies of interest-rate-sensitive securities on the specification of the term structure of volatility.

Hull and White (1990) combine the arbitrage-free approach with the Cox-Ingersoll-Ross specification of mean reversion. Specifically, in their model:

$$dr = (\theta(t) - ar)dt + \sigma dz \qquad (18)$$

where a and s are constant. The bond price at time t can be determined as a function of the short rate.

Arbitrage-free analytical solutions are important because they enable us to achieve a precise valuation, in contrast to the approximate valuations obtained using a binomial model or a finite difference methodology. Analytical solutions of some standard bond options have been derived for these one-factor normal models.

The arbitrage-free approach takes the yield curve as given. Ho and Lee also suggest estimating the term structure of volatility by fitting the implied volatilities to observed interest rate contingent claim prices, for example, the prevailing prices of caps and floors. The securities used to derive the yield curve and the term structure of volatility are called benchmark securities (the set of benchmark securities is called a bellwether portfolio). Today, this procedure is called "calibration." The theory of arbitrage-free modeling justifies this calibration methodology. In essence, by using calibration, we are valuing a security relative to the value of the benchmark securities.

In contrast, one can fit an interest rate model to the term structure by estimating a market price of risk that can best fit the observed yield curve. However, the model will determine a specific market price of risk as well as the real (not implied) probability distribution of the short-term rate.

The concept of relative valuation on which the arbitrage-free model is based can sometimes involve counterintuitive situations. For example, during 1993 the yield curve was historically steep (positively sloped). As a result, the implied forward rates rose sharply. Many fixed-income investment professionals attributed the steepness of the yield curve to a significant imbalance of supply and demand in the bond market. They therefore viewed the implied forward rates as very poor predictors of future interest rates.

Suppose the arbitrage-free model was calibrated to market bond prices in such an environment. Caps, for example, would be priced on a risk-neutral basis (i.e., assuming a zero term premium). But the caps had high values, even though many investment professionals did not expect market interest rates to reach the cap strike prices. How could the arbitrage-free model provide correct prices in such a situation? How should investment professionals interpret the prices obtained from the model?

In using an arbitrage-free model, the cap is priced relative to the yield curve and the assumed volatilities. The price of the cap is therefore the cost of replicating the cap by using the bonds along the yield curve. When the yield curve is considered "steep," the long bond is "cheap" relative to a short-term bond. In replicating a cap, we need to short the long bond and buy the short-term bond. As a result, hedging becomes expensive. That is to say, roughly speaking (ignoring Jensen's inequality and other technical issues), when the forward rates differ from the investor's predicted rates, part of the cost of the interest rate option (inherent in its calculated value) is this "hedge cost."

ARBITRAGE-FREE MODELS: LOGNORMAL FORM

Thus far we have discussed an arbitrage-free model involving a one-factor Gaussian process. The Ho-Lee model with constant volatility tends to have negative interest rates, a feature many fixed-income professionals found undesirable. However, this problem can be eliminated by allowing for time-dependent volatility. Ritchken and Boenawan (1990) and Pedersen, Shiu, and Thorlacius (1990) discuss appropriate modifications of the Ho and Lee model to eliminate this problem.

Alternatively, one can use a lognormal model. Black, Derman, and Toy (1990), and Black and Karasinski (1991) propose that short- term interest rates follow the process:

$$d(logr) = (\theta(t) - f(t)logr)dt + \sigma(t)dz, \qquad (19)$$

where $\theta(t)$, $f(t)$, and $\sigma(t)$ are arbitrary functions that fit the current Treasury yield curve. Such an interest rate process assures that all interest rates are positive (since it is not acceptable for the log function to take a negative argument). However, there are other somewhat undesirable features of this model for some applications. First, the lognormal model may not permit negative forward rates, and such a situation might happen when the yield curve is steeply downward-sloping. Second, if the mean-reversion speed is very low, forward interest rates might rise very quickly. Third, the lognormal model does not usually lead to an analytical solution for some basic interest-rate-sensitive securities, in contrast to the normal model.

ARBITRAGE-FREE MODELS: N-FACTOR MODEL

A third arbitrage-free approach involves utilizing a two-factor model. Instead of focusing on long rates and short rates, the model simply focuses on an extra degree of freedom in the movement of interest rates. In particular, the yield curve can move up and down as well as steepen or flatten. The characterization two factor refers to the two possible movements of the yield curve.

Heath, Jarrow, and Morton (1990, 1992) describe a framework for developing an n-factor model. They suggest specifying all the forward rates in the future in such a way that the forward rates fit both the yield curve and the term structure of volatility. This approach does not base the movement of the yield curve on a short-term rate or a long-term rate. The only requirement for these yield curve movements is that they be arbitrage-free.

Two-factor models have many possible applications. A one-factor model is often used for valuing mortgages. However, a two-factor model may be more appropriate because prepayment behavior tends to depend more on the long-term rate, while the discount rates will depend on the short-term rate. The two-factor model may also be more appropriate for callable bonds: The bond value on which the value of the embedded option rests will depend on the long-term rate, while the discount rates may depend on the short-term rate, particularly when the bond is likely to be called soon. A change in the shape of the yield curve can change the value of a callable bond significantly. U.S. securities such as spread options, whose value depends on the spread between the long-term rate and the short-term rate, require two-factor models since the value of such options is sensitive to the changing shape of the yield curve.

While an n-factor model can clearly provide a more complete description of yield curve movements, such a model requires more inputs for calibration. Often, unfortunately, all the needed information is not easily available. Also, the model may require significant computing time.

RELATIVE VALUATION AND HEDGE RATIOS

As discussed previously, central to the relative valuation process is the assumption regarding dynamic hedging, continually replicating a derivative using basic bonds. For an arbitrage-free model, how do we calculate the hedge ratios for derivatives?

In principle, when we use a one-factor model, we only need one basic bond to hedge the derivative because the model asserts that all bond and derivative price movements are perfectly correlated. While a one-factor model, in general, provides a reasonable value, we cannot make the same assumption for hedging purposes. In formulating a hedge of a derivative using basic bonds, we have to consider all the possible instantaneous movements of the yield curve.

One approach, called key rate duration, has been proposed by Ho (1990, 1992). Along similar lines, Reitano (1990) proposes partial duration, and Peng and Dattatreya (1995) propose Treasury key rate duration. In brief, key rate duration calculates the proportional change in price of any interest-rate-sensitive security to a small change in a key rate. We can calculate the key rate duration for each of a set of key rates along the yield curve.

Theoretically, the sum of the key rate durations is the "effective duration" measure, which is the price sensitivity measure to a parallel shift of the yield curve. That is, key rate duration involves a decomposition of the effective duration measure, identifying a bond's value sensitivity to each key rate. For example, a T-year zero coupon bond has zero key rate duration for all the key rates except for the T-year rate. For the T-year rate, the key rate duration is the duration of the bond, T years.

We can calculate the key rate durations of a derivative. And we can always determine a portfolio of basic bonds (the hedging instruments) such that the portfolio has the same set of key rate durations and the same value

FIGURE 4-1

Evolution of Models

Model	Normal	Lognormal
Interest rate		
1-factor	Vasicek (1977)	Cox-Ingersoll-Ross (1985)
2-factor		Brennan-Schwartz (1979)
Arbitrage-free		
1-factor	Ho-Lee (1986)	Black-Derman-Toy (1990)
2-factor	Brace-Musiela (1995)	Heath-Jarrow-Morton (1992)

as the derivative. When the yield curve moves, the movement must have the same effect on the hedging portfolio and the derivative. If we continually revise this hedging portfolio, we can replicate the derivative. The effectiveness of this replicating strategy is an empirical issue. McCoy (1994) empirically replicates a two-year call option on a 10-year current coupon bond, and also replicates a corporate callable bond. His results lend support to the usefulness of the key-rate-duration approach to determining appropriate hedge ratios for derivative instruments.

CONCLUSION

This chapter provides a brief overview of the available models to value interest-rate-sensitive securities. It explains that there are three main basic classes of models: the modified Black-Scholes model, interest-rate models, and arbitrage-free models. Within the latter two classes, we can assume either a lognormal rate process or a normal rate process. Each class of models includes one-factor, two-factor, or n-factor models. Figure 4–1 indicates the evolution of models for valuing interest-rate-sensitive securities. I have discussed the strengths and weaknesses of each of these types of models, but I have not discussed any implementation issues, such as continuous time versus discrete time models. The interested reader is referred to Cox, Ross, and Rubinstein (1979).

Another area of research with growing importance is the econometric estimation of term structure models. Campbell, Lo, and MacKinlay (1994) provide an extensive survey of the work in this area to date.

What is a good model? The answer to this question necessarily depends on the intended use. Traders often prefer a simple bond model that offers them speed and intuitive understanding of the formulation. They also need to know the values of their trades relative to the benchmarks that they continually monitor. In these cases, often relatively simple models are required.

In managing a portfolio, or performing asset/liability management, we need to value and manage the risk exposure. It is therefore important to have a consistent framework for valuing a large cross-section of bonds. In general, an arbitrage-free model is preferred because such a model is calibrated to benchmark bonds that portfolio managers can observe. The choice between a one-factor model and a two-factor model has to depend on the nature of the portfolio.

In formulating portfolio strategies where the values of certain selected economic parameters are important, we should consider n-factor models or general equilibrium models, which can also take the economic factor into account. Arbitrage-free models do well in interpolating values based on the observed values of the selected benchmark securities. General equilibrium models enable us to extrapolate the values, guided by the modeling of the economic behavior.

For insurance companies and banks, interest rate models are used for more than the valuation of securities. They are also used to generate interest rate scenarios for cash flows modeling or preparing income simulations.

Also, interest rate models are used to formulate crediting or rate-setting strategies for their products. Babbel, Stricker, and Vanderhoof (1990), Griffin (1989), and Ho, Scheitlin, and Tam (1995) discuss these issues and show that the arbitrage-free models enable financial institutions to value their products (which are not traded) relative to publicly traded bonds.

Interest rate models have numerous applications in the fixed income market, and research will continue to progress along many avenues. For example, recent research concerning the relative movement of foreign and domestic yield curves has made it easier to value quantos and other cross-currency instruments. Brace and Musiela (1995) and others have proposed new approaches to building n-factor models. Also, progress is being made in combining interest rate risks with credit risks, equity risks, or currency risks (see, for example, Kishimoto 1989, Lesseig and Stock 1995, Wei 1994, and Hull and White 1994).

In the end, interest-rate models are tools for making decisions. As our tools are refined and improved, we must still bear in mind that selecting the most appropriate tool is usually more important than using the most sophisticated model.

REFERENCES

Abken, P. A. 1990. "Innovations in Modeling the Term Structure of Interest Rates." *Federal Reserve Bank of Atlanta Economic Review* (July/August).

Babbel, D., R. Stricker, and I. Vanderhoof. 1990. "Performance Measurements for Insurers." New York, NY: Goldman, Sachs & Company.

Ball, C. A., and W. N. Torous. 1983. "Bond Price Dynamics and Options." *Journal of Financial and Quantitative Analysis* (December): 517–31.

Black, F. 1976. "The Pricing of Commodity Contracts." *Journal of Economics* (March).

Black, F., E. Derman, and W. Toy. 1990. "A One-Factor Model of Interest Rates and Its Application to Treasury Bond Options." *Financial Analysts Journal* (January/February): 33–39.

Black, F., and P. Karasinski. 1991. "Bond and Option Pricing When Short Rates Are Lognormal." *Financial Analysts Journal* (July/August): 52–59.

Black, F., and M. Scholes. 1973. "The Pricing of Options and Corporate Liabilities." *Journal of Political Economy* 81: 637–59.

Brace, A, and M. Musiela. 1995. "A Multifactor Gauss Markov Implementation of Heath, Jarrow, Morton." Working paper.

Brennan, M. J., and E. S. Schwartz. 1979. "A Continuous Time Approach to the Pricing of Bonds," *Journal of Banking and Finance:* 133–55.

Campbell, J. Y., A. W. Lo, and A. C. MacKinlay, 1994. "The Econometrics of Financial Markets: Models of the Term Structure of Interest Rates." Massachusetts Institute of Technology working paper (May).

Courtadon, G. 1982. "The Pricing of Options on Default-Free Bonds." *Journal of Financial and Quantitative Analysis* 17 (March): 75–100.

———.1991. "A Survey of Bond Option Pricing Models." New York: CIBC working paper.

Cox, J. C., J. E. Ingersoll, and S. A. Ross. 1985. *Econometrica* (March) 363–84.

———.1981. "A Re-Examination of Traditional Hypotheses about the Term Structure of Interest Rates." *Journal of Finance* (September): 769–99.

Cox, J. C., S. A. Ross, and M. Rubinstein. 1979. "Option Pricing: A Simplified Approach." *Journal of Financial Economics:* 229–63.

Dothan, L. U. 1978. "On the Term Structure of Interest Rates." *Journal of Financial Economics* (January): 59–69.

Dybvig, P. H. 1989. "Bond and Bond Option Pricing Based on the Current Term Structure." Washington University working paper (February).

Griffin, M. 1989. "The Excess Spread Approach to Pricing and Designing the SPDA." New York: Morgan Stanley Research.

Heath, D., R. Jarrow, and A. Morton. 1992. "Bond Pricing and the Term Structure of Interest Rates: A New Methodology." *Econometrica* 1: 77–105.

———. 1990. "Bond Pricing and the Term Structure of Interest Rates: A Discrete Time Approximation." *Journal of Financial and Quantitative Analysis* 4 (December): 419–40.

Ho, T. S. Y. 1992. "Key Rate Durations: Measures of Interest Rate Risks." *The Journal of Fixed Income* (September).

———. 1990. Strategic Fixed-Income Investment. New York: Dow Jones Irwin.

Ho, T. S. Y., and S. B. Lee. 1986. "Term Structure Movements and Pricing Interest Rate Contingent Claims." *The Journal of Finance* 5 (December): 1011–29.

Ho, T. S. Y., A. G. Scheitlin, and K. O. Tam. 1995. "Total Return Approach to Performance Measurement." In *The Financial Dynamics of the Insurance Industry*, E. I. Altman and I. T. Vanderhoof, eds. Burr Ridge, IL: Irwin.

Hull, J., and A. White. 1990. "Pricing Interest-Rate-Derivative Securities." *The Review of Financial Studies* 4.

———. 1993. "One-Factor Interest-Rate Models and the Valuation of Interest-Rate Derivative Securities." *Journal of Financial and Quantitative Analysis* 2 (June): 235–53.

———. 1994. "Numerical Procedures for Implementing Term Structure Models II: Two-Factor Models." *The Journal of Derivatives* (Winter): 37–47.

Jamshidian, F. 1989. "An Exact Bond Option Formula." *Journal of Finance* 1 (March): 205–09.

Kishimoto, N. 1989. "Pricing Contingent Claims under Interest Rate and Asset Price Risk." *Journal of Finance:* 571–89.

Lesseig, V. P., and D. Stock. 1995. "The Impact of Correlation of Firm Value and Interest Rate Changes Upon Bond Risk Premia." Working paper (February).

Litterman, R., and J. Scheinkman. 1991. "Common Factors Affecting Bond Returns." *Journal of Fixed Income* (June): 54–61.

Longstaff, F. A., and E. S. Schwartz. 1992. "Interest Rate Volatility and the Term Structure: A Two-Factor General Equilibrium Model." *Journal of Finance*: 1259–82.

McCoy, W. 1994. "Bond Dynamic and Return Attribution." *Journal of Portfolio Management* (Winter).

Merton, R. C. 1973. "The Theory of Rational Option Pricing." *Bell Journal of Economics and Management Science* (Spring): 141–83.

———. 1974. "On the Pricing of Corporate Debt: the Risk Structure of Interest Rates." *Journal of Finance:* 449–70.

Pedersen, H., E. Shiu, and A. Thorlacius. 1990. "Arbitrage-Free Pricing of Interest Rate Contingent Claims." *Transactions of the Society of Actuaries:* 41.

Peng, S. Y., and R. E. Dattatreya. 1995. *The Structured Note Market*. Chicago, IL: Probus.

Reitano, R. 1990. "Nonparallel Yield Curve Shifts and Durational Leverage." *The Journal of Portfolio Management* (Summer): 62–67.

Richard, S. F. 1978. "An Arbitrage Model of the Term Structure of Interest Rates." *Journal of Financial Economics* (March): 33–57.

Ritchken, P., and K. Boenawan. 1990. "On Arbitrage-Free Pricing of Interest Rate Contingent Claims." *Journal of Finance* (March): 259–64.

Ritchken, Peter, and L. Sankarasubramanian. 1994. "The Volatility of the Term Structure and the Pricing of Interest Sensitive Claims." Working paper (April).

Schaefer, S. M., and E. S. Schwartz. "A Two-Factor Model of the Term Structure: An Approximate Solution." *Journal of Financial and Quantitative Analysis* (December): 413–24.

Vasicek, O. 1977. "An Equilibrium Characterization of the Term Structure." *Journal of Financial Economics:* 177–88.

Wei, J. Z. 1994. *"Valuing Differential Swaps."* The Journal of Derivatives (Spring) 64–76.

CHAPTER 5

Default Risk-Based Pricing in a Two-Asset Setting

Duen-Li Kao
Director of Investment Research
General Motors Investment Management Corporation

Over the last two decades, the evolution of fixed-income asset pricing has centered around term structure theories and option valuation techniques. Conventionally, these pricing processes are driven solely by the information embedded in interest rate movements and market prices (e.g., volatilities, Treasury yield curve, and yield spreads). The riskiness and mispricing (cheap/richness) of a security are implied by its rating, sector, and maturity (or duration). The appropriateness of this basic pricing framework becomes questionable when dealing with securities that have very limited liquidity and high credit risks, or whose payoffs also heavily depend upon bond covenants and collateral values. Examples include lower-quality bonds, privately placed bonds, convertible bonds, commercial mortgages, commercial mortgage-backed securities, and options on two risky assets (rainbow options).

The author would like to thank Tom Ho and Pat Corcoran for their helpful comments and discussion.

Junk bonds provide an excellent case for why the standard interest rate option pricing model needs additional building blocks. Market participants have long been aware that the term "option adjusted spread" bears little relevance to the valuation of junk bonds for the following reasons:

1. Market price quotes either are not available or are not very reliable for most lower-quality, illiquid bonds;

2. The firm's specific risk and equity risk can be the dominant factors; and

3. The values of options often are not driven by interest rates but by factors such as operating results.

To solve analytical difficulties in valuing these bonds, we need to incorporate two additional elements into the standard interest rate option pricing framework: default risk (default probabilities and losses), and the relationship between interest rates and other pricing factors. By calculating default probabilities and credit losses, we assess the financial fundamentals and intrinsic value of the asset directly, without relying on the availability of "right" market prices and yield spreads. By specifying the relationship (the correlations) between assets, we consider all the risky assets relevant to pricing simultaneously. The result is a dynamic multi-variate contingent claim asset pricing model that emphasizes the importance of analyzing the firm's financial risk and prosperity.

Extending the works of Corcoran and Kao (1994) on assessing credit risk of commercial mortgage-backed securities (CMBS) and Ambarish and Subrahmanyam (1989) on high-yield bond valuation, this chapter presents a two-asset binomial pricing model in a risk-neutrality framework. This method can be applied easily to analyze credit risk of illiquid corporate bonds or mortgage securities.

THE CONCEPT OF A DEFAULT RISK-BASED PRICING METHOD

The major difference between default risk-based pricing and the standard interest rate option pricing rests on how credit risk is assessed and adjusted. The conventional method of fixed income valuation requires market credit spread (or option adjusted spread) and quality rating as inputs to adjust *yield measure* upward in discounting promised cash flows. Instead of adjusting the discount rates for credit risks, we can downward-adjust promised cash flows for the issuer's default likelihood and losses in the event of default. The discount rate under this framework would be the risk-free rate, or a rate adjusted for non-credit-risk-related factors (e.g., illiquidity premium). These two approaches to the bond valuation are essentially equivalent from the viewpoint of risk certainty.

The concept of risk neutrality as applied to fixed income valuation and risk measures is nothing new.[1] In fact, recently there has been renewed interest in academic literature as to how the bankruptcy (or default) process can be incorporated *explicitly* and/or *exogenously* into the conventional interest rate option pricing for default-free debt.[2] This is in contrast to the more traditional contingent claim pricing model whereby the bankruptcy is determined *implicitly* by comparing the two sides of the firm's balance sheet (e.g., Merton 1974).

---

1. See Kao (1993a) for a more detailed discussion of the development of the default risk-based pricing approach, and Kao (1993b) for the comparison with other pricing methodologies as applied to the valuation of private securities.
2. For examples, refer to Longstaff and Schwartz (1995), Jarrow, Lando, and Turnbull (1995), Leland (1994), Kim, Ramaswamy, and Sundaresan (1989) on corporate bonds; Ginzburg, Maloney, and Willner (1994) on floating rate debt; Toft (1995) on equity derivatives; Titman and Torous (1989) on commercial mortgages; Madan and Unal (1994) on certificates of deposit; and Nadler (1995) on emerging market debt.

However, while the bankruptcy (or default) process may be treated explicitly and exogenously in those recent models, its specification still heavily relies on the default trigger assumption,[3] the availability of credit yield spread information, and credit ratings. As a result, these models can still be difficult to apply to the pricing of illiquid and privately placed securities. The misspecification of the default trigger assumption in particular can generate delinquency and recovery results significantly different from those empirically observed in the market.

Alternatively, one can follow the normal process that a credit analyst in a real-world setting would use in evaluating the firm's default likelihood and financial risks: directly evaluating items on balance sheets, income statements, and collateral underlying the security; analyzing financial and business risk of related industry and economic sectors; etc. The resulting assessment of default probability and recovery over the holding time period should provide more useful inputs to a default risk-based pricing model, especially in evaluating illiquid and privately placed securities. By doing so, the model can produce an intrinsic value that is not subject to the short-term trading noise or the availability and reliability of market information. By retaining the essential elements of an interest rate option pricing, a default risk-based debt pricing model can still properly evaluate conventional optionality embedded in a security.

EMPIRICAL EXAMPLES OF DEFAULT RISK-BASED PRICING

Perhaps the most direct way to test a pricing methodology is to compare the "fair value" computed by the model with

---

3. Default trigger assumption specifies the critical asset value at which default option is exercised. For example, one can assume that the borrower will be in default when the property price is below the value of a mortgage.

FIGURE 5-1

Pricing Comparison: Default Risk-Based Valuation

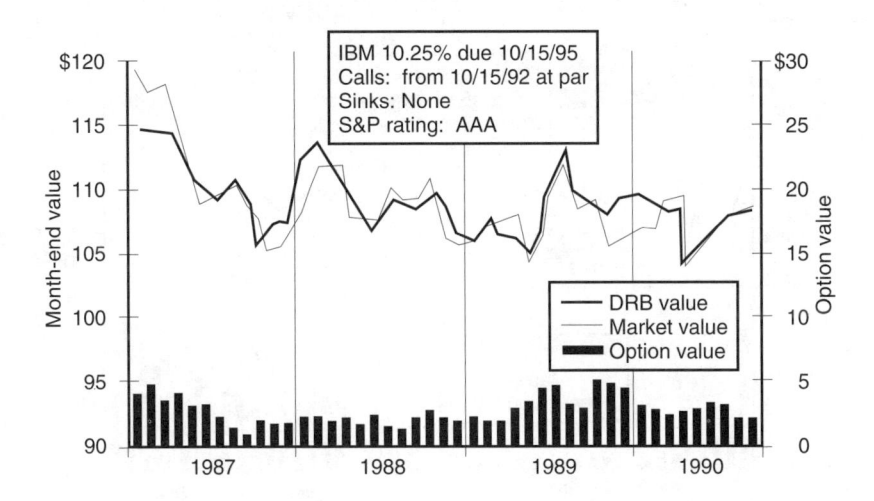

IBM 10.25% due 10/15/95
Calls: from 10/15/92 at par
Sinks: None
S&P rating: AAA

— DRB value
— Market value
■ Option value

the actual price paid in a transaction. Regardless of the underlying theory of valuation, the fair value of a security cannot be sustained if no one is willing to buy or sell at this price. Fair value often deviates from the transacted price. The magnitude of this deviation largely depends on:

1. The accuracy of the methodology and/or assumptions;

2. The short-term trading noise in public trading places;

3. The price concession in a private negotiation; and

4. The misperception of the company's fundamentals.

While the deviation is expected, a very large deviation over a long term cannot simply be explained away by market imperfection or price concession. Thus, the merit of a valuation approach is the only cause of this large deviation.

Figures 5-1 and 5-2 demonstrate how intrinsic values obtained from the default risk-based valuation ap-

FIGURE 5-2

Pricing Comparison: Default Risk-Based Valuation

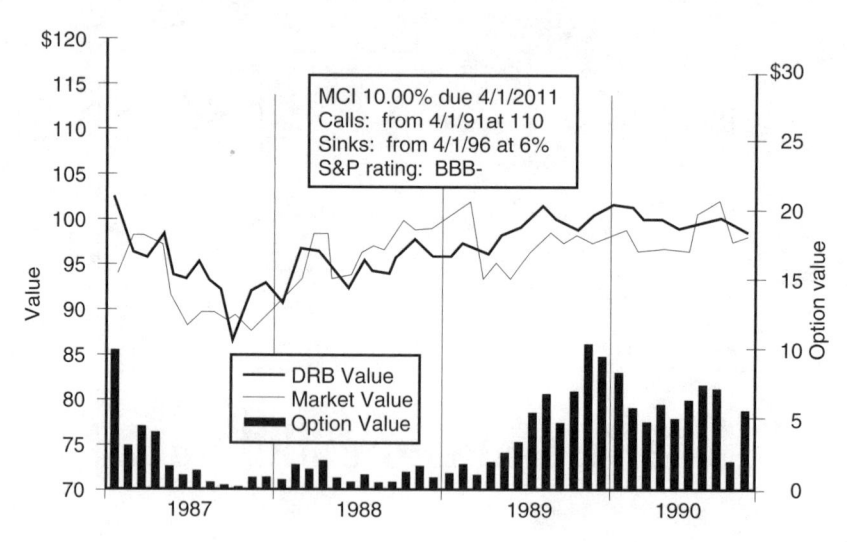

MCI 10.00% due 4/1/2011
Calls: from 4/1/91 at 110
Sinks: from 4/1/96 at 6%
S&P rating: BBB-

— DRB Value
— Market Value
■ Option Value

proach converge with observed market prices. In both cases, the valuation does not require bond ratings from rating agencies or yield spreads from bond market trading information. Instead, the inputs to the credit risk assessment for the purpose of bond valuation were based on quarterly or annual financial statements, and historical bond default experience. Here, Zeta credit risk scores and associated default probabilities over time are used as a basis for credit risk adjustment.[4] The interest rate option pricing methodology follows the basic form of Ho and Lee

---

4. Credit risk scores were computed by Zeta Services, Inc., based on quarterly or annual financial statements. While applied to the default risk pricing, these scores were assumed to be updated a month after the end of each quarter. Here we used monthly default probability curves covering the settlement date to a security's maturity, instead of constant default probability. See Kao (1993a) for the discussion of this issue.

(1986). In addition, the valuation also takes into account capital structure and bond convenants.

Figure 5–1 plots data for IBM 10.25%s due 10/15/95 which were rated AAA by S&P. The intrinsic values estimated from the default risk-based pricing model tracked actual market values very well during the period of 1987 to 1990 with slightly less price volatility. The value of the call option (callable from 10/15/92 at par, no sinking fund provision), shown at the bottom of the figure, fluctuated between $0.90 and $4.70 per $100. Without considering call options, the price of this bond derived from the default risk-based valuation can be significantly higher than the transacted price (approximately by the amount of option values).

Figure 5–2 plots similar data for MCI 10.00%s due 4/1/11, rated BBB- by S&P. As expected, the price differentials between the default risk-based valuation and market place were substantial at times, given the issuer's lower credit quality. However, market prices tended to drift back to the intrinsic values. This bond had complicated call and sinking fund provisions (callable from 4/1/91 at $110 and sinkable from 4/1/96 at 6 percent per annum). As shown at the bottom of the exhibit, the ability to estimate the value of these options would have a great impact on the accuracy of bond valuation.

APPLYING THE DEFAULT RISK-BASED PRICING TO CMBS

Corcoran and Kao (1994) applied the concept of a default risk-based pricing approach to analyzing the impact of credit risk on the pricing of commercial mortgage-backed securities. They specified the changes of interest rates and collateral values (underlying real estate properties) as two static and independent processes. They did, however, discuss important obstacles in applying a default risk-based pricing:

First, empirical studies such as Vandell (1993) have shown that "ruthless" default is not a reliable delinquency decision rule, and thus is not very useful for modeling the collateral default process. Moreover, there is no publicly available data set for commercial mortgage markets with regard to outstanding individual mortgages' detailed fundamental characteristics (e.g, net operating income, historic loan to value ratio, and debt service). As a result, it is difficult to study the fundamental factors underlying each mortgage's delinquency. Delinquency and credit losses may be easier to evaluate on the basis of aggregate market experience. Based on the actual default experience in the overall mortgage market, Corcoran and Kao (1994) constructed an "empirical" default model that relates default probability to the price changes of real estate properties by region as well as sector.

Using this empirical default model, Figure 5–3 demonstrates how the ruthless default rule can result in default probabilities substantially different from the empirical data under certain real estate scenarios. Here, it is assumed that mortgages have an average maturity of 10 years, 20-year amortization schedule, and initial LTVs of 72 percent with dispersion (standard deviation) of 15 percent to 20 percent.[5] The figure shows that, over the 10-year period, the ruthless default assumption tends to over-

---

5. In order to make delinquency probabilities estimated by the empirical model and ruthless default assumption comparable, we need to have an adjustment. As discussed in Corcoran (1995), the reported LTVs during 1988–1992, the time period covered by Corcoran and Kao's empirical model, understated reality due to problems such as loans being involuntarily rollovered and lagged appraisal valuation. Corcoran (1995) estimated that the underestimation of LTVs during that period was approximately 7 percent. This implies that when applying to the calculation of theoretical ruthless default probabilities, we should use an LTV of 79 percent in order to equal the average LTV of 72 percent reported by National Association of Insurance Commissioners (NAIC) in the mid-1980s.

FIGURE 5-3

The Sensitivity of Ruthless Default Probabilities

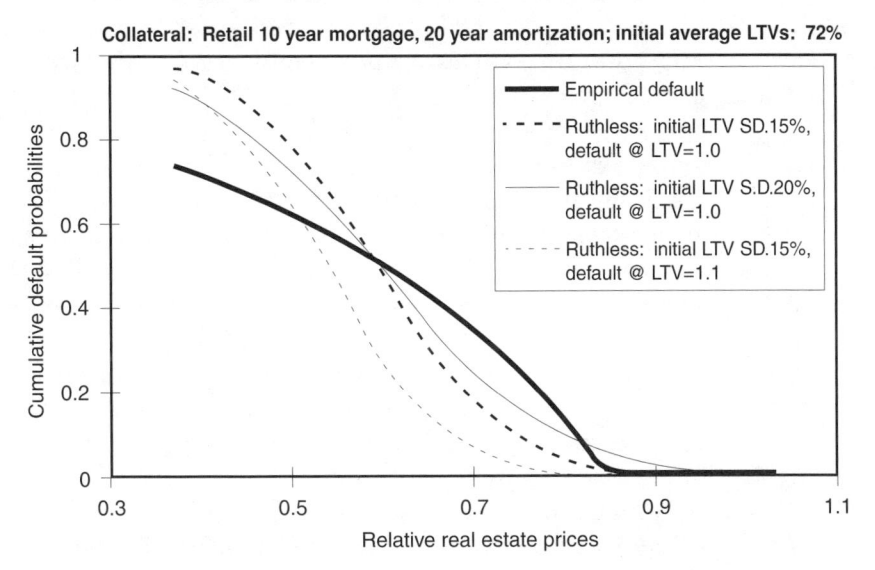

Collateral: Retail 10 year mortgage, 20 year amortization; initial average LTVs: 72%

- Empirical default
- Ruthless: initial LTV SD.15%, default @ LTV=1.0
- Ruthless: initial LTV S.D.20%, default @ LTV=1.0
- Ruthless: initial LTV SD.15%, default @ LTV=1.1

estimate cumulative default probabilities, except for the modest declining real estate scenarios (about 2 percent to 4 percent per year). As expected, a higher default trigger (e.g., at LTV of 1.1) would push the cumulative default probability curve lower. A more disperse distribution of LTVs at the beginning period (e.g., 20 percent) would generate a flatter default curve.

TWO-ASSET BINOMIAL PRICING MODEL

The default risk pricing model presented in Corcoran and Kao (1994) can be further enhanced via a multivariate binomial valuation framework. A multivariate contingent claim model can effectively evaluate asset prices affected by two or more relevant-state variables, as in the case of commercial mortgages or CMBS (real estate and interest rate movements). As shown in Ho et al. (1993) and Nielson et al. (1993), the specification of covariance characteristics among assets is a critical factor in pricing efficiency of this type of model. As for Corcoran and Kao's CMBS valuation model, we need to add three more ingredients: a real estate pricing tree, an interest rate binomial tree, and the relationship of these two processes.

As shown in the left panel of Figure 5–4, the Real Estate Price Tree specifies the changes of real estate prices over time, given an expected price volatility (10 percent). Based on the Corcoran and Kao empirical default model, we can calculate a cumulative default probability for the expected real estate price in each node of this tree. For example, at the end of the third year, if the price of a property declines 10 percent, the cumulate default probability is estimated to be 13.5 percent. This default probability curves, along with the loss assumptions, are used in the risk neutrality pricing calculation.

For simplicity in the Interest Rate Binomial Tree, we assume a flat yield curve and a basic CIR (Cox-Ingersoll-Ross) CIR interest rate pricing model with a single volatility factor of 9 percent.

After the real estate and interest rate pricing trees are constructed, we need to specify the relationship (i.e., correlation) of these two processes.[6] From the two trees in Figure 5–4, let us take the interest rate scenario of 5.9 percent at the end of year three (the lowest node of the right panel) as an example. If the changes in interest rates and real estate prices were perfectly positively correlated (+1), the corresponding real estate scenario would be a decrease of 26 percent (a relative real estate price of 0.74). If the two processes were perfectly negatively correlated (−1), the corresponding real estate scenario would be an increase of 35 percent (a relative real estate price of 1.35).

---

6. Like the pricing volatility assumption for constructing a binomial tree, the correlation assumption can vary by the time horizon (see Ho, Stapleton, and Subrahmanyam 1993). Again, for simplicity we assume a single correlation factor.

FIGURE 5-4

Two-Asset Binomial Tree

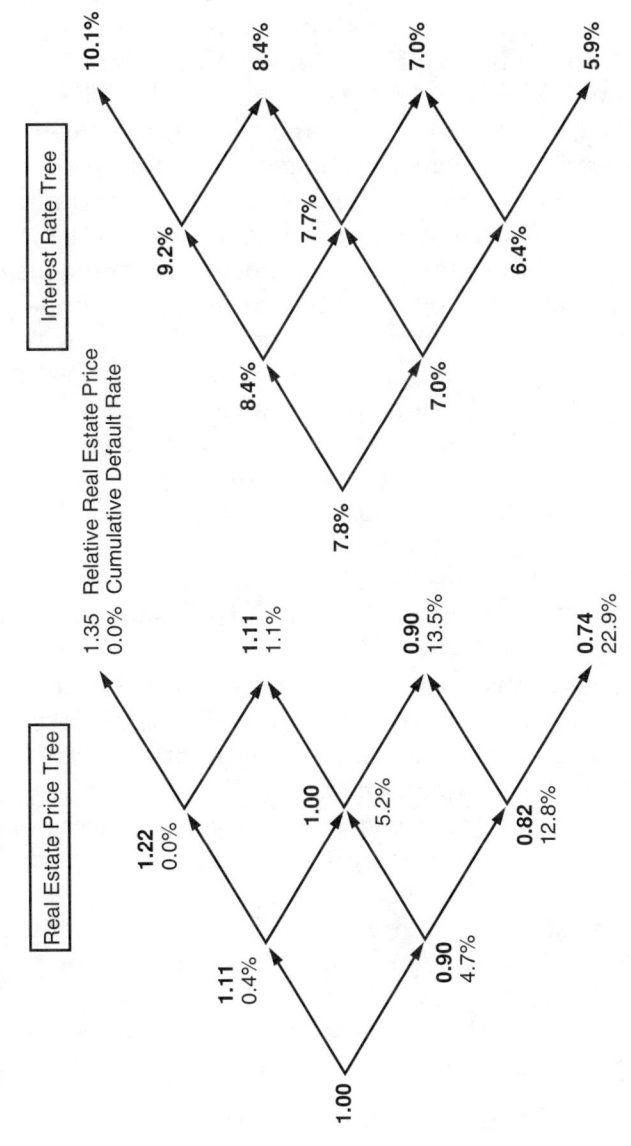

Real Estate Price Tree

- 1.35 — Relative Real Estate Price
- 0.0% — Cumulative Default Rate

1.22
0.0%

1.11
0.4%

1.11
1.1%

1.00

1.00
5.2%

0.90
4.7%

0.90
13.5%

0.82
12.8%

0.74
22.9%

Interest Rate Tree

10.1%

9.2%

8.4%

8.4%

7.8%

7.7%

7.0%

7.0%

6.4%

5.9%

Real Estate Volatility: 10%
Mortgage Collateral: Retail
No Amortization

Interest Rate Volatility: 9%
Flat Yield Curve

For a correlation between these two extreme cases, the calculation has to take into account all four possible real estate scenarios. However, since each tree has its own mean and variance, both trees have to be "standardized" first (i.e., mean = 0 and variance = 1). Once viewing these two trees from an equal footing, we can follow the calculation methodology for a standard bivariate normal density function presented in Rubinstein and Reiner (1993).

While computationally cumbersome, the concept behind this methodology is rather intuitively simple. Again, viewing from an interest rate scenario of 5.9 percent at the end of year three, each of the four possible real estate price scenarios has to be adjusted to reflect the correlation relationship.[7] The "true" real estate price change corresponding to the 5.9 percent interest rate scenario is merely the probability weighted sum of all four real estate price changes after adjustment.

In essence, the correlation relationship changes the range and the shape of a binomial tree when viewing from the other binomial tree. Figure 5–5 compares the real estate price paths under two different correlation assumptions while viewing from the interest rate process. With a correlation of 0.5, the real estate binomial tree becomes more compact symmetrically.

After the trees are constructed and adjusted for their relationship, one can simply follow the "backward" valuation procedure of a conventional binomial option pricing model. That is, for each node, cash flow is first adjusted for default probability from the real estate pricing tree and the assumed recovery rate. Second, the adjusted cash flow is discounted back to the previous period by the rate specified in the interest rate binomial tree. The lockup and

---

[7]. Mathematically, the adjusted value is $\rho * u + (1 - \rho^2)^{1/2} * v$, where ρ is correlation, and u and v are the standardized values of the two assets.

FIGURE 5-5

Real Estate Price Paths and Correlation with Interest Rates

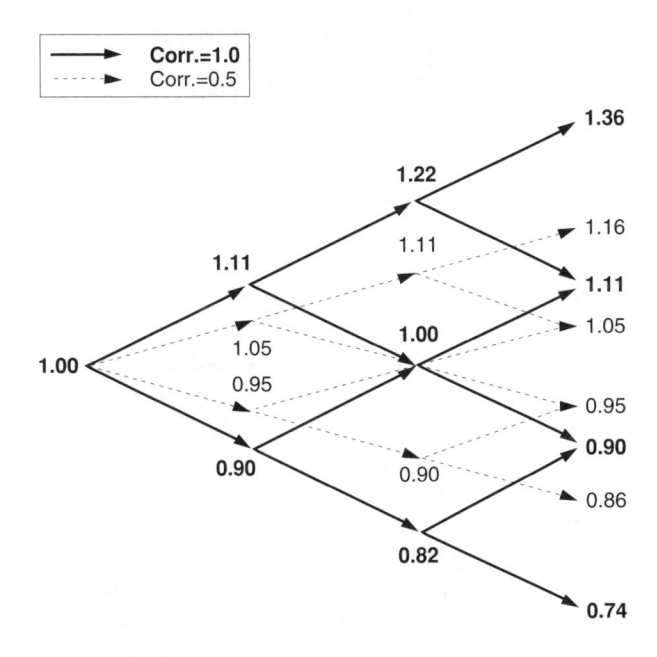

→ Corr.=1.0
⇢ Corr.=0.5

yield maintenance provisions, as well as other optionalities, can be examined against the probability weighted present value of the security at that time period.

ANALYZING CREDIT RISK OF COMMERCIAL MORTGAGE-BACKED SECURITIES

Following a CMBS structure similar to the one presented in Corcoran and Kao (1994), we apply the default risk-based pricing in a framework of two-asset binomial trees to analyze the credit risk of a CMBS. Bond market and real estate market assumptions are shown in the middle

TABLE 5-1

Risk-Neutral Valuation of CMBS

Security Information	
Maturity: 10 years	Coupon rate: 10.0%
Amortization: 20 years	Nominal spread: 240 b.p. (s.a.)
Average life: 7.0 years	Subordination: 25%
Collateral: 100% retail	Rating: BBB

Market Information

Bond	Real Estate
Treasury rate: 7.81%	Volatility: 10%
Volatility: 9% p.a.	Forecl/restrt: 50%–50%
Flat year curve	Credit loss:
	Foreclosure: 36%
	Restructured: 18%

Tree up-down probability: 50%–50%

Correlation	Expected Credit Losses	Net Credit Spread
1	33	207
0.5	26	214
0	24	216
−0.5	26	214
−1	32	208

panel of Table 5–1. If the interest rate movement and real estate price changes are perfectly positively correlated (+1), the estimated credit losses would be 33 basis points. The nominal credit spread of 240 b.p. for this BBB-rated CMBS would become a net spread of 207 b.p. Changes in the correlation assumption have little impact on the net credit spreads, since the probabilities of up and down movement for each tree were assumed to be equal and the prepayment risk is assumed to be nil due to the lockup and yield maintenance provisions.

FIGURE 5-6

Split a Binomial Tree

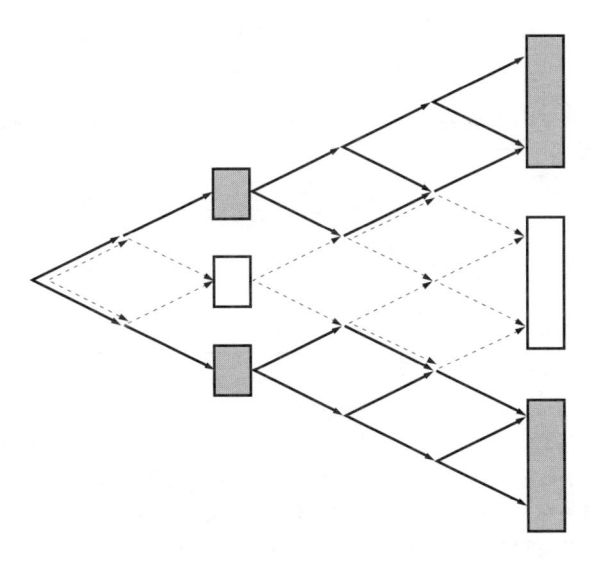

We can further extend this analysis to examine the structure's credit risk sensitivity under various interest rate scenarios. A simple three-scenario test is presented showing rising, stable, and declining interest rate environments. Splitting a binomial tree into regional components can be tricky since a few interest rate paths can go through the same node. In the spirit of the concept of linear path space developed by Ho (1992), Figure 5-6 depicts how three interest rate scenarios are defined in the context of a binomial tree. First, we select the time periods where the number of nodes can be subdivided evenly into three interest rate regions: rising, stable, and declining. These interest rate time zones are the end of year two, year five, or year eight, etc. Those interest rate paths passing a particular "block" are considered belonging to the same interest rate scenario regardless of how they "travel" between the two interest rate time zones.

TABLE 5-2

Net Credit Spreads of CMBS

| | Net Credit Spreads (b.p.) | | | |
| | Given Interest Rate Scenarios | | | |
Correlation	Rising	Stable	Declining	Overall
1	237	211	−37	207
0.5	232	216	159	214
0	214	216	218	216
−0.5	150	213	233	214
−1	−40	206	238	208

Nominal Credit Spread: 240 b.p. (s.a.)

Table 5–2 presents interest rate scenario testing of the credit risk of a CMBS under various correlation assumptions. In a rising interest rate environment, a CMBS can experience significant credit loss if the values of real estate properties decline (i.e., correlation is negative). In fact, the net credit spread can contrast from 240 b.p. to −40 b.p. if rising interest rates accompany severe declines in real estate prices.

Table 5–3 compares the net credit spread analysis of CMBS under the assumptions of "ruthless default" and empirical default. As demonstrated in Figure 5–3, the ruthless default assumption tends to overestimate the severity of default probability of a commercial mortgage in most real estate environments. Table 5–3 shows that, while applied to value CMBS with a first loss subordination structure, the ruthless default assumption can result in underestimations of net credit spread (ranging from 13 b.p. to 28 b.p.) in various real estate and interest rate scenarios.

TABLE 5-3

Net Credit Spreads of CMBS: Empirical versus Ruthless Default

Interest Rate Scenarios

Correlation	Overall Empirical	Overall Ruthless	Rising Empirical	Rising Ruthless	Stable Empirical	Stable Ruthless	Declining Empirical	Declining Ruthless
1	207	186	237	222	211	192	−37	−50
0.5	214	193	232	213	216	196	159	147
0	216	196	214	192	216	196	218	199
−0.5	214	194	150	134	213	192	233	217
−1	208	187	−40	−68	206	184	238	225

Initial LTV 0.72
Initial LTV Std Dev. 0.15
Ruthless Default LTV 1.00

Nominal Credit Spread: 240 b.p. (s.a.)

113

SUMMARY

The evaluation of illiquid, lower-quality or privately placed fixed income securities requires special attention to proper assessment of the firm's financial risk, default and recovery likelihood, and the impact of collateral and financial covenant provisions. A conventional interest rate option pricing model handles these analytical difficulties via simple and static assumptions or risk indicators implied from available market prices (e.g., rating and yield spread). Recently, several academic research papers in the area of fixed income pricing focus on (1) the specification of bankruptcy (or default) as an explicit and exogenous process, and (2) option valuation in a multi-variate contingent claim framework. In conjunction with fundamental analysis of the firm's credit risk, these models can effectively evaluate illiquid, lower-quality, or privately placed bonds. This chapter uses empirical examples to demonstrate how a default risk-based pricing model combining with a simple two-asset binomial process can be applied to analyze risky debt and commercial mortgage-backed securities.

REFERENCES

Ambarish, Ramasastry, and Martin G. Subrahmanyam. 1989. "Default Risk and the Valuation of High-Yield Bonds: A Methodological Critique." Working paper No. 519, New York University Salomon Center.

Corcoran, Patrick J. 1995. "Debt and Equity in the New Real Estate Markets." Chapter 8 in this volume.

Corcoran, Patrick J., and Duen-Li Kao. 1994. "Assessing Credit Risk of CMBS." *Real Estate Finance* (Fall): 29–40.

Ginzburg, Alex, Kevin J. Maloney, and Ram Willner. 1994. "Risk Rating Migration and the Valuation of Floating Rate Debt." Working paper presented in the 3rd Annual GAT Fixed Income Conference.

Ho, Thomas S. Y. 1992. "Managing Illiquid Bonds and the Linear Path Space." *The Journal of Fixed Income* (June): 80–94.

Ho, Thomas S. Y., and S. Lee. 1986. "Term Structure Movement and Pricing Interest Rate Contingent Claims." *Journal of Finance:* 1011–29.

Ho, T. S., Richard C. Stapleton, and Marti G. Subrahmanyam. 1993. "Multivariate Binomial Approximations for Asset Prices with Non-Stationary Variance and Covariance Characteristics." Working paper, New York University Salomon Center.

Jarrow, Robert A., David Lando, and Stuart M. Turnbull. 1995. "A Markov Model for the Term Structure of Credit Risk Spreads." Working paper presented at the 13th Annual Conference of the Western Finance Association.

Kao, Duen-Li. 1993a. "Illiquid Securities: Issues of Pricing and Performance Measurement." *Financial Analysts Journal* (March–April). Also in Thomas S. Y. Ho, ed. 1993. *Fixed-Income Management: Issues and Solutions.* Homewood, IL: Business One Irwin.

———. 1993b. "Fair Trading." *Balance Sheet* (Winter): 15–19.

Kim, In Joon, Krishna Ramaswamy, and Suresh Sundaresan. 1989. "The Valuation of Corporate Fixed Income Securities." Working paper No. 32, R. L. White Center for Financial Research, Wharton School, University of Pennsylvania.

Leland, Hayne E. 1994. "Corporate Debt Value, Bond Covenants, and Optimal Capital Structure." *The Journal of Finance* 49, 1213–52.

Longstaff, Francis A., and Eduardo S. Schwartz. 1995. "A Simple Approach to Valuing Risky Fixed and Floating Rate Debt." *The Journal of Finance* 50, 789–819.

Madan, Dilip B., and Haluk Unal. 1994. "Pricing the Risks of Default." Working paper 94–16, The Wharton Financial Institutions Center, the University of Pennsylvania.

Merton, Robert C. 1974. "On the Pricing of Corporate Debt: The Risk Structure of Interest Rates." *Journal of Finance:* 449–70.

Nadler, Dan. 1994. "Valuing Risky Floaters: Lessons for the Emerging Debt Markets." Goldman Sachs Fixed Income Research.

Nielsen, Lars T., Jesus Saa-Requejo, and Pedro Santa-Clara. 1993. "Default Risk and Interest Rate Risk: The Term Structure of Default Spreads." Working paper presented at the 12th Annual Conference of the Western Finance Association.

Rubinstein, Mark, and Eric Reiner. 1993. "Exotic Options." Unpublished manuscript.

Titman, Sheridan, and Walter Torous. 1989. "Valuing Commercial Mortgages: An Empirical Investigation of the Contingent-Claims Approach to Pricing Risky Debt." *Journal of Finance:* 345–73.

Toft, Klaus B. 1995. "Options on Leveraged Equity with Default Risk." Working paper presented at the 13th Annual Conference of the Western Finance Association.

Vandell, Kerry D. 1992. "Handing Over the Keys: A Perspective on Mortgage Default Research." *Journal of the American Real Estate and Urban Economic Association* 21: 211–46.

CHAPTER 6

Implied Prepayments: A New Perspective on Mortgage-Backed Securities Analysis

Si Chen
Portfolio Manager
Fischer Francis Trees & Watts

The early 1990s have been a turbulent period for the mortgage-backed securities market. This was a period of high interest rate volatility which brought about extremes in prepayments. In December 1993, for example, it was common to see prepayment speeds in excess of 70 percent Constant Prepayment Rate, which translated to over 2000 percent of the Public Securities Association prepayment curve, or PSA, for some pools. Only a year later, speeds under 50 percent PSA were common. Such turbulence in the market has highlighted the need for rigorous valuation systems and risk management tools. An important trend of recent years has been the development of option-adjusted spread, or OAS, models to satisfy these needs. In their present form, however, most OAS models do not adequately capture the risks of mortgage-backed securities. To fully understand the risks and rewards of the mortgage market, therefore, we must go beyond OAS and examine the mortgage market from a new perspective: implied prepayments.

THE STATE OF THE ART: OAS ANALYSIS

Today's state of the art in mortgage analysis are the OAS models, which date back to the mid-1980s.[1] Although there are now many versions, all such models share some common themes. In essence, they seek to derive the value of mortgage cash flow risk from options prices by combining a bond option pricing model with a prepayment model. The bond option pricing model is calibrated to the observed yield curve and given a set of assumptions about the volatility of interest rates. The prepayment model is usually constructed from historical prepayment data and serves to establish a link between interest rates and mortgage prepayments.[2]

A decade of research and development has produced increasingly refined OAS models. Their bond option pricing models have evolved from simple one-factor models with flat volatility assumptions to multi-factor arbitrage-free models which capture the implied volatility of the options market. The prepayment models, likewise, have evolved from simple "S-curves" to complex models which capture many causal factors of prepayments.[3]

Despite all these advances, however, many portfolio managers and traders continue to be skeptical because OAS models frequently fail either to identify correctly relative value or to predict correctly the price behavior of mortgage-backed securities. As a result, relatively primitive techniques such as price spreads and empirical durations continued to be relied upon as heavily as OAS analysis.

---

1. The earliest form of option-based analysis for mortgage-backed securities that I know of is in Diller (1984). Only four years later, OAS models similar to those of today were available. See Askin, Hoffman, and Meyer (1988).
2. For more information on OAS and mortgage analysis, see, for example, Davidson and Herskovitz (1994).
3. For example, see Patruno (1994) and Hayre and Rajan (1995).

BEYOND THE STATE OF THE ART: IMPLIED PREPAYMENTS

There is a reason why OAS models have not fulfilled their initial promise to the mortgage market. Even though some models can capture the market pricing of term structure and volatility risk by calibrating the bond option pricing model to the observed yield curve and observed options prices, *they still arbitrarily value prepayment risk*. All prepayment models, no matter how sophisticated, implicitly establish an arbitrary link between interest rates and prepayments. Such a link is based upon one interpretation of historical prepayments under various interest rate environments. The market, however, may assume an entirely different relationship between interest rates and prepayments. When that happens, the OAS model would value prepayment risk differently than the market, and thus project a price behavior of mortgage-backed securities which is inconsistent with actual market observations. As a result, the output from such models becomes less valuable.

Another subtle problem with current OAS models is that they assume that prepayment behavior will be fixed over time. That is, the same type of mortgage, given the same incentives, would produce the same prepayment behavior. For example, if FHA/VA borrowers with 10-year-old 30-year loans who had never had a significant refinancing opportunity were given an x percent lower rate, y percent of them could be expected to prepay.[4] This would be as true in 1996 as it would be in 2006. In reality, however, prepay-

---

4. Some models use the percentage savings from refinancings rather than the absolute saving in mortgage rate as the parameter for rate incentive to refinance. Such models only define the stimulus function differently and make similarly strong assumptions about the stimulus-response relationship.

ment behavior has changed over time. The market prices of mortgage-backed securities often reflected such changes before they were incorporated into prepayment models. Relying exclusively on prepayment models built upon historical behavior can sometimes be almost like driving with a rear-view mirror.

The use of implied prepayments attempts to resolve the problem of arbitrarily valuing prepayment risk, primarily by turning traditional OAS models upside down. Whereas traditional models use a fixed prepayment assumption, the implied prepayments approach changes the prepayment assumptions to reflect the prices of actual mortgage-backed securities. Because traditional models assume that prepayment behavior is fixed, differences in the performance of mortgage-backed securities and Treasuries and options are reflected as a change in spread or change in OAS. Under these models, therefore, prepayments are fixed and spread or risk premium is a variable.

In contrast, the implied prepayments approach assumes that mortgage spreads are stable over time and that the underlying prepayment assumptions are variable. In other words, mortgages are not becoming "cheaper" or "richer"—only the market's views on housing turnover and refinancing behavior are changing. Given a yield curve and volatility assumption, the prepayment function is altered such that a set of benchmark mortgage securities have the same OAS.[5] Thus, the value of prepayment risk is "calibrated" so that it is consistent with market prices. This prepayment function could then be used to evaluate

---

5. In reality, there is often enough noise in the pass-throughs or strips market to make it highly difficult to produce the "same" OAS. Nevertheless, fairly simplistic prepayment functions could be fitted to produce OAS statistics on benchmark securities which are within the typical bid/offer and model error.

nonbenchmark mortgage securities. As the prices of the benchmark securities change, the prepayment function is recalibrated over time to reflect different assumptions.

WHY IMPLIED PREPAYMENTS?

Implied prepayments satisfy three needs of mortgage analysis. First, the spreads of mortgage-backed securities *should* be stable, and volatile OAS points to probable model error. Option-adjusted spread analysis was initially designed to measure the credit and liquidity premium of mortgage-backed securities. The credit premium should obviously be fairly stable for agency-quality securities. It is also difficult to argue that any generic mortgage security could command a significant liquidity premium, because the mortgage market is the second-largest component of the U.S. bond markets and has liquidity to rival U.S. Treasuries. What is more likely: that the liquidity premiums of pass-throughs really expands in a market rally, or that the model is simply wrong about prepayments?

Second, the implied prepayments approach creates a risk management system based upon the market prices of mortgage securities. Many practitioners believe that market prices are more powerful predictors of mortgage price risk, and therefore use price spreads and empirical durations rather than OAS models for risk management. Such a risk management system has two strong merits. First, it allows various mortgage products to be hedged effectively with other mortgage products. Second, it provides a disciplined framework for examining one's risk management assumptions versus market realities.

Third, the implied prepayments approach is a more effective tool for identifying relative value opportunities in the mortgage market. Many OAS models often generate OAS differences between benchmark mortgage securities which are really the residual values of prepayment risk that is not captured by the model Under the implied prepayments approach, however, OAS ceases to be the "rug" under which misvalued prepayment risk is shoved. Instead, OAS differences point to tangible rich/cheap differences under the market's pricing assumptions. Thus, the OAS model can value less-liquid mortgage product, such as collateralized mortgage obligations (CMOs), using prepayment assumptions from liquid mortgage securities.

APPLICATION: IMPLIED PREPAYMENTS THROUGH TIME

The mortgage market of 1993–1994 has been viewed as a period of high spread volatility. In fact, much of what happened could be captured by changes in the market's implied prepayments during different points of this period. Figure 6–1 shows the prepayment response function implied in the pass-through market for a current coupon FNMA pass-through on different dates from this period. In essence, significant changes in mortgage valuation occurred as the market repeatedly changed its assumptions about turnover and refinancing risk.

In September 1993, as the market rallied to historic lows in yields, prepayment fears plagued the market. These fears are reflected in market prices, which implied that any pass-through over par would experience explosive prepayments. Thus, even with a 50 bp rally, the then-current coupon mortgage security could be assumed to prepay at 30 percent CPR for life. For the higher coupon pass-throughs, the market believed that burnout would be nonexistent. Hence, long-term speeds on these pass-throughs were projected to be 45 percent CPR.

By December 1993, as signs of slowing prepayments emerged, the market became less penalizing on premium

FIGURE 6-1

Prepayment Model Projections, FNMA $99 30-Year Pass-Through

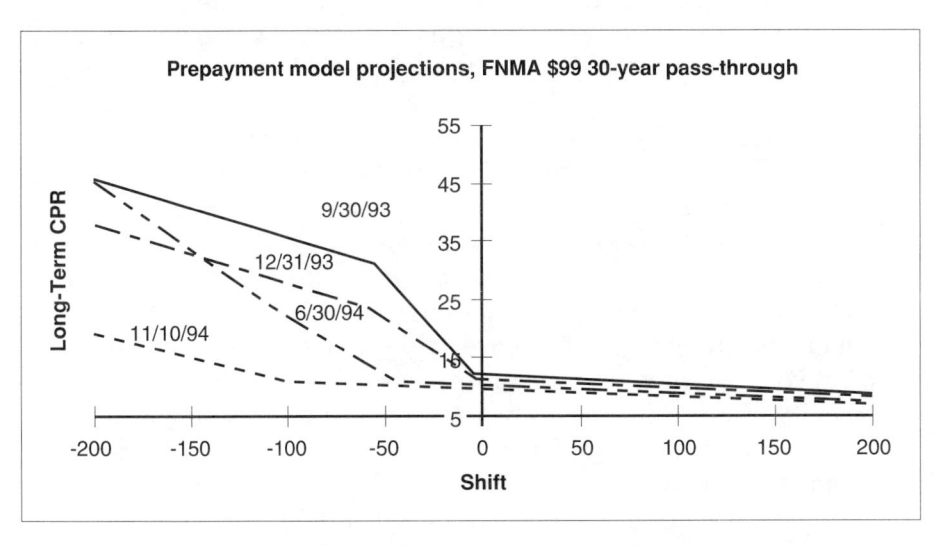

[Chart: Prepayment model projections, FNMA $99 30-year pass-through. Y-axis: Long-Term CPR (5 to 55). X-axis: Shift (-200 to 200). Curves labeled 9/30/93, 12/31/93, 6/30/94, 11/10/94.]

Source: Analysis performed on the Salomon Brothers *Yield Book* using the Salomon Brothers' "prepayment dials."

pass-throughs. As a result, long-term implied prepayment projections on high coupon pass-throughs fell from 45 percent CPR to about 35 percent CPR. By June 1994, the elbow of the prepayment function shifted outwards further, implying that a greater-than-50 b.p. rally was required to cause meaningful prepayments.

Finally, by November 1994, a completely different prepayment function was implied in the market. After a severe bear market and fears about historic *slow* prepayments, the implied prepayments on high coupon pass-throughs were not even half of what they were only a year ago. By this time, a 100 b.p. rally was projected to have no effect on current coupon pass-throughs, and even a 200 b.p. rally would only ignite prepayments of 20 percent CPR. In contrast, the market's long-term turnover speed on current coupon pass-throughs fell from 12 percent CPR to 10 percent CPR. For FNMA 30-year 6.5 percent pass-throughs, which went from a current coupon to a deep discount during this time, this meant that pricing speeds fell in half—from 200 percent PSA to 100 percent PSA.

Changes in implied prepayment assumptions can lead to significant differences in mortgage duration and convexity. The price behavior of mortgage-backed securities is a function of the yield curve shape, volatility, and prepayment assumptions. There are two important relationships between prepayment assumptions and duration and convexity. First, a flatter prepayment curve implies longer durations and less negative convexity, or duration drift. Second, the elbow of the prepayment function is the point of greatest negative convexity in pass-throughs.

In Figures 6–2 and 6–3, we see that this is indeed the case. Using the yield curve and mortgage prices of March 30, 1994, the duration and convexity for all pass-throughs were calculated with prepayment assumptions implied from other dates for which an implied prepayment function was available.[6] The effects could be dramatic. Under the steepest and flattest prepayment functions (from September 1993 and November 1994), the implied durations on some premium pass-throughs were as much as two years or 100 percent apart. Similarly, the convexity of the current pass-through was implied to be −1.5 using the September 1993 prepayment function, but barely negative

---

6. March 30, 1994, was selected because it was one of the rare days when there were as many discounts as there were premium coupons. The point of the analysis is not to examine how the duration of a specific mortgage pass-through changes over time. Rather, it is to highlight the changes to the duration and convexity of all pass-throughs under different prepayment assumptions but using the same yield curve and volatility assumption.

FIGURE 6-2

Effective Duration and Implied Prepayment Assumptions

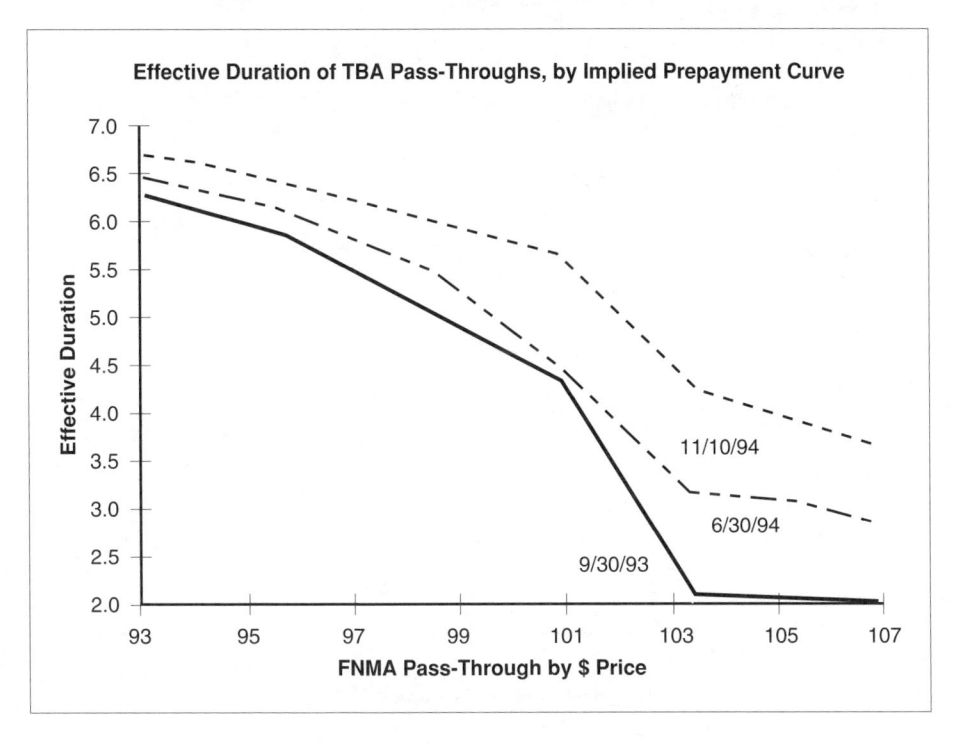

Effective Duration of TBA Pass-Throughs, by Implied Prepayment Curve

[Chart showing effective duration vs FNMA Pass-Through by $ Price, with curves labeled 11/10/94, 6/30/94, and 9/30/93]

Source: Analysis performed on the Salomon Brothers *Yield Book* using 3/31/94 prices and market data. UST 10-yr. yield 6.733%, volatility 13%.

using the November 1994 function. Over time, the elbow of the prepayment function has pointed to the coupon with the greatest convexity risk. In contrast, when the prepayment function was exceptionally steep, high premium pass-throughs were positively convex.[7]

The fact that duration and convexity of pass-throughs are functions of the market's price spread between coupons

---
7. This implies that under September 1993 prepayment assumptions, high coupon interest only (or IOs) were *positively* convex, contrary to results from many OAS models.

FIGURE 6-3

Effective Convexity and Implied Prepayment Assumptions

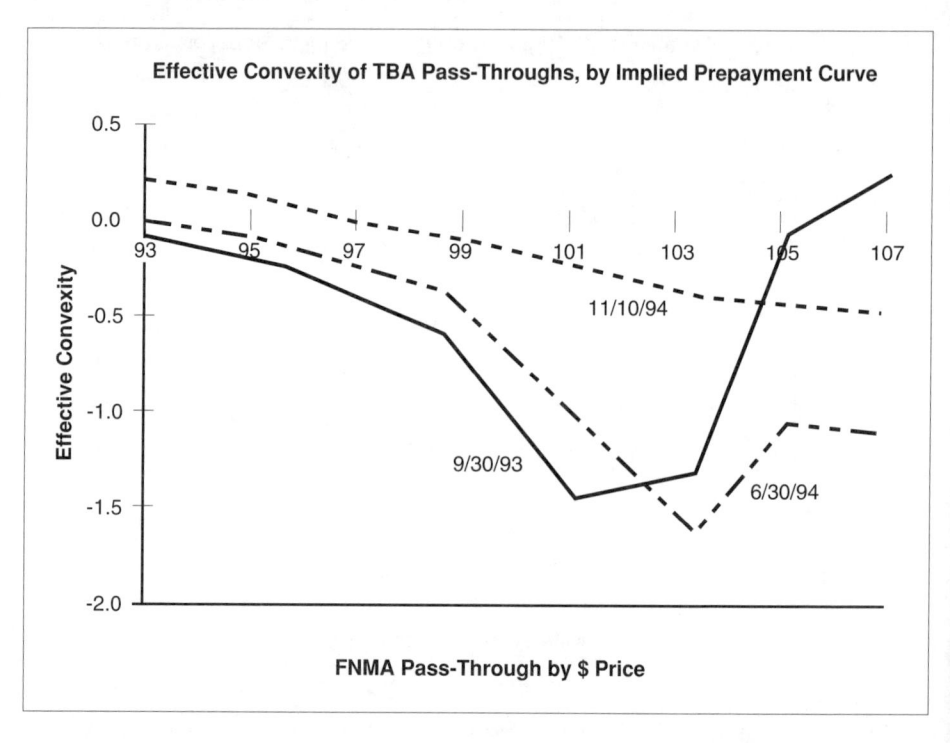

Effective Convexity of TBA Pass-Throughs, by Implied Prepayment Curve

[Chart showing Effective Convexity (y-axis, from -2.0 to 0.5) vs FNMA Pass-Through by $ Price (x-axis, from 93 to 107), with three curves labeled 11/10/94, 9/30/93, and 6/30/94]

Source: Analysis performed on the Salomon Brothers *Yield Book* using 3/31/94 prices and market data. UST 10-yr. yield 6.733%, volatility 13%.

is not a new discovery. Many practitioners already rely upon price spreads rather than OAS models to manage pass-throughs. The implied prepayments approach, however, does bring together the option-based valuation method from OAS models and the market-driven approach from traditional price spread analysis. Further, an implied prepayments approach based upon the general OAS framework allows us to identify the impact of changes in the shape of the yield curve and volatility on mortgage valuation, which is difficult for a methodology that uses only price spreads. Finally, whereas traditional price spread analysis is limited only to the liquid pass-through markets, implied prepayments could also be applied to less-liquid markets, such as CMOs.

APPLICATION: ANALYZING THE RELATIVE VALUE OF CMOS

The structuring of CMOs redistributes the prepayment risk of the underlying pass-through collateral. Many investors purchase CMOs because they offer performance characteristics not found in pass-throughs. Nevertheless, it is still helpful to ask whether the CMOs are "cheap" relative to pass-throughs; that is, whether the cash flows and prepayment risks are cheaper in the CMO or pass-through market.

The OAS model should be well suited to answer such a question. If, however, the OAS differences between various pass-throughs are not due to model error rather than accurate rich/cheap valuations, then how could the OAS difference between CMOs and the underlying collateral be reliable indicators of relative value? For example, an OAS model could say that a premium support bond is cheap relative to its collateral. The same model, however, could also be biased such that premium pass-throughs usually have higher OAS than discount pass-throughs. In that case, is the premium support bond *really* cheap, or is the model merely undervaluing call risk?

To illustrate this, let us look at a discount sequential with premium underlying collateral. On January 17, 1995, FNMA 91–140 D, a sequential bond with a 6 percent coupon backed by FNMA 9.5 percent collateral, is priced at 83 3/32. OAS analysis for this bond and comparative benchmark pass-throughs are shown in Table 6–1. On the surface, this is a rich bond because FNMA 9.5 percent

TABLE 6-1

Option-Adjusted Spread (OAS) of Collateralized Mortgage Obligations (CMS) and Pass-Throughs Using Traditional OAS Model

	\multicolumn{6}{c}{*Coupon*}
	6.5%	7.5%	8.5%	9.5%	10%	FN 91–140 D
Price	88–27	91–20	99–4	103–20	105–18	83–3
OAS	34	36	46	61	59	42
Duration	6.65	6.07	5.09	3.9	3.48	7.83
Convexity	0.13	−0.21	−0.75	−0.74	−0.96	0.00

Analysis performed on the Salomon Brothers *Yield Book* using 1/17/95 market data and a 12% volatility.

collateral offers an OAS of 61 b.p., almost 20 b.p. higher. On closer inspection, however, the fact that the OAS model believes that FNMA 9.5 percent pass-throughs are cheaper than FNMA 6.5 percent pass-throughs may mean that the model is undervaluing convexity. By the same token, then, FNMA 91–140 D, which offers better convexity than FNMA 9.5 percent collateral, may be undervalued.

The implied prepayments approach allows us to adjust our assumptions to value convexity consistently with the pass-through market. Using prepayment assumptions implied in the pass-through market, FNMA 91–140 D offers an OAS of 69 b.p., as shown in Table 6–2. Compared to a "pass-through surface" whose OAS is on average 45 b.p., the CMO offers 24 b.p. of liquidity premium and could be considered a cheap bond.

APPLICATION: ANALYZING IO/PO STRIPS

Interest-only and principal-only strips, or IOs and POs, should not be analyzed only with traditional OAS models. Small changes in prepayment assumptions can cause large swings in the theoretical values of such bonds. Given their prepayment leverage and the amount of potential error in

Implied Prepayments: A New Perspective

TABLE 6-2

Option-Adjusted Spread (OAS) of Collateralized Mortgage Obligations (CMS) and Pass-Throughs Using Implied Prepayments OAS Model

	Coupon					
	6.5%	7.5%	8.5%	9.5%	10%	FN 91–140 D
Price	88–27	91–20	99–4	103–20	105–18	83–3
OAS	46	41	45	41	50	69
Duration	6.37	5.77	4.73	3.44	2.92	7.56
Convexity	0.04	−0.30	−0.88	−0.90	−1.17	0.08

Source: Analysis performed on the Salomon Brothers *Yield Book*. Prepayment parameters were calibrated to produce an OAS of approximately 45 b.p. on TBA FNMA 30-year 6.5% through 10% collateral using 1/17/95 yield curve and 12% volatility. CMO OAS calculated with the same volatility and yield curve and the implied prepayment parameters.

prepayment assumptions, IO/PO strips have much more price risk from prepayment assumptions than from interest rates or volatility. This is why their OAS have tended to be the most volatile, and why most OAS models show differences of several hundred basis points of OAS between different IO strips. Because of the importance of prepayment assumptions in their valuation, implied prepayment is a much more powerful tool than traditional OAS when analyzing IO/PO strips.

For example, Table 6–3 shows the OAS difference between three benchmark IO strips and their underlying pass-throughs. The prepayment assumptions of the OAS model have already been calibrated to the pass-through market, so that 7 percent, 8.5 percent, and 9.5 percent pass-throughs all have the same OAS. Table 6–3 shows that there are significant OAS pick-ups available to investors who are willing to substitute IO strips for pass-throughs.

Or are there?

An alternative to comparing the OAS between IOs and pass-throughs is to compare the implied prepayment

TABLE 6-3

Comparing OAS of Pass-Throughs and IO Strips

	Coupon		
	7%	8.5%	9.5%
TBA pass-through OAS	46	44	46
TBA pass-through price	91–21	99–9	103–31
Trust IO strip OAS	148	209	393
IO OAS advantage	+102	+205	+353

Source: All analysis performed on the Salomon Brothers *Yield Book* using 1/17/95 market data and a 12% volatility. OAS are calculated using a prepayment model whose parameters are calibrated to produce approximately 45 b.p. OAS for all TBA FNMA 30-year pass-throughs from 6.5% to 10%.

TABLE 6-4

Comparing Prepayments Implied from Pass-Throughs

	Yield Shift						
	–200	–100	–50	0	+50	+100	+200
Pass-through market	749	203	181	165	151	139	118
IO/PO Market	1021	232	188	171	156	144	122
PSA difference	+272	+29	+7	+6	+5	+5	+4

Prepayments are long-term PSA speeds for a $99 FNMA TBA pass-through.

Source: All analysis performed on the Salomon Brothers *Yield Book* using 1/19/95 market data and a 12% volatility. The prepayment model for pass-throughs is calibrated to produce OAS of approximately 45 b.p. with 5 b.p. of error, whereas the prepayment model for strips is calibrated to produce OAS of approximately 50 b.p. with 50 b.p. of error.

assumptions in the two markets. In other words, is the IO/PO market really being priced with more aggressive prepayment assumptions? Table 6-4 compares the implied prepayment assumptions in the IO/PO strips market versus those in the pass-through market. Both sets of prepayment assumptions are used to generate long-term PSA speeds for a current coupon pass-through.

The results are startling: only premium IOs are meaningfully cheap to pass-throughs. Whereas the IO/PO market assumes significantly faster speeds for premium securities, as shown in the projections for the −200 b.p. rally scenario, the prepayment speeds for current coupon and discount securities are the same in the IO/PO and pass-through markets. Therefore, using the implied prepayment approach, it seems that one logical strategy would be to combine current coupon or discount pass-throughs or POs with premium IOs as substitutes for premium pass-throughs.

THE IMPLIED PREPAYMENTS APPROACH AND RISK MANAGEMENT

Interest rate risk is only one dimension of a two-dimensional problem in the mortgage market. Strategies which manage only the interest rate component of portfolio risk but not its prepayment risk will produce volatile results, even if the underlying long-term prepayment assumptions ultimately prove to be sound. As Figure 6–1 showed, the market's prepayment assumptions have been highly volatile over time. Further, assuming that prepayment behavior will remain constant is dangerous. Any prepayment model could only establish a link between interest rates and prepayments subject to the environment variables when the observed prepayments actually occurred. As those environment variables change over time, the forecasts from such models could become increasingly less reliable. The market's implied prepayment assumptions could thus serve as a valuable reality check.

CONCLUSION

OAS models have made tremendous contributions to the mortgage market. By establishing a link between mortgage and option valuation, they have enhanced investors' ability to manage mortgage portfolios more effectively and perhaps indirectly contributed to the growing liquidity of the mortgage market. The link between interest rates and prepayment behavior, however, is not always certain, and the implied prepayments approach should be used to address this second dimension of mortgage risk.

The implied prepayments concept does not challenge the option-based valuation of mortgage-backed securities. Instead, it enhances the power of such valuation techniques by capturing the "price" of prepayment risk, just as traditional bond option pricing models capture the "price" of term structure risk and volatility risk. Further, the implied prepayments approach focuses on risk-neutral valuation rather than risk premiums. While the mortgage market may indeed command risk premium in the form of OAS for bearing prepayment risk, such a hypothesis is difficult to express in a valuation model. The popularity of arbitrage-free term structure models seems to indicate that we should begin to explore risk-neutral mortgage valuation tools.

REFERENCES

Askin, David J., Woodward C. Hoffman, and Steven D. Meyer. 1988. "Evaluation of the Option Component of Mortgage Securities." *The Handbook of Mortgage-Backed Securities,* 2nd ed. Chicago, IL: Probus Publishing.

Davidson, Andrew and Michael Herskovitz. 1994. *Mortgage-Backed Securities: Investment Analysis and Advanced Valuation Technique.* Chicago, IL: Probus Publishing.

Diller, Stanley. 1984. "Parametric Analysis of Fixed Income Securities." New York: Goldman, Sachs & Co. (June).

Hayre, Lakhbir, and Arvind Rajan. 1995. "Anatomy of Prepayments: The Salomon Brothers Prepayment Model." New York: Salomon Brothers Inc. (June).

Patruno, Gregg N. 1994. "Mortgage Prepayments: A New Model for a New Era." New York: Goldman, Sachs & Co. (June).

CHAPTER 7

Finding Value in Mortgage Derivatives:
A View from the Trenches

Laurie S. Goodman
Managing Director

Linda L. Lowell
First Vice President
and

Jeffrey Ho
Vice President
PaineWebber Mortgage Strategy

Investors evaluate inverse floating rate mortgage products—inverse floaters and inverse IOs—from a variety of approaches, each of which has strengths and weaknesses. No single approach tells the whole story. Five major approaches are often used to gauge relative value:

- Traditional—yield and average-life profile,
- Re-creation value,
- Option-adjusted spread analysis,
- Yield to forward LIBOR, and
- Unbundling of options.

During the 1990–93 rally, inverse floating rate product traded very rich by most measures, but investors were not purchasing it as a relative value play. They looked at it as a way to express bullish sentiment in a steep yield curve environment. After the bull market ended, these securities cheapened dramatically, reigniting the interest of some large, sophisticated mortgage players. The surge of interest in mortgage derivatives on the part of the more

TABLE 7-1

Yield Curve and Forward LIBOR as of March 13, 1995

Treasuries		1–Month LIBOR Forwards	
3 mo.	5.93	now	6.1250
6 mo.	6.19	03/96	6.3734
1 yr.	6.39	03/97	6.9303
2 yr.	6.75	03/98	7.3513
3 yr.	6.87	03/99	7.6519
5 yr.	7.01	03/00	7.8494
10 yr.	7.18	03/01	7.9611
30 yr.	7.46	03/02	8.0029
		03/03	7.9892
		03/04	7.9319

sophisticated investors, particularly in inverse floaters and inverse IOs (IIOs), has generated some lively discussion about the application, and limitations, of these different approaches to valuation.

In this chapter, we review the various approaches and compare the advantages and disadvantages of each. We do this for each of two bonds: FHG 24 SE, an inverse floater backed by GNMA 7s evaluated at a price of 52, and FHG 21 S, an inverse IO also backed by GNMA 7s and evaluated at a price of 3:26. Both bonds are indexed off one-month LIBOR. (Prices are offerings as of March 13, 1995. The curve and LIBOR forwards on selected securities for that date are provided in Table 7–1.) We will see that each approach can both add to a basic understanding of the complex securities. behavior and indicate where good relative values exists. Evaluating both securities across all measures, a picture emerges that the first bond was fairly priced, while the second bond represented excellent relative value. We recommend that all measures of relative value be employed by investors in this market sector.

TRADITIONAL MORTGAGE CASH-FLOW MEASURES: THE YIELD AND AVERAGE-LIFE PROFILE

Investors first approached mortgage derivatives by evaluating them the same way they would other mortgage products, using a price/yield table or an inverse table (index/yield table). The first is widely used with fixed-rate MBSs, displaying yields and average lives, given different prices on one axis and prepayment speeds on the other (or, alternatively, displaying prices, with yield as a variable on one axis). In the case of variable-rate securities, the coupon at the current level of the index rate is assumed. Alternatively, inverse tables display yields, given a price, with different levels of the index on one axis and different prepayment speeds on the other axis. These tables indicate the sensitivity of the security's average life and yield to different prepayment speeds. Given an average life, it is an easy matter also to evaluate the sensitivity of yield spread to Treasuries for different prepayment speeds.

Table 7–2 provides an example of an inverse table for FHG 24 SE, the inverse floater backed by 30-year GNMA 7s (again, all prices are as of 3/13/95, for settlement 3/21/95). The coupon on this inverse floater resets according to the formula: 18.95 percent – (2.16667 × 1-month LIBOR). At the 3/13/95 1-month LIBOR rate of 6.125 percent, the security has a coupon of 5.68 percent. In the base case, at 85 percent PSA—the Bloomberg median of prepayment projections supplied by mortgage dealers for this collateral (often referred to as Street consensus speed for this collateral)—the security has an average life of 22.39 years and, priced at 52 points, a yield of 12.08 percent. This base case yield is shown in the center box (LIBOR = 6.125 percent, 85 percent PSA). If LIBOR were unchanged, and speeds were to come in at 150 percent PSA (corresponding to the consensus projection for this collateral for

TABLE 7-2

Inverse Floater Yield Table
FHG 24 SE (Px = 52 on 3/13/95)*

LIBOR Scenario	Interest Rate Scenario						
	+300	+200	+100	Unchanged	−100	−200	−300
	\ \ \ \ \ Percent PSA						
	57%	65%	75%	85%	115%	150%	470%
3.125%	24.66	24.67	24.68	24.71	24.90	26.60	large
4.125	20.21	20.23	20.26	20.30	20.60	22.59	large
5.125	15.94	15.97	16.01	16.08	16.48	18.74	195.41
6.125	11.89	11.93	12.00	12.08	12.59	15.06	189.27
7.125	8.12	8.17	8.26	8.36	8.95	11.55	183.21
8.125	4.67	4.73	4.82	4.94	5.57	8.20	117.24
9.125	2.68	2.74	2.83	2.95	3.58	6.20	173.55
Avg. Life	24.61	24.08	23.3	22.39	18.48	10.82	0.58
Duration	8.55	8.52	8.47	8.40	7.99	6.18	0.23
Window	2/19–6/20	7/18–1/20	8/17–5/19	7/16–8/18	1/12–5/15	5/02–7/08	4/95–1/96

*3/21/95 settle; coupon = 18.95% − 2.16667 × 1-month LIBOR; 30-yr. GNMA 7 collateral.
Source: Bloomberg Financial Markets and PaineWebber Mortgage Strategy.

a 200-basis-point decline in interest rates), the security's yield would increase to 15.06 percent and the average life would contract to 10.82 years. A more likely scenario, however, would have been if faster prepayments were accompanied by a lower LIBOR rate: For instance, at LIBOR of 4.125 percent, the expected yield on this security is 22.59 percent. Accordingly, most investors look at the diagonal from lower left-hand corner (high LIBOR, slow prepayments) to upper right-hand corner (low LIBOR, fast prepayments) to gain an idea of how the security behaves. The scenarios implied by the diagonal to the other corners are fairly unlikely—fast speeds such as 470 percent PSA accompanied by a dramatic rise in LIBOR (reflecting a steeply inverted yield curve) or a sharp fall in LIBOR and very slow speeds.

Finding Value in Mortgage Derivatives: A View from the Trenches 137

TABLE 7-3

Inverse IO Yield Table
FHG 21 S (Px = 3:26 on 3/13/95)*

	Interest Rate Scenario						
	+300	+200	+100	Un-changed	−100	−200	−300
1-month	Percent PSA						
LIBOR	57%	65%	75%	85%	115%	150%	470%
3.125%	153.41	152.24	150.76	149.27	144.71	139.20	77.92
4.125	113.82	112.71	111.30	109.88	105.50	100.16	39.06
5.125	77.67	76.60	75.24	73.85	69.54	64.17	1.72
6.125	44.54	43.46	42.07	40.63	36.07	30.26	−35.73
7.125	12.95	11.66	9.97	8.21	2.53	−4.74	−77.70
8.125	n/a	n/a	n/a	n/a	n/a	n/a	n/a
9.125	n/a	n/a	n/a	n/a	n/a	n/a	n/a
Avg. Life	7.55	7.00	6.40	5.89	4.71	3.802	1.35
Window	3/95-12/10	3/95-1/10	3/95-1/09	3/95-1/08	3/95-9/05	3/95-9/03	3/95-2/98

*Coupon = 8.0% − 1-month LIBOR; 30-yr GNMA 7 collateral.
Source: Bloomberg Financial Markets and PaineWebber Mortgage Strategy.

The term *yield leverage* is often used as a thumbnail measure of the risk of the security. Yield leverage is the difference between the base-case yield and the yield at LIBOR 100 basis points higher. In this instance, the base-case yield is 12.08 percent. If LIBOR rises 100 basis points, the yield falls to 8.36 percent. The difference (12.08 percent − 8.36 percent) amounts to a yield leverage of 3.72.

The yield and average life table for FHG 21 S is shown in Table 7-3. As can be seen from this yield table, the inverse IO backed by GNMA 7s has a yield of 40.63 percent and an average life of 5.89 years in the base case (85 percent PSA, 6.125 percent LIBOR). Even if LIBOR rises 100 basis points, with prepayment rates unchanged, the bond still has a yield of 8.21 percent. Note also that the security has a very different payoff structure from the inverse floater in Table 7-2. The best scenario for the inverse floater along the lower-left-to-upper-right diagonal was the upper right—low rates and fast prepayments. The best scenario for the inverse IO (Table 7–3) along the same diagonal is also lower rates and faster prepayments, but if the prepayments get too fast, the yield begins to decline because the security disappears too quickly. This can actually be seen best by assuming that LIBOR is set at 6.125 percent. Reflecting the discount price, the yield increases on the inverse floater as prepayments increase and principal is returned more quickly. On the notional IIO, the security actually yields less as prepayments increase, because it is outstanding less long. That is, because there is no principal payment, the amount of cash flow received depends entirely on how long the underlying principal is outstanding. The investor is hoping that, in actuality, prepayments are no faster than indicated by the Street consensus.

The problem with inverse tables or yield tables is that they cannot indicate how much an investor should be compensated for the complex risks in an inverse floater or an inverse IO. For one thing, these are leveraged positions, and we know that investors in leveraged positions should be compensated for the additional risk. Is a yield of 12.08 percent on the inverse floater adequate compensation for the higher leverage and average-life variability? Is the yield of 40.63 percent adequate compensation on the inverse IO? We tend to focus on the yield tables primarily to understand the average life variability on the security. It is very difficult to make a relative value judgment on the basis of a yield table.

RE-CREATION ANALYSIS

Given the limitations of inverse tables in determining relative value, it was natural that investors should want a measure of relative value that could also be used as a pricing guide. One of the first approaches widely used in the market was to determine the "re-creation" or recombination value. This technique takes advantage of the fact that inverse floaters are created by dividing the cash flows of an underlying fixed-rate bond into a floating-rate and inverse-floating-rate security. Theoretically, the market value of the underlying is equal to the sum of the market values of the floater and the inverse floater. Many investors use re-creation values for month-end marking; others use the recombination technique to evaluate the month-end marks they get from dealers. Furthermore, dealers often use re-creation value as a guide when bidding a security. To perform this analysis, the floater and the inverse are recombined to form the underlying fixed-rate tranche. If this underlying security—a Planned Amortization Class (PAC), Targeted Amortization Class (TAC), or companion structure of some type—is traded, then it can be priced. The prices of both the underlying and the floater uniquely determine the recombination value of the inverse.

In order to see how this approach is implemented, we use our inverse floater example, FHG 24 SE . This bond was created by taking a 6.5 percent TAC backed by 30-year GNMA 7s and tranching it into a floater and an inverse. This is shown in Figure 7–1. The floater, FHG 24 FE, pays LIBOR + 75 basis points up to an 9.5 percent cap (corresponding to a LIBOR strike of 8.75 percent, or 9.5 percent − 75 basis points). We evaluated this floater at a dollar price of 94:14 points (again, as of March 13, 1995), which corresponds to a discount margin of 125 basis points at 75 percent PSA. The underlying bond would have traded at +80 to the old long bond at 85 percent PSA. As of the close on March 13, 1995, the old long bond had a yield of 7.51 percent. Thus, the underlying bond would yield

FIGURE 7-1

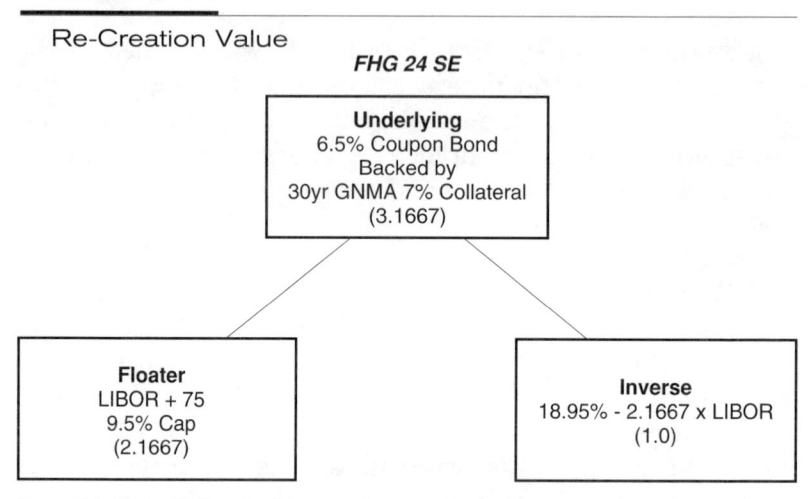

Re-Creation Value

FHG 24 SE

```
         Underlying
      6.5% Coupon Bond
          Backed by
     30yr GNMA 7% Collateral
           (3.1667)
         /          \
        /            \
   Floater          Inverse
  LIBOR + 75     18.95% - 2.1667 x LIBOR
   9.5% Cap            (1.0)
   (2.1667)
```

Source: PaineWebber Mortgage Strategy.

8.31 percent, at 85 percent PSA, corresponding to a price of 82:28 points. Using a little algebra, we can easily find the price of the inverse floater. We know:

$$(2.1667(\text{Price FE}) + \text{Price SE}/(1+2.1667) \quad (1)$$
$$= \text{Price of the underlying fixed-rate tranche}^1$$
$$(2.1667\,(94{:}14) + \text{Price SE})/3.1667$$
$$= 82{:}28$$

Solving for Price SE, we get a recombination price of 57.82 points, considerably higher than the offered price of 52 points, indicating this inverse is very cheap to its re-creation value.

However, this is too optimistic a way to look at this security. In order to recombine the floater and the inverse floater in an economic fashion, as we have seen done frequently in the market, the underlying bonds would have to

---

1. The multiplier, 2.1667 in this case, expresses the ratio of floater principal to inverse floater principal.

be purchased 20 basis points cheaper (a combination of two or more CMO tranches is called a re-REMIC). The explanation is that re-REMIC tranches trade 10 basis points behind; costs add another 10 basis points. Thus, the underlying bond would not be sold at a price of 82:28, it would be sold at a price 20 basis points cheaper. This would be an 8.51 percent yield at a speed of 85 percent PSA, corresponding to a price of 81:06. Assuming the price of the floater is 94:14, the re-REMIC bid for the inverse floater would be 52.38. This is insignificantly different from the actual price of 52:00.

Finding the re-creation value of FHG 24 SE, the inverse, assumes that we know where the floater and the underlying fixed-rate tranche trade with a fair degree of certainty, and we are merely finding the re-creation price of the inverse. In many cases—particularly in situations in which the security is less well-structured—there can be considerable pricing uncertainty on both the underlying fixed rate and the floater. When solving for the price of the inverse floater, this pricing uncertainty is magnified by the degree of leverage.

Another common problem with determining re-creation value occurs when the underlying bond is divided into three on more bonds rather than just a floater and an inverse floater or a floater and an inverse IO. One common variation is to divide the underlying bond in this case into three bonds: a floater, an inverse floater, and a two-tiered index bond (TTIB). The inclusion of TTIBs was a very common structuring strategy in 1993 deals. The collateral used to create such structures was primarily 6.5s and 7s. With coupons this low, it was difficult to simultaneously create both a floater with a cap high enough to be salable *and* an inverse floater with enough leverage—and hence enough yield—to be salable. The solution, as it turned out, was the introduction of TTIBs.

FIGURE 7-2

Determining Re-Creation Value Is Difficult (and Not Very Meaningful) on FHG 21 S

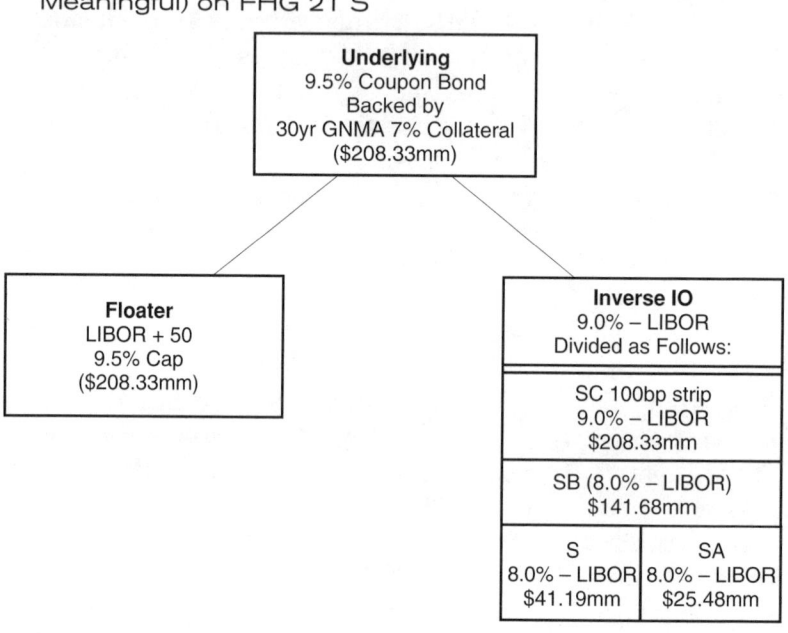

```
                    Underlying
               9.5% Coupon Bond
                    Backed by
              30yr GNMA 7% Collateral
                   ($208.33mm)
```

```
      Floater                          Inverse IO
    LIBOR + 50                        9.0% – LIBOR
     9.5% Cap                       Divided as Follows:
   ($208.33mm)
                                   SC 100bp strip
                                    9.0% – LIBOR
                                      $208.33mm

                                   SB (8.0% – LIBOR)
                                       $141.68mm

                                    S             SA
                               8.0% – LIBOR  8.0% – LIBOR
                                 $41.19mm      $25.48mm
```

Source: PaineWebber Mortgage Strategy.

When a TTIB is also part of the structure, we can still perform the recombination, but the analysis is less useful, as there is considerable uncertainty as to where the TTIBs are actually trading; these bonds are much less liquid and harder to value than the inverses. In this case, then, a re-combination analysis should be viewed as "garbage in, garbage out."

In some structures, the underlying bond is divided into a floater/inverse floater pair or a floater/IIO pair, but then the inverse floater or inverse IO is further subdivided, making recombination analysis difficult. Our representative inverse IO, FHG 21 S, was created in this fashion. Figure 7–2 shows how the underlying bond, a 9.5 percent coupon bond backed by 30-year GNMA 7 percent collateral, was divided into a floater paying LIBOR + 50, and an IIO paying 9% − LIBOR. This IIO was in turn divided into four pieces. One of these, tranche SC, is a 100-basis-point strip off the underlying IIO; the remainder pays 8 percent − LIBOR and is divided three ways, to create tranches S, SA and SB. Tranche SB is an IIO paying 8 percent − LIBOR. Tranches S and SA together have the same cash flows as tranche SB; only tranche S receives the earlier cash flows, and tranche SA receives the later cash flows. The only way to back out the value of FHG 21 S is to determine the value of each of the other pieces—a nearly impossible job.

The most important objection to re-creation value is that it only prices the bonds (the underlying, the floater, and the inverse) relative to each other. For this reason, it is not a guide to relative value within the mortgage market. For example, consider a situation in which the underlying bond is inherently rich and the floater too cheap. The fact that the inverse falls out cheap to creation value may not indicate relative value. The investor may still be purchasing a rich security relative to the universe of alternatives.

The final problem with recombination analysis is that there is no reason why an inverse floater (or any bond, for that matter) cannot trade cheap to re-creation value for a long period of time. When, as is currently the case, there is an adequate supply of secondary bonds trading cheap to re-creation value, the selling of new inverses is precluded. If inverses were trading expensive to recombination values, the pace of new issuance would be such that the price of the securities would quickly realign.

OPTION-ADJUSTED SPREAD ANALYSIS

Recombination allows investors to appraise an inverse relative to its re-creation value, but it does not allow investors to gauge relative value in inverses against other securities, especially long-duration alternatives. By contrast, the option-adjusted spread (OAS) was introduced into the mortgage market specifically to allow comparisons between securities. Before discussing the advantages and disadvantages of this approach for inverses, we provide a brief review of OAS analysis.

To calculate option-adjusted spreads for mortgage securities, market participants use a Monte Carlo, stratified sampling, or similar approach. Different approaches can cause the results to vary from firm to firm, but the two major sources of variation are the way the probability distribution of interest rates is determined and the way each firm specifies and estimates the prepayment function.

The first step in an OAS analysis is to generate a probability distribution of interest rates over time. This is done first by deriving spot and implied forward rates for Treasury securities of different maturities. Some firms use on-the-run Treasury securities for this derivation; other firms use all Treasury coupon securities; still others use all coupon issues plus Treasury strips. (Generally, the more market information incorporated, the better. However, the result can occur that individual on-the-run Treasuries are rich to the generalized Treasury yield structure when run through the model—which some users of OAS models may find disconcerting the first time they encounter it.) After the spot-rate yield curve is calculated, a probability distribution is selected for short-term Treasury rates. This probability distribution is selected so that it is consistent with current spot rates. Loosely speaking, this means it will be centered near today's forward rates. The selection of the probability distribution can be very different across models; implicit in the distribution is the volatility and the degree of mean reversion. Some models assume a normal distribution of rates, others a log-normal distribution. Using a log-normal distribution ensures that interest rates will never be negative; a normal distribution coupled with mean reversion ensures that interest rates will never get very negative. The variance of the distribution can either be assumed or estimated.

The probability distribution is then used to generate interest rate paths. In Monte Carlo simulations, for instance, a large number of interest rate paths are chosen randomly from the interest rate distribution. For each path, the cash flows of the mortgage security are generated, using an embedded proprietary prepayment model, which gives the prepayment rate at each point in time. The OAS is found using an iterative search. A spread is assumed (guessed) and the present value along each path is calculated. The present values are then averaged and compared to the market price of the bond. If they are equal, the assumed spread is the option-adjusted spread. If the values are not equal, other spreads are tried until one is found which equals the market price of the bond.

OAS is a powerful tool for relative value analysis. It is the only methodology that is internally consistent and captures both the shape of the yield curve and the value of the embedded options in a single summary number. Moreover, by running a large number of interest rate paths, both favorable and unfavorable to the security, the structure of the tranche is fully taken into account. Any priority switches, rapid call or extension, or strange behavior under certain interest-rate-prepayment scenarios will be captured. The problem with OAS lies not in the number, but in the interpretation.[2]

It is very easy to misinterpret OAS numbers. First, OAS users must bear in mind that OAS is heavily model

---

2. An excellent and very readable discussion of the disadvantages of OAS analysis can be found in Robert Kopprasch, "Option Adjusted Spread Analysis: Going Down the Wrong Path?" in the *Financial Analysts Journal,* May/June 1994.

TABLE 7-4

Sensitivity of OAS to Prepayment Model

FHG 24 SE (Px = 52:00)			
	OAS	OAD	Convexity
80% of PW prepayment model	87	44.49	2.100
100% of PW prepayment model	109	42.01	2.367
120% of PW prepayment model	157	41.77	3.740
FHG 21 S (Px = 3:26)			
	OAS	OAD	Convexity
80% of PW prepayment model	1112	60.52	11.580
100% of PW prepayment model	835	60.04	8.580
120% of PW prepayment model	551	59.67	11.990

Source: PaineWebber Mortgage Strategy.

dependent. Small differences in the prepayment model can make large differences in the OAS. Table 7–4 shows the OAS, as well as the option-adjusted duration and convexity of FHG 24 SE and FHG 21 S, the inverse floater and inverse IO, respectively, at different multiples of the PaineWebber prepayment model. At 100 percent of the prepayment model, FHG 24 SE has an OAS of 109; an OAS of 157 at 120 percent of the model, and an OAS of 87 at 80 percent. In fact, at 80 percent of the prepayment model, the inverse floater has a lower OAS than some pass-throughs (at a normal multiple of 100 percent). Moreover, this is a fairly tame example; FHG 21 S is much more sensitive. The IIO has an OAS of 835 at 100 percent of the model, an OAS of 551 at 120 percent of the model, and an OAS of 1112 at 80 percent of the model. This sensitivity to the prepayment function should make investors wary of relying exclusively on OAS analysis. There are wide differences in prepayment models at different firms, and they can make very large differences in the results.

TABLE 7-5

Divergence in Prepayment Models (GNSF 7%)

	\multicolumn{9}{c	}{Interest Rate Scenario}
	−300	−200	−100	−50	Unchanged	+50	+100	+200	+300
PSA projection									
Street median	464	155	114	97	86	77	73	63	57
PaineWebber	464	151	114	101	91	88	85	80	77
Absolute deviation from street median									
Eleven-firm average	67	28	9	10	10	9	9	10	12
PaineWebber	0	4	0	4	5	11	12	17	20
Absolute deviation as percentage of street median									
Eleven-firm average	14	18	8	10	12	11	12	16	21
PaineWebber	0	3	0	4	6	14	16	27	35

Source: Bloomberg Financial Markets and PaineWebber Mortgage Strategy.

Furthermore, by making some simple comparisons, we can show that 10–20 percent is a normal variation between prepayment models. Table 7–5 shows Bloomberg Street consensus speeds on GNMA 7s for nine interest rate scenarios. It also indicates the amount the individual projections of the 11 firms contributing to the consensus differed, on average, from the consensus. These differences are summarized as the mean absolute deviation and mean percentage deviation across firms. Thus, in the base case, the Bloomberg median is 86 percent PSA. The average absolute deviation was 10 percent PSA—that is, firms were, on average, different from the consensus by 10 percent PSA. The difference amounts to 12 percent of the consensus speed. (Obviously, some firms were higher and some were lower.) Note also that the mean percentage deviation on the security is smaller in the base case and for modest interest rate shifts and higher in cases in which interest rates go up or down substantially. More importantly, looking at the average of prepayment models versus the Street median understates the degree any individual firm can vary from consensus. For instance, in the table we also compare the PaineWebber results to the Street median numbers. In the base case, PaineWebber is higher than the Street average by 6 percent. When yields shift up 300 basis points, it is 35 percent higher than the Street average. To summarize, a 10–20 percent difference between prepayment models is realistic as an estimate of model uncertainty. Applied to the OAS analysis of volatile derivatives, however, this normal variation in prepayment models can make the difference between the security looking very attractive, marginally attractive, or unattractive.

A second disadvantage is that OAS is a less-meaningful number for leveraged securities. Clearly, any model error is magnified as a result of the leverage. Moreover, the OAS on a leveraged security should be higher, as the OAS on the financing should be low. For example, if the OAS on GNMA 7s is 40 and we are able to finance at 0 OAS, then the OAS on a position in which we own 3.167 GNMA 7s and finance 2.167 of them would be 126.7 (40 × 3.167). This is actually higher than the OAS on FHG 24 SE, the inverse floater, which has similar leverage.

Third, a security will never actually earn its OAS. In fact, depending on the path that materializes, the security can significantly outperform or significantly underperform Treasury securities. Thus, the OAS will not correspond to the *ex post* profit on the trade. More important, the distribution of path-dependent prices is never provided with OAS numbers, so that one does not have a good idea of how wide the variation is across paths. If the path-dependent prices were highly concentrated, the security would have less risk than if the path-dependent prices were all over the map. This uncertainty is not priced.

Our conclusion regarding OAS numbers is that they should be used cautiously as measures of relative value.

TABLE 7-6

Price Change for an Instantaneous Change in Interest Rates (OAS Constant)

FHG 24 SE (Coupon = 18.96 − 2.167 × 1-month LIBOR; OAS = 109)								
Interest Rate Scenario								
	−200	−100	−50	Unchanged	+50	+100	+200
Price	100.92	74.77	62.44	52.00	42.64	34.44	22.04
Duration	10.16	38.86	37.66	42.00	46.87	49.65	54.70
Convexity	−2.63	8.92	2.78	2.39	4.02	8.46	11.36

FHG 21 S (Coupon = 8.00 − 1.00 × 1-month LIBOR; OAS = 853)								
Interest Rate Scenario								
	−200	−100	−50	Unchanged	+50	+100	+200
Price	7.46	6.15	4.94	3.81	2.84	1.99	0.87
Duration	−18.42	40.30	50.99	60.03	71.54	86.11	91.41
Convexity	−68.65	−9.11	2.55	8.21	7.14	15.76	39.97

Source: PaineWebber Mortgage Strategy.

Run the prepayment model at different multiples and test the sensitivity. The less sensitive the OAS output is to multiplying the prepayment model, the more credence that can be placed in the results.

Despite its limitations, we believe that OAS can serve as a very valuable guide (1) to the price risk of the security and (2) to the possible upside on the security if interest rates remain at current levels. By holding OAS constant and calculating instantaneous price changes under different scenarios, we can get an idea of the price risk and the convexity of a security. For instance, on FHG 24 SE, if interest rates go up 100 basis points, holding the OAS constant, the price of the security would decline by 17.56 points (52 − 34.44) or 33.8 percent. The instantaneous price changes under different interest rate scenarios are shown in Table 7–6. Investors should make sure they can handle this degree of risk. This analysis also illustrates the positive convexity of the security. Note that if rates fall 100 basis points, the security will rise in price by 22.77 points. This is notably larger than the price drop of 17.56 points if rates rise 100 basis points. This analysis is even more interesting in the case of the IIO, because it allows investors to see how negatively convex the security is. The IIO actually behaves as if it has positive convexity. If rates fall 100 basis points, the price of the security rises from 3.81 to 6.15 for a gain of 2.34, whereas if rates rise 100 basis points, the price, OAS-constant, drops from 3.81 to 1.99 for a change of 1.82 points.

Finally, OAS analysis allows investors to gauge the impact of mispricing. If, for example, with the market at these levels, we thought the OAS on FHG 24 SE could tighten 100 basis points, from 108.7 to 8.7, we could determine that the security would instantaneously increase in price from 52:00 to 56:24-points. Is a 4:24-point gain enough compensation for the bid-ask spreads in the market? The investor must decide.

YIELD-TO-FORWARD LIBOR

Many investors have been frustrated in a steep-yield-curve environment by the ambiguity that surrounds the evaluation of inverses using yield or inverse tables. When the curve is upward-sloping, a more highly leveraged portfolio should have a higher yield. This can be seen by using the swap market to convert an inverse floater into a fixed-rate bond (in effect, swapping out the implied LIBOR financing).[3] That is, the investor would receive floating and pay a fixed rate on an amortizing swap. The net payment

---

3. Such a transaction follows from viewing an inverse floater as a leveraged position in the underlying fixed-rate bond funded at the coupon rate of the sibling floater plus some caps on the implied floating-rate expense.

(fixed rate minus floating rate) would reflect the forward rates implied by current market rates. The fixed rate paid on the swap is subtracted from the yield on the inverse, so that the yield on the swapped inverse floater would be far lower, for instance, than the base-case yield indicated in Table 7–2. The differential will be far greater in a steeper curve than in a flatter curve environment.

That we can treat the inverse as a leveraged position and swap out the short-term funding provides us with another technique for evaluation. We make use of the fact that entering into a swap is equivalent to using Eurodollar futures to convert the LIBOR component of each cash flow into a fixed-rate component; the fixed rate that would be received at each point in time would be forward LIBOR. In turn, we can replicate the economic effect of this series of transactions by using forward LIBOR to set the coupons on the inverse floater at each date under various prepayment assumptions; the yields generated by these cash flows are then often compared to those of fixed-rate structures with similar average lives.

The mechanics of the yield-to-forward-LIBOR calculation are actually quite simple: Each coupon is converted to a fixed-rate equivalent by assuming that LIBOR is equal to forward LIBOR as of each coupon reset date. For example, the coupon formula for FHG 24 SE is 18.95% − 2.167 × 1-month LIBOR. Thus, if forward LIBOR for a particular month were 6.5 percent, the bond would be assumed to pay a coupon rate of 4.86 percent to generate a monthly interest payment equal to 4.86 percent divided by 12 and multiplied by the outstanding amount of the tranche. The assumed fixed coupon will be different each month depending on forward LIBOR implied for that date. Finally, the yield-to-forward LIBOR is simply the internal rate of return on this cash-flow stream.

Table 7–7 provides an example of this analysis for FHG 24 SE and FHG 21 S under the same prepayment

TABLE 7-7
Yield-to-Forward LIBOR versus Yield-to-Current LIBOR

FHG 24 SE (price = 52)

Percent PSA

	57%	65%	75%	85%	115%	150%	470%	PW Prepay Model
Yield-to-forward LIBOR	7.05	7.11	7.20	7.31	7.96	10.93	187.81	7.57
Yield-to-current LIBOR*	11.89	11.93	11.99	12.08	12.59	15.06	189.27	12.28
Avg. Life (yrs.)	24.61	24.08	23.30	22.39	18.48	10.82	0.58	20.64

FHG 21 S1 (price = 3:26)

Percent PSA

	57%	65%	75%	85%	115%	150%	470%
Yield-to-forward LIBOR	8.32	7.00	5.31	3.57	−1.56	−6.63	−69.32
Yield-to-current LIBOR*	44.54	43.46	42.07	40.63	36.07	30.26	−35.73
Avg. Life (yrs.)	7.55	7.00	6.40	5.89	4.71	3.80	1.35

*LIBOR = 6.125% on 3/13/95.
Source: PaineWebber Mortgage Strategy.

speeds used in Tables 7–2 and 7–3, as well as projected speeds from the PaineWebber Prepayment Model. The table indicates that for FHG 24 SE, the inverse floater, the yield-to-forward LIBOR is lower than the yield-to-current LIBOR (Table 7–2) at all prepayment speeds, but the differential increases in the slower prepayment scenarios, where the inverse is heavily dependent on coupon income for its cash-flow performance. Note that FHG 24 SE has a 0 percent coupon as long as LIBOR is 8.75 percent or above. (We call 8.75 percent the LIBOR "strike.")

FHG 21 S, the inverse IO, has very high yields-to-current LIBOR but very modest yields-to-forward LIBOR. At 115 percent PSA and higher speeds, the yield to forward LIBOR is actually negative. The explanation is simple: The bond pays a coupon of 8% – LIBOR. Forward LIBOR rates are somewhat higher than the current LIBOR level of 6.125 percent (as of March 13, 1995), which sharply reduces the cash flow from the coupon. Since this is a low-dollar-price security, and all expected cash flow is coupon income, the yield differences between current and forward LIBOR are quite large.

The problem with a yield-to-forward-LIBOR analysis is that many investors believe they have created a fixed-rate bond in which the yield profile is readily comparable to a Treasury security or a fixed-rate bond with a similar structure. This is not true, for two reasons. First, even an amortizing swap (what we have, in effect, replicated here) does not reflect the uncertainty of the mortgage cash flows. If yields rise, slowing prepayments, the inverse would be under-swapped, and additional swaps would have to be added, but at a greater cost reflecting the higher fixed rate. On the other hand, if yields decline, accelerating prepayments, the combination is now over-swapped, and some swaps would have to be paired off but at a lower fixed rate.

Either outcome will always hurt the inverse. It follows, then, that in the absence of other considerations, inverse floaters should trade cheaper than fixed-rate cash flows.

The other reason that the swapped inverse position is not fully comparable to a fixed-rate bond is that the inverse contains a valuable embedded LIBOR option that is not priced by this procedure. This option can be viewed as a cap on the implied LIBOR funding if we construe an inverse floater as equivalent to a long position in the underlying fixed-rate bond funded at the coupon rate of the sibling floater. Consider the fixed-rate bond underlying FHB 24 SE, a 6.5 percent coupon bond backed by GNMA 7 percent collateral. If we had a 3.16667 long position in this fixed-rate bond, and a 2.16667 short position in the sibling floater, and interest rates went up to 9 percent, the investor would be paying more to fund the position than he is receiving on the fixed-rate bond. However, on an inverse floater, the coupon can never go below zero. Thus, we can think of this inverse floater as containing a cap on LIBOR struck at 8.75 percent. Similarly, on the inverse IO, FHG 21 S, we can think of a cap struck at LIBOR = 8 percent. Given the presence of such valuable options, the yield-to-forward LIBOR on an inverse should be lower than on a comparable fixed-rate bond.

In other words, when we compare an inverse floater's or inverse IO's yield-to-forward-LIBOR profile to that of a similarly structured fixed-rate bond under the same prepayment profiles, our view of relative value is obscured by two contradictory effects: The value of the inverse floater is overstated because we miss the added cost to the swap imposed by average life variability, and the value of the inverse floater is understated because we ignore the value of the LIBOR option. As a result, yield-to-forward LIBOR is a better indicator of value in those situations where both problems are minimized. The effect of implicitly over- and under-swapping is minimized for bonds with cash flows that are stable over a wide range of interest rate scenarios—for example, inverses backed by low-coupon balloon collateral and inverses backed by 30- or 15-year collateral with stable structures such as PACs. The value of the LIBOR cap is minimized in bonds with high LIBOR strikes; these correspond to inverses in which the cap on the sibling floater is high. That is, the 0 percent floor on the inverse coupon is exercised when the floater hits its cap and is receiving all interest cash flow from the underlying fixed-rate bond. The higher the cap on the floater and the shorter its average life, the less valuable it is— and the less important, then, is determining the value of the floor on the inverse. In the case of the inverse floater FHG 24 SE, an 8.75 percent strike on the floater cap is relatively high. In many cases, the caps are struck at 7 percent, or even slightly lower.

UNBUNDLING THE OPTIONS

We have pointed out the difficulties that arise when we try to use swaps (or, equivalently, forwards) to evaluate inverse floaters with volatile average lives. Swap-based analyses also have the drawback that they fail to capture the PO-like optionality in many inverse floaters. To account for this option value, as well as the value of the LIBOR option, we take a different approach to decomposing the inverse floater into its economic constituents: We divide an inverse floater into its coupon payment stream and its principal payment stream. It should be immediately apparent that the principal cash flows represent a structured PO. We then show that the coupon payment stream is an IO inverse, which, in turn, is equivalent to a floor. Once again, we base our example on FHG 24 SE. Assume an amount of $10 million, which we strip into two parts as follows:

1. The $10 million in principal. This is a scheduled (TAC) PO backed by 30-year GNMA 7s.

2. The interest, which is computed according to the formula 18.95% − (2.1667 x 1-month LIBOR) on a notional balance of $10 million.

Now we can easily create the same interest cash flows by thinking of a security with a larger notional amount and less leverage as follows:

Receive 18.95		Receive 8.75
Pay 2.1667 × LIBOR	=	Pay LIBOR
on $10 million		on $21.667 million

The cash flows from this second security are precisely those of an inverse IO (8.75% − LIBOR, 0% floor). Notice, as well, that the interest payments on the bond are equal to those on $21.667 million interest rate swaps, with one important difference: *The cash flows from the inverse can never be negative.* The reason: the investor is long a 8.75 percent cap, acquired from the floating-rate tranche.

Now it can easily be shown that an IIO is a floor. Table 7–8 shows the payment structure on a floor. If the index (LIBOR) is less than the strike (8.75 percent), the position will pay the strike less the index (8.75 percent − index). If the index is higher than the strike, the position will pay zero. This is exactly the payout on a floor.

It can also be shown, as we do in Table 7–8, that a floor is equal to a swap plus a cap. That is, a long swap position nets the investor the fixed rate minus the index, regardless of the index level. The cap pays the index minus the fixed rate as long as the index is above the fixed rate. Thus, a swap (S) plus a cap (C) pays 0 if the index is

TABLE 7-8

Cap/Floor/Swap Parity

	Condition	Payment
Floor	IF index > X%	0
	IF index < X%	X% − index
Cap	IF index > X%	index − X%
	IF index < X%	0
Swap		
(Receive X	IF index > X%	X% − index
Pay Index)	IF index < X%	X% − index
Conclusion	$F - C = S \geqq F = S + C$	

Source: PaineWebber Mortgage Strategy.

greater than the fixed rate, and pays the fixed rate minus the index if the index is less than the fixed rate. This is equivalent to a floor (F). We can summarize these notions in equation form below.

$$F = S + C$$
$$\text{or } F = IIO$$

This analysis tells us that an inverse floater is a structured PO plus a floor, or a structured PO plus an inverse IO. The difficulty with this methodology is that now that we have done the decoupling, we need to determine where each of the component parts trade to evaluate the market price of the inverse floater. We know where the PO trades, but it is very difficult to value the IIO with these characteristics. However, we can easily value a floor which has a maturity equal to the average life of the security, or alternatively, we can value an amortizing floor with matching cash flows. The former can be done on Bloomberg.

Many investors assume that if they are really long a floor, they should be able, in effect, to sell it, reducing the purchase price of the inverse by its market value and implicitly valuing the PO. The implicit value can be compared to the fair value determined by pricing principal cash flows at the yield or spread where they would trade in the market.[4] Similarly, the yield profile of the principal cash flows can be evaluated at the implied PO value. Table 7–9 shows this analysis for FHG 24 SE. We assume that we have sold off 2.1667 floors with a 8.75 percent strike and received 14.8 points for each of them. The purchase price of the PO is then reduced by 32.06 points (14.8 × 2.1667), from its original price of 52 to 19.94 points. The price-yield table for this PO, assuming a price of 19.94, is also shown in Table 7–9. By comparison, the fair value of the structured PO cash flows is 20.38. Pricing out the floor puts us virtually on top of fair value of this security.

This approach is intuitively appealing because it allows the investor to break out the options, and evaluate directly the bets that are implicit in the security. The problem with this approach is that the floor, which is embedded in the inverse floater and which we are implicitly long, is not identical to the floor we can write in the derivatives market. The floor we can write has a fixed maturity and average life, while the implied floor in the security is prepayment-rate dependent. As rates fall, the floor we are implicitly long disappears, limiting its potential for price appreciation, while the floor we can write increases in value dramatically. For example, if rates fall 100 basis points, the average life of the inverse floater FHG 24 SE shortens from 22.39 years to 18.48 years. If rates fall 300 basis points, the IIO component disappears, while the long-term amortizing floor, which the security is being priced against, will still be outstanding. Similarly, as rates rise, the implicit floor (IIO) extends, depreciating less in price than it would if its average life were fixed. The inverse floater FHG 24 SE has modest extension risk,

---

4. To do this in the price-yield table calculator, we set LIBOR high enough to force the coupon to zero so that, in effect, we are valuing the PO.

TABLE 7-9

Valuation of an Inverse Floater as a Structured PO and Floor (FHG 24 SE)

Floor Cost Per $100		Price of PO	
Single 8.0% floor	14.8	Orig. Px of inverse floater	52.00
× 2.1667	32.06	Gain from writing floors	32.06
		Price of structured PO	19.94
		Fair value of structured PO	20.38

Interest Rate Scenario

	+300	+200	+100	Unchanged	−100	−200	−300
PSA	57	65	75	85	115	150	470
Yield*	6.68	6.83	7.06	7.35	8.96	15.82	1250.00
Avg. Life	24.61	24.08	23.30	22.39	18.48	10.82	0.58

*This yield table was calculated assuming the bond is a PO with a price of 19.94, long bond = 7.46.
Source: Bloomberg Financial Markets and PaineWebber Mortgage Strategy.

going from 22.39 years average life in the unchanged scenario to 24.61 years if rates rise by 300 basis points. In general, reflecting the prepayment uncertainty, the prepayment-linked floor should be worth less than a non-prepayment-linked floor. In this case, if we attribute the fair value of 20.38 to the PO, the floors have a value of 31.62 (52 − 20.38), or 0.44 of a point less than where we could write amortizing floors with the same cash flows. This is not enough of a discount to make up for the relative unattractiveness of a prepayment-linked floor versus a non-prepayment-linked floor.

This point can be seen even more clearly with FHG 21 S, the inverse IO. In the unchanged scenario, the IIO's average life is 5.89 years, and its floor value (or price of an amortizing swap with matching cash flows) 6.84 points. If interest rates go down 200 basis points, the average life of the security will contract to 3.80 years. Table 7–10 shows the floor values (again assuming March 13, 1995, market levels) at different speeds. As can be seen, the market

TABLE 7-10

Floor Valuation on FHG 21 S (Price = 3:26)

	\+300	\+200	\+100	unch	-100	-200	-300	Breakeven
	\+300	\+200	\+100	unch	-100	-200	-300	Floor Value
	57%	65%	75%	85%	115%	150%	470%	200%
Avg. life	7.55	7.00	6.40	5.89	4.71	3.80	1.35	2.97
Floor value	8.38	7.88	7.33	6.84	5.68	4.72	1.77	3.79

Headers above: Interest Rate Scenario / Percent PSA

Source: Bloomberg Financial Markets and PaineWebber Mortgage Strategy.

clearing price for this security (3:26 points) is lower than the floor value consistent with a speed of 150 percent PSA. As a matter of fact, the break-even prepayment speed on this security—that is, the speed at which the cost of an IIO is equal to its floor value—is 200 percent PSA. While IIOs should be cheap to floors of the same average life, this looks so cheap as to be a very good buy. In other words, if one were to buy a non-prepayment-linked floor, paying 8 percent – LIBOR, at the same price as the IIO, the average life of the floor would be 2.97 years, much shorter than the 5.89-year average life of the IIO.

To summarize, an inverse floater or IO investor is implicitly long a floor, but the value of the floor cannot be fully realized in the interest rate derivatives market, and pricing it in the derivatives market attributes to it too much premium income. When inverse floaters are evaluated, this excess premium is then used to reduce the cost of the PO. In effect, the PO is purchased too cheaply in this analysis. Alternatively, the investor could start by determining fair value for the PO and finding the actual floor value (the difference between the price of the inverse floater and the fair value of the PO). This can then be compared to where an IIO could be purchased or to an equivalent floor. In the latter case, the IIO component should trade cheap to an amortizing floor, as it is prepayment linked. In the case of the inverse floater, FHG 24 SE, it is not trading cheap enough.

Similarly, investors can evaluate an inverse IO as a prepayment-linked floor, and look at how cheaply this prepayment-linked floor can be purchased. It should always be cheap to the non-prepayment-linked floor value. In the case of FHG 21 S, rates could have gone down more than 200 basis points before expected prepayments reached levels where investors would have been better off purchasing a non-prepayment-linked floor.

CONCLUSION

There are at least five different approaches to evaluating inverse floaters and inverse IOs: the traditional yield and average life tables, recombination (or re-creation) analysis, OAS analysis, yield-to-forward-LIBOR (or swap-based) analysis, and unbundling the options. Each of these methods adds to our understanding of the instruments, and each has a set of well-defined problems. Table 7–11 sums up the major advantages and disadvantages of each. The important point is that each method contributes to a clearer evaluation of the security, and they should be used together. If a security appears to represent good relative value on all measures, investors should feel comfortable that they have purchased a cheap bond. This is true of the inverse IO discussed in this chapter. If, on the other hand, the security looks cheap on some measures and less appealing on others, further work must be done to see if the techniques by which the security looks good are those techniques in which we are upwardly biasing the answer, or if the techniques by which the security looks poor are techniques in which we are downwardly biasing the answer. In the case of the inverse floater in this paper, a picture emerges that it is fair value but not a compelling buy.

TABLE 7-11

Inverse Floating Rate Mortgage-Backed Securities Summary of the Advantages and Disadvantages of Different Evaluation Methods

Method of Evaluation	Advantages	Disadvantages
Traditional: Yield and average-life profile	• Readily available on Bloomberg.	• Difficult to use for analysis; • Doesn't tell what the security should yield in the base case as compensation for its risk.
Re-creation value	• Valued in light of underlying structure; • Options in the inverse do not have to be valued explicitly.	• Often hard to realistically price on the floater or underlying, further complicated when a TTIB is present; • Doesn't reveal anything about relative value—the price on the underlying or floater may be rich or cheap.
Option-adjusted spread analysis	• Captures option values and the shape of the Treasury yield curve in a consistent manner; • The structure of the bond is explicitly considered.	• Heavily dependent on prepayment model.
Yield-to-forward LIBOR	• Captures the impact of the forward curve on the coupon.	• Security really can't be swapped as a result of the average life variability as prepayment rates change; • Doesn't take account of the implicit long cap; • Doesn't tell what base-case yield should be.
Unbundling the options	• Captures the options and turns the inverse into a less-complicated PO plus floor. Turns the IIO into a floor.	• Tends to overstate the value of the floor, making the inverse or IIO look too attractive.

Source: PaineWebber Mortgage Strategy.

CHAPTER 8

Debt and Equity in the New Real Estate Markets

Patrick J. Corcoran
Vice President
Nomura Securities International, Inc.

As the United States real estate cycle has bottomed and the recovery has strengthened in 1994 and 1995, traditional real estate investments have priced in these sharply improved fundamentals. Property cap rates and real estate investment trust (REIT) dividend yields have fallen dramatically, and commercial mortgage lending spreads have narrowed.

While spreads in commercial mortgage-backed securities (CMBS) have also narrowed somewhat, pricing in this sector continues to reflect substantially more pessimism about real estate risk. In the language of option-based bond models, it is always possible to assign real estate a sufficiently high "volatility" that today's wide CMBS spreads are rationalized. Implicitly, however, this assigns excessive weight to remote and gloomy real estate scenarios.

Indeed, if investors' views about today's real estate risk are shaped by real estate fundamentals, one thing is clear: large further downside of the kind that occurred in 1988–1992 appears to be ruled out. Investors whose focus is disciplined by fundamentals will be interested in total return in scenarios ranging from moderate declines to moderate/strong increases in net operating income (NOI) and property values. Here, subordinate CMBS dominate direct property ownership, both on an unleveraged and a moderately leveraged basis; i.e., they do better in nearly all the relevant scenarios. Thus, traditional real estate investors should consider supplementing their real estate portfolios with subordinate CMBS.

Importantly, subordinate CMBS, in contrast to traditional real estate investments, offer pension funds a way to achieve superior real estate returns in mediocre real estate scenarios. For life insurance companies, subordinate CMBS offer the prospect of earning returns exceeding those from direct property investments and, at the same time, avoiding the huge risk-based capital penalty of direct property ownership.

The first section of this chapter lays out the spectrum of alternative real estate investments which we will be considering. The second section briefly reviews a credit loss model, which is used to simulate losses for both commercial mortgages and CMBS. This model is described more fully elsewhere (Corcoran and Kao 1994, 1995). The third section examines prospective returns in a wide range of real estate scenarios.

A BROADER RANGE OF REAL ESTATE INVESTMENTS

Traditional real estate investments include both direct property ownership and commercial mortgages (Figure 8–1). Pension funds may own properties directly or through investment vehicles such as commingled funds. As with equity investments generally, there is often separation of ownership and control with real estate operating companies managing properties and pension funds as equity partners. The middle panel of Figure 8–1 shows a 65

FIGURE 8-1

Traditional Real Estate Investments and CMBS

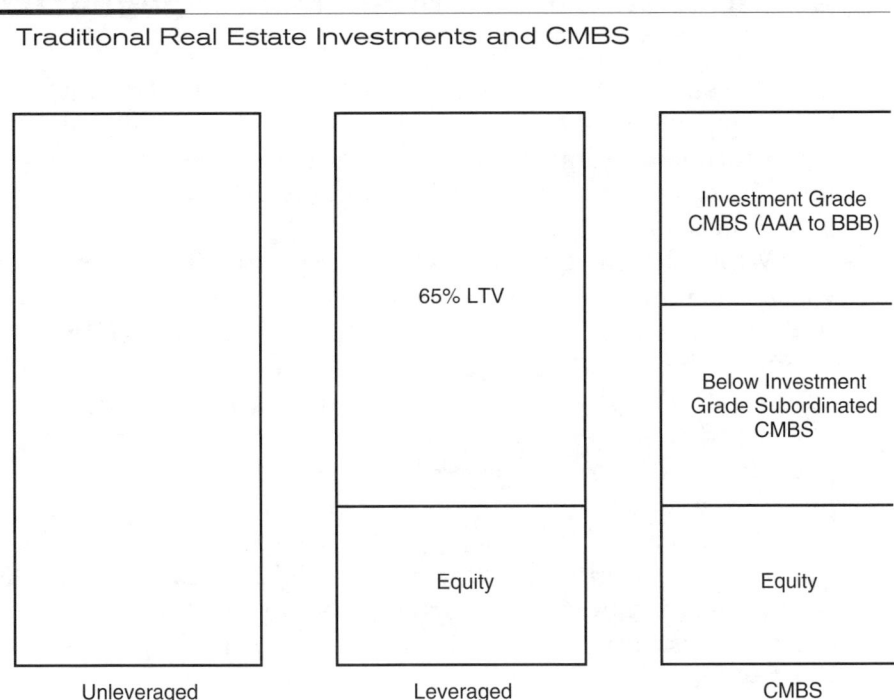

| Unleveraged Real Estate | Leveraged Real Estate (65% LTV / Equity) | CMBS (Investment Grade CMBS (AAA to BBB) / Below Investment Grade Subordinated CMBS / Equity) |

percent loan-to-value (ltv) commercial mortgage with the borrower's leveraged equity position of 35 percent. The right-hand panel shows how commercial mortgage-backed securities would be created by "credit tranching" the commercial mortgage whole loan, or a pool of such loans. This is done by sequentially subordinating each bond class to the ones above it. This results in a prioritization of payment from available cash flow. The senior classes are paid first, then the intermediate-rated classes, then the junior classes. Finally, the cash flow left over after the bondholders are paid goes to the equity holder.

Credit Losses for Commercial Mortgages and CMBS

The flip side of this payment prioritization is that credit losses are allocated from the bottom up. This means that the principal and interest due the most junior bondholder must be completely exhausted before any loss is allocated to the class above it.

While the bond structure allocates losses among the various bond classes, the total losses experienced by the pool of commercial mortgage loans depend on the performance of the underlying real estate. Figure 8–2 shows the empirical default relationships estimated in an earlier study and used here to simulate both commercial mortgage and CMBS credit losses. As shown, the earlier study linked commercial mortgage defaults to changing property values (left panel). In so doing, it built in the average initial ltv for loans originated during the difficult 1988–1992 period. While this ltv is reported to be about 72 percent, there is substantial reason to believe the reported figure is too low (see below). Our operating assumption for purposes of this study is that the true average ltv in 1988–1992 is about 79 percent. We will examine projected losses for a pool of loans originated in today's environment with an initial average ltv of 72 percent.

What are the reasons to think that reported ltvs in the earlier period are too low? First, there is a basic quality problem in the loan-to-value ratios (and coverage ratios) which insurers report to the American Council of Life Insurance (ACLI).

For example, in a hot lending market such as the mid-1980s, underwriting standards come under pressure and reported loan-to-value ratios understate reality. (Conversely, with today's much more conservative underwriting standards, reported loan-to-values likely overstate reality.)

FIGURE 8-2

Sector Delinquency Rates, Real Estate Values, and LTV Ratios

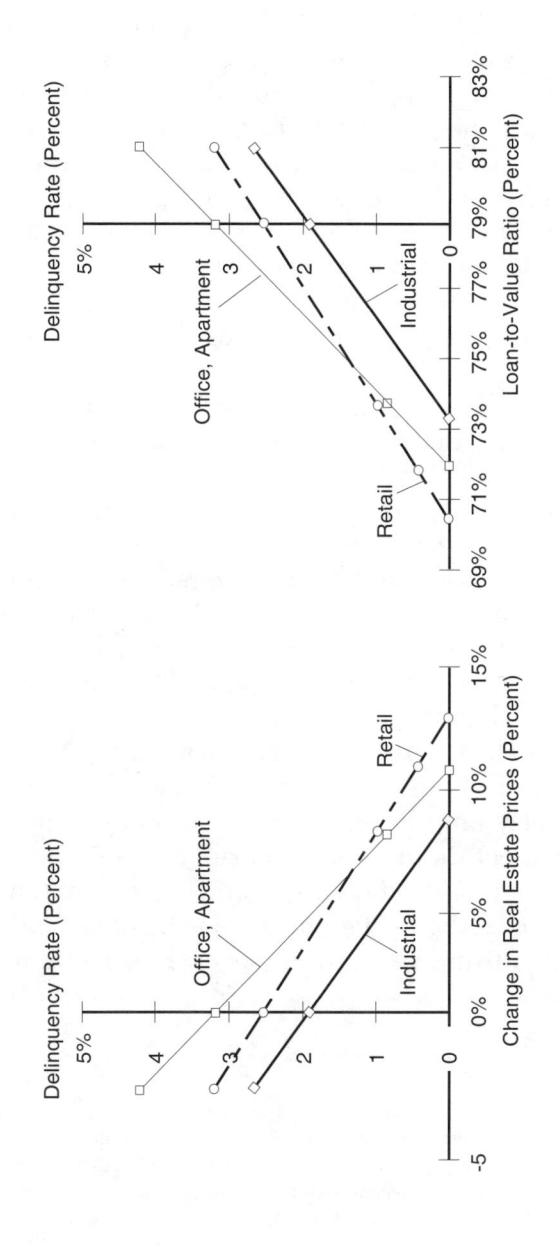

In the mid-1980s, Prudential might have offered a borrower a loan of $105 million on a property appraised at $150 million, implying a loan-to-value of 70 percent. If the Travelers had made a competitive bid to lend $140 million on the same property and won the bid, the commitment form reported to the ACLI would likely have shown a loan of $140 million on a property appraised at $200 million, implying a loan-to-value ratio of 70 percent.

In addition, once real estate values began to decline dramatically in the second half of the 1980s, appraisals lagged way behind, so loan-to-values are overstated on this account as well. Thus, while 72 percent is the average reported loan-to value for new loans originated in the 1980s, it likely is too low for this reason.

There is a second—and more important—problem in applying the 1988–1992 model estimates literally to today's new loans. During this adverse period, a very substantial amount of loan origination consisted of refinancing loans already on the books of the insurer. Many of these loans had suffered substantial erosion in loan-to-value terms, but these borrowers typically could not find refinancing elsewhere. The result was an unusually large share of "new" high loan-to-value loans. These loans performed poorly and find no parallel in today's market or in normal real estate markets generally.[1] While there are no publically available data highlighting the magnitude of this problem in the 1980s, the author has had the opportunity to look at internal data at several large life insurance companies.

---

1. These high loan-to-value loans experienced much higher defaults and loss severities than loans in the same year of origination but in a more normal loan-to-value range. while technically these "involuntary rollovers" were new loans, in reality they were modified loans. For a recent study on the much higher loss severities of modified loans, see Ciochetti and Riddiough (1994).

Notice in Figure 8–2 that the different default curves come down to zero at an average ltv of about 72 percent. This means that, in scenarios where NOI and property values are flat or rising, projected losses will be zero because the average ltv will remain at or below 72 percent. In scenarios where NOI and property values are falling, we will be encountering losses as the average ltv rises and we move up the default curve.

A CMBS Example

Next, we look at a hypothetical CMBS example with a large pool loan structure, and utilize our empirical credit loss model to allocate losses. Since our credit losses are estimated from life insurer lending experience, the loan collateral is assumed to reflect life insurer loan characteristics. Our collateral consists of newly originated loans with average ltvs of 65 percent. By property type, the loans are $25 million of retail mortgages, $25 million multifamily mortgages, $25 million industrial property mortgages, and $25 million of office property mortgages, for a total loan pool of $100 million. The loans are all assumed to have 10-year maturities with 30-year amortization schedules. The geographical distribution of the loans is representative of new life company origination.

Table 8–1 shows information on the bond structure. The general form of the structure follows guidelines as suggested in a recent publication by Duff & Phelps (1994).[2] The most junior bond is a $2.5 million unrated

---

2. The size of the unrated bond reflects rating agency requirements for loans which are not cross-collateralized and cross-defaulted. The assumed mortgage pool average ltv is 72 percent, roughly in line with recent reported insurance company ltv's. Selecting a rating agency ltv of 72 percent while our model ltv is 65 percent captures today's relatively tough underwriting relative to the 1980s. See discussion in text above.

TABLE 8-1
Hypothetical CMBS Structure*

Tranche		Amount (millions)	Coupon (percent)	Price (percent)	T-Yield (percent)	Spread (b.p.)	Yield (percent)	WAL (year)	Begin (date)	End (date)
Collateral		$100.0	8.28%	100.37%	6.5390%	181	8.3482%	9.49	7/4/95	6/4/05
A-1A	AAA	18.5	7.70	102.98	6.4580	78	7.2451	7.24	7/4/95	6/4/05
A-1B	AAA	39.0	7.75	103.00	6.5800	85	7.4297	10.01	6/4/05	6/4/05
A-2	AA	12.2	7.83	102.52	6.5800	100	7.5802	10.01	6/4/05	6/4/05
A-3	A	5.6	8.08	102.55	6.5800	125	7.8292	10.01	6/4/05	6/4/05
A-4	BBB	6.9	8.08	99.19	6.5800	175	8.3304	10.01	6/4/05	6/4/05
B-1	BB	10.9	8.08	85.00	6.5800	415	10.7287	10.01	6/4/05	6/4/05
B-2	B	4.3	8.08	75.22	6.5800	615	12.7273	10.01	6/4/05	6/4/05
B-3	UR	2.5	8.08	45.94	6.5800	1542	22.0011	10.01	6/4/05	6/4/05

*Coupon strips created in this structure are ignored here and in the text.

piece, Class B-3, which occupies the first loss position. Only when allocated losses exceed $2.5 million will any loss be allocated to the next-most junior bond, the $4 million B-rated Class B-2.

In our example, all the loans pay out at maturity at 10 years. The bond structure is designed to match the cash flows accruing from the loan collateral. With fairly slow amortization at a 30-year rate and no loans scheduled to pay out prior to 10 years, only the AAA-rated Class A-1A is scheduled to receive principal payments prior to 10 years. All the other bonds which receive both principal and interest receive all their scheduled principal in year 10, and hence show a weighted average life (wal) of 10 years.

THE REAL ESTATE OUTLOOK AND CHOOSING REAL ESTATE SCENARIOS

Since no real estate investment outperforms other real estate investments in every scenario, identifying the relevant and likely scenarios is very important. This is where the real estate outlook comes in. In recent papers, we have emphasized a positive view for commercial real estate investments generally in the aftermath of the 1980s overbuilding boom (Corcoran and Kao 1994, 1995). Here we don't want to emphasize a point estimate forecast of real estate returns, but rather a general absence of further downside risk.

Our scenarios are defined by specifying a constant annual rate of growth of property NOI and property value appreciation. For example, in a +1 percent scenario, both NOI and property values grow 1 percent per year for 10 years. In our worst-case scenario, NOI and property values decline 3 percent per year for a cumulative drop of almost 30 percent, similar to retail and apartment property declines in 1988–1992.

While worse scenarios can be imagined, further generalized downside is effectively precluded by the current state of the real estate cycle. With property values well below replacement cost levels in many sectors and markets following the overbuilding boom of the 1980s, new supply is likely to remain at the low end of the historic range. In a number of markets and sectors around the country, rents have reached levels where new construction can be justified. In our view, however, this signals a return to demand-supply balance in these markets and not a replay of the generalized 1980s overbuilding. Indeed, more-cautious pricing of commercial real estate is likely to be the legacy of the 1980s overbuilding boom, just as a more-cautious approach to stock ownership was the legacy of the Great Depression for a generation.

In this setting, the persistence of inflation pressures at or above 2 percent per year is important. Over time, even modest continuing inflation will put upward pressure on construction costs and ultimately on rents and property values. Over investment horizons ranging from 5 to 10 years, the likelihood of different real estate scenarios is shifted. The "–3 percent" scenario looks even more remote because in inflation-adjusted terms, it is really "–5 percent." Similarly, the "+3 percent" scenario looks a lot more likely because it is really only "+1 percent."

"DEFAULT-ADJUSTED" YIELDS AND CREDIT SPREADS

For simplicity, we assume that losses are resolved instantly at the point where default occurs.[3] The first column (left-hand side) in Table 8–2 shows the "no loss" yield spread for each CMBS in the structure. The remaining columns show

---

3. In reality, a default in a loan would take some time to resolve either as a foreclosure or as some kind of modification. In the interim, credit would typically be extended by the servicer to the bondholders. For more on the servicer, see Jacob and Duncan (1995) and Gichon (1995). As discussed in Corcoran and Kao (1994, 1995), we assume an average loss severity for defaults of 27 percent.

TABLE 8-2
Default-Adjusted Credit Spreads*

Annual Growth in NOI/Property Values (in basis points)

Bonds/Mortgages		No loss scenario	−3	−2	−1	0	+1	+2	+3
Commercial Mortgage		185	152	168	182	185	185	185	185
Class A-1A	AAA	71	63	67	70	71	71	71	71
Class A-1B	AAA	83	83	83	83	83	83	83	83
Class A-2	AA	98	98	98	98	98	98	98	98
Class A-3	A	122	122	122	122	122	122	122	122
Class A-4	BBB	171	171	171	171	171	171	171	171
Class B-1	BB	402	402	402	402	402	402	402	402
Class B-2	B	593	487	593	593	593	593	593	593
Class B-3	UR	1462	−1718	509	1335	1462	1462	1462	1462

*Credit spreads are spreads to the spot Treasury curve.

default-adjusted credit spreads in each of the real estate scenarios. The default-adjusted spread debits the "no loss" spread by the average annual loss posted over 10 years in the scenario. This is computed by first taking the present value of losses using the Treasury yield curve.

If the bond's actual price is debited by the value of the loss, the default-adjusted yield is the yield which discounts the bond's "no loss" cash flows into the debited current value.[4] Default-adjusted yields may be expressed either as yields or as spreads to the Treasury curve. In addition, we may think of the default-adjusted yields as roughly corresponding to projected total returns over our 10-year holding period on the assumption that cash flows are reinvested at the default-adjusted yield.

In the worst scenario (−3 percent), the cumulative default rate on the pool of commercial mortgages is about 13 percent. In the "−2 percent" scenario, cumulative loan defaults amount to 5.4 percent. In scenarios where NOI and property values are rising, there are no defaults because of the substantial equity cushion initially in place. As shown in Table 8–2, the worst scenario reduces the credit spread for the commercial mortgages from 185 basis points in the "no loss" scenarios to 152 basis points, a loss equivalent to 33 basis points per year.

A glance at Table 8–2 shows that none of the bonds from AAA on down to BB sustain any losses in any of the scenarios. This shows up because the default-adjusted credit spreads for these bonds are the same as the assumed "no loss" credit spreads. The CMBS spreads and the Treasury yield curve represent market pricing as of early June 1995.

Table 8–3 compares the worst-case default-adjusted yields, expressed as spreads to Treasuries, to those for cor-

---

4. See Fons (1987, 1994).

TABLE 8-3

Default-Adjusted Credit Spreads: Corporates versus CMBS (10-year maturity, in basis points)

	Corporates*	CMBS Adverse Scenario
AAA	26	83
AA	37	98
A	51	122
BBB	54	171
BB	119	402
B	163	487

*Source: Nomura Securities International and Fons (1994).

porate bonds. The substantially wider CMBS spreads testify to the sector's relative value. While corporate markets generally have more liquidity than CMBS, they also lack the very strong call protection present in CMBS.[5] Thus, the wider default-adjusted credit spreads in CMBS arguably represent "excess value" rather than the pricing of other characteristics of the bonds.

The brunt of default losses are borne by the unrated bond, which represents the first loss position. This bond has a 22 percent yield to maturity, representing a 1462 basis point spread to the Treasury curve (Table 8–2). As losses begin to hit this bond in the "–1 percent" scenario, the default-adjusted credit spread drops to 1335 basis points, to 486 basis points in the "–2 percent" scenario, and to –1718 basis points in the "–3 percent" scenario. In the worst scenario, total losses of about $3.2 million (relative to

---

5. Commercial mortgages generally have very strong call protection through some combination of prepayment prohibition (lockouts) and yield maintenance provisions. However, the structure of a CMBS deal includes the allocation of yield maintenance penalties to the various bond classes. Hence, it is also necessary to look at the deal structure to ensure that adequate compensation is received in the event of prepayment.

a loan pool of $100 million) exceed the principal of $2.5 million owed on the unrated bond. Thus, in this scenario the B-rated bond also sustains some losses, which reduce its default-adjusted credit spread by about 100 basis points (from 593 basis points to 487 basis points in Table 8–2). At the same time, the unrated bond's overall performance strongly commends it as an "equity" investment because it generally registers a huge outperformance of the other bonds in the other scenarios. This invites a comparison of the subordinate CMBS with traditional equity real estate, the subject to which we now turn.

EQUITY REAL ESTATE VERSUS SUBORDINATE CMBS

At a basic level, the total return for equity investments in real estate consists of the income return and the capital gain or loss arising from the change in the value of the property. In addition, returns to property ownership can be leveraged up by financing the purchase with borrowed funds. An important issue at the outset is to properly define the income component in relation to NOI and market cap rates. In computing the income component relevant for total return calculations, we need to subtract from NOI normal wear and tear and obsolescence of the properties. In addition, normal outlays in connection with tenant improvements also need to be debited against NOI.

Two recent studies have provided historical comparisons on this issue using the pool of NCREIF (National Council of Real Estate Investment Fiduciaries) properties.[6] One study suggests that historical outlays in this category ranged from 15 percent of NOI for apartments to 45 percent of NOI for large retail malls. While these numbers are high, they are muddied by the overbuilding boom

---

6. See Young et al. (1995) and Fisher (1995).

of the 1980s, which likely forced many property owners wishing to stay competitive in the leasing market to keep capital and related expenditures unusually high. In addition, the interaction of technological, environmental, and regulatory factors created one-time charges which will not be repeated. Our view is that the required amount going forward may be significantly lower. Thus, in our base case below, we shall take 10.5 percent as the relevant cap rate for a representative pool of properties and assume that required outlays are 1 percent, or about 10 percent of NOI. This produces a net income of 9.5 percent.

Figure 8–3 compares an "unleveraged equity" position in a pool of commercial properties with total returns for the subordinate bonds.[7] This unleveraged equity could include a pension fund investment in properties either directly or through an investment vehicle such as a commingled fund. Notice first that the unleveraged equity position underperforms the B-rated bond in every case in adverse and improving scenarios ranging from "–3 percent" to "+3 percent." Only in the "+4 percent" and "+5 percent" scenarios does unleveraged equity surpass the B-rated bond. Similarly, the equity underperforms the BB-rated bond in scenarios from "–3 percent" to "+1 percent."

At first blush, it might appear that comparing unleveraged equity with the unrated bond in Figure 8–3 scores some points for the equity. After all, in the "–3 percent" scenario, the unrated bond does very poorly and underperforms the equity. In fact, however, there are also scenarios in which the BB-rated bond (and the BBB, and the A, and the AA . . .) does very poorly. The reason that

---

7. Bond total returns over the 10-year maturity period are measured as the default-adjusted yield. Since prepayments are not considered, the strong call protection of the commercial mortgages and CMBS is presumed. In deals where call protection is weak, prepayments would have to be considered explicitly.

FIGURE 8-3

Unleveraged Equity Total Returns versus Subordinated CMBS

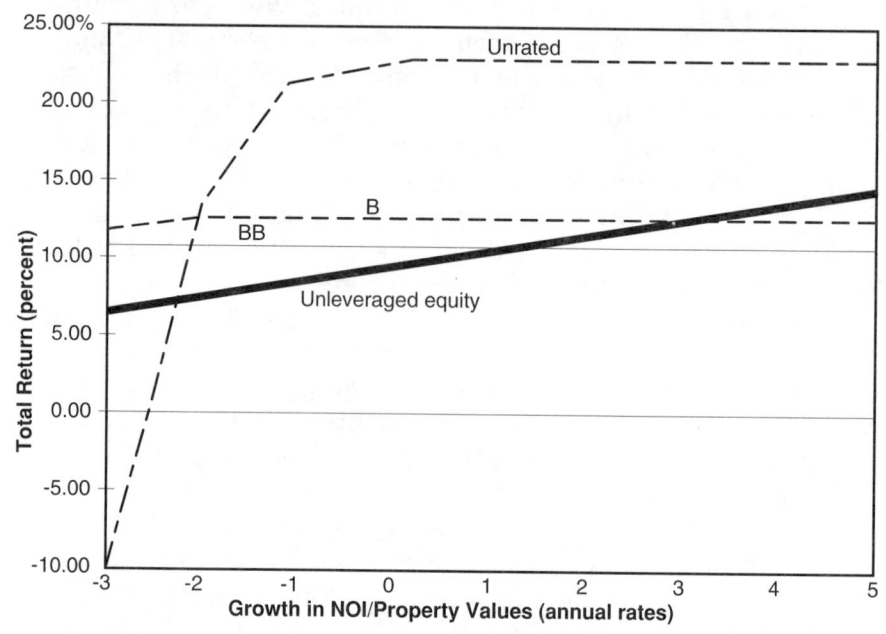

CMBS:	−3	−2	−1	0	1	2	3	4	5
BB	10.73	10.73	10.73	10.73	10.73	10.73	10.73	10.73	10.73
B	11.67	12.73	12.73	12.73	12.73	12.73	12.73	12.73	12.73
Unrated	−9.80	12.49	20.73	22.00	22.00	22.00	22.00	22.00	22.00
Unleveraged equity*	6.75	7.66	8.58	9.50	10.42	11.35	12.27	13.20	14.13

*Assumptions: cap rate = 10.5%; depreciation reserves = 1%; all equity cash reinvested at 9.5% rate.

they are not on the chart is that it requires 6 percent declines per year for 10 years before the BB-rated bond experiences any losses.

So the issue is what is the likelihood of the "−3 percent" scenario or the "−6 percent" scenario. If, as we have

Debt and Equity in the New Real Estate Markets

suggested, they have negligible probability, then the unrated bond dominates the equity and everything else. In addition, for those who think the "middle ground" in Figure 8–3 represents the likely outcomes, but who worry a bit about the downside, the B and BB-rated bonds dominate the equity in the lower and middle outcomes without giving up too much to the equity at the low-probability high end. To pick the equity over the subordinate CMBS is, in our view of the real estate fundamentals, to pay an expensive "insurance premium" against the risk of remote and hugely improbable scenarios. This insurance premium equals the shortfall of direct property performance in all the most probable scenarios.

Consider another investor who believes that each of the scenarios from "–3 percent" to "+1 percent" has a 20 percent probability of occurrence, and all the other outcomes have zero probability. This investor will dislike the unrated bond because of its poor return in "–3 percent." Logically, it might be pointed out that such an investor has no business in real estate equity. This could be a valid argument for traditional real estate equity, but not for the B and BB-rated CMBS, which shine in these mediocre scenarios.

Figure 8–4 shows a "leveraged equity" position in which the investor has financed an ownership in property, directly or indirectly, with a 65 percent ltv commercial mortgage. In weak scenarios, leveraged equity performs poorly. Clearly the reason to take a leveraged equity position is because you are bullish on real estate and don't think there is meaningful downside. Indeed, Figure 8–4 shows the clear outperformance of leveraged equity over the B and BB-rated bonds from "+1 percent" to "+5 percent". Once again, however, the unrated CMBS is a tough act to follow in the strong scenarios. It outperforms the leveraged equity except in the "+5 percent" (and stronger) scenarios.

FIGURE 8-4

Leveraged Equity Total Returns versus Subordinated CMBS

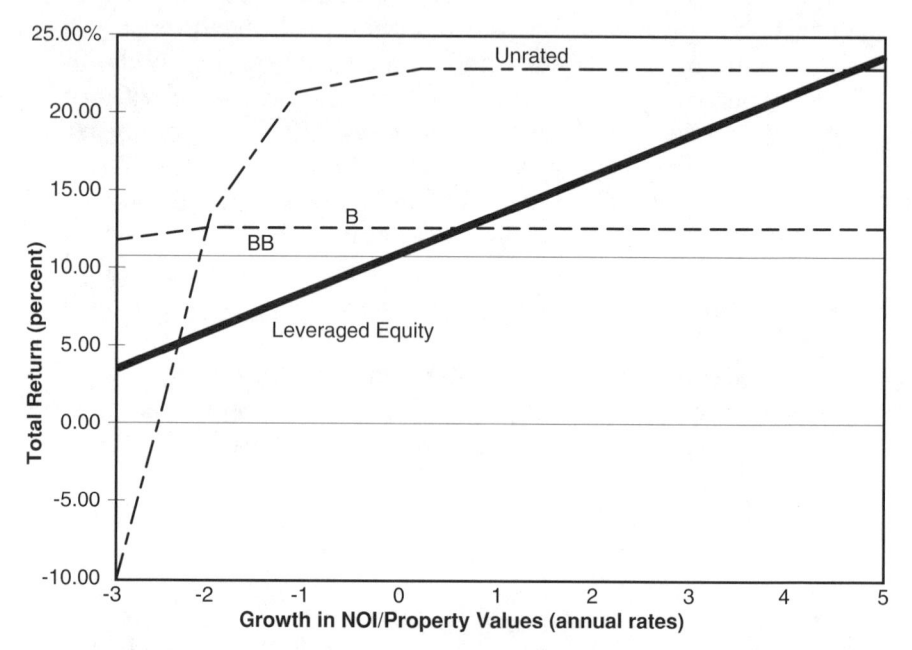

CMBS:	-3	-2	-1	0	1	2	3	4	5
BB	10.73	10.73	10.73	10.73	10.73	10.73	10.73	10.73	10.73
B	11.67	12.73	12.73	12.73	12.73	12.73	12.73	12.73	12.73
Unrated	-9.80	12.49	20.73	22.00	22.00	22.00	22.00	22.00	22.00
Leveraged equity*	2.97	5.95	8.72	11.33	13.79	16.14	18.38	20.50	22.62

*Assumptions: cap rate = 10.5%; depreciation reserves = 1%; commercial mortgage loan is 65% ltv for a 20-year mortgage with yield of 8.38%.

Leveraging up the equity has the effect of steepening the slope of the return line relative to the unleveraged equity (Figure 8–3). So with higher leverage than 65 percent the leveraged equity line would cut above the unrated

CMBS in scenarios with slower NOI/ property value growth than 5 percent.

However, the dominance of the unrated bond over leveraged equity (with 65 percent ltv) in a wide range of weak and strong scenarios serves to highlight once again the relative value in subordinate CMBS. Indeed, when the leveraged equity (Figure 8–4) results are put side by side with the unleveraged equity (Figure 8–3), the results are even stronger than viewing them separately. This is because the leveraged equity investment would generally be considered only by investors who were very bullish on real estate. These investors would tend to focus exclusively on scenarios from "–1 percent" and higher. The flip side of this point is that these bullish investors are less interested in unleveraged equity (Figure 8–3). In other words, the unleveraged equity comparisons with CMBS will be of greatest interest to investors whose real estate probabilities are more concentrated in the middle outcomes. For such investors, the dominance of subordinate CMBS is very strong indeed.

QUALIFICATIONS AND LOAN STRUCTURE

Our CMBS example reflects the characteristics of a pooled loan structure rather than either a single-asset deal or a pool of loans with cross-collateralization and cross-default provisions. For example, in a single-asset deal, it could never happen that a subordinate CMBS underperforms the leveraged equity, as happens in our "–3 percent" scenario (Figure 8–4). The reason it could never happen is that the leveraged equity itself is the "equity cushion" protecting the bondholders. As long as there is any cushion remaining, the bondholders are protected from loss.

In the pooled loan structure, this result still holds, for example, if all the properties move up and down together perfectly. However, if several loans do very poorly while others perform strongly, the equity cushion on the strong properties does not support the weak loans. In this case, losses passing through to the first loss CMBS may cause underperformance relative to the leveraged equity. Essentially, this result arises because of dispersion in the performance of the pool properties and loans. Our empirical model, estimated in the adverse 1988–1992 period, builds in dispersion, which may or may not be relevant in particular portfolios.

In the case of a cross-collateralized pool of loans, the pool effectively acts as a single large loan secured by a single collective property. Thus, the subordinate CMBS will always outperform the leveraged equity, just as in the case of a single-asset deal. In addition, the sharply reduced variability of the collection of properties will contribute to sharply lower defaults relative to loan pools which are not crossed.

The reduction in the property variability and expected loss in a "crossed" pool of loans will depend on the typical correlation between pool properties. Intuitively, the higher the correlation, the less variability can be diversified away because the correlation reflects a set of common factors which are impacting all the property returns. For example, if this correlation were 0.5, the variability of the average property's performance would be reduced to 50 percent of the typical single property.[8] Moreover, for loans in the 70 percent to 80 percent ltv range, this decline in variability would produce a parallel 50 percent drop in expected defaults and losses (see results by Childs, Ott, and Riddiough 1994).

In terms of our scenario analysis above, a 50 percent drop in expected defaults represents the difference be-

---

8. If the variance of a single property's returns is S^2, then the limit in the average property variance as the number of (equally sized) properties becomes large is ps^2, where p is the typical correlation. So a single property variance of 100 could be ultimately reduced to 50 when $p = 0.5$. with 10 properties, the variance would be reduced from 100 to 55. A recent

tween the "–3 percent" and "–2 percent" scenarios. Thus, with loans crossed, subordinate CMBS returns in the "–3 percent" scenario look like uncrossed subordinate CMBS returns in the "–2 percent" scenario. In other words, even in our most adverse scenario, all the subordinate CMBS handily outperform real estate equity when the loans are crossed.

Thus, in comparing the performance of subordinate CMBS to real estate equity, the pooled loan structure used in our example above is less favorable to subordinate CMBS than the other two loan structures. Indeed, while the rating agencies set different requirements for different loan structures, we believe that the market has generally substantially underpriced the advantages of crossed loan structures.

A separate issue that heavily influences the relative and absolute performance of the unrated CMBS is this bond's pricing. Unrated CMBS tend to vary within a substantially wider range than other subordinate CMBS. If we had a larger discount in the unrated CMBS initial price so that it traded at a yield to maturity of, say, 35 percent instead of 22 percent, this makes a big difference. In this case, it is obviously much easier for the unrated bond to outperform both unleveraged and leveraged equity, even in the most adverse scenarios. While this initial yield may seem high, some unrated CMBS have indeed been sold on such terms.

The CMBS example presented above uses a cap rate assumption of 10.5 percent. Obviously, many large regional malls and multifamily properties have cap rates well below this figure. Some properties, such as hotels,

---

study by Graff and Young (1995) points to correlations between NCREIF properties averaging about 0.2. While such correlations can obviously vary over time, and even long-term real estate correlations need to be better established, we deliberately choose a value well above the Graff and Young estimates.

would generally trade at cap rates above it. In general, lowering the cap rate assumption will shift down the equity curves in Figures 8–3 and 8–4, thereby increasing the range of subordinate CMBS dominance.

CONCLUSION

At bottom, subordinate CMBS represent equity-like risk exposure. This suggests that these securities, like traditional real estate investments, are amenable to all the tools of portfolio analysis. The primary conclusion from portfolio theory applied to traditional real estate speaks to the benefits of diversification. This conclusion also applies to subordinate CMBS, which could be pooled or combined in other ways with traditional real estate investments to reduce risk.

No single real estate investment will dominate others in all real estate scenarios. Hence, we see the importance of the real estate outlook in determining which outcomes are possible and likely. From a fundamental perspective, we have argued that large additional downside is ruled out. Yet wide CMBS spreads seem to weight such downside heavily. If we rule out the worst 1980s-style outcomes, subordinate CMBS outperform traditional equity investments over a wide range of real estate scenarios ranging from negative to fairly bullish. This should commend subordinate CMBS to traditional real estate investors.

Subordinate CMBS may differ from traditional real estate investments in other ways, such as control or liquidity. But these differences also exist among traditional investments. The current pricing of real estate risk in CMBS makes them a beacon of relative value compared to direct property ownership or fixed-income benchmarks. As of this writing, the huge relative value in CMBS is the first-order issue, while the other issues are distinctly second order.

REFERENCES

Altman, Edward I. 1994. "Defaults and Returns on High Yield Bonds: Analysis through 1993." New York: Merrill Lynch & Co.

Childs, Paul D., Steven H. Ott, and Timothy J. Riddiough. 1994. "The Value of Recourse and Cross-Default Clauses in Commercial Mortgage Contracting." Forthcoming in *Journal of Banking and Finance.*

Ciochetti, Brian A., and Timothy J. Riddiough. 1994. "Loss Severity and Its Impact on Commercial Mortgage Performance." Mimeographed.

Corcoran, Patrick J. 1991. "Commercial Mortgage Risk and Regional Property Performance." *Investing* (Spring): 67–73. Also, "Commercial Mortgage Risk, Regional Property Performance and Portfolio Management." In *Real Estate Portfolio Management,* B. R. Bruce, ed. Chicago, Il: Probus Publishing Co.

———. 1994. "Assessing the Risks for New Real Estate Loans." *Real Estate Review* (Spring): 10–14.

Corcoran, Patrick J., Dale Fathe-Aazam, and Alberto Perez-Pietri. 1994. "The Role of Commercial Mortgages in Fixed Income Investing." *Pension Real Estate Association Quarterly* (January): 26–30.

Corcoran, Patrick J., and Duen-Li Kao. 1994. "Assessing Credit Risk in CMBS." *Real Estate Finance* (Fall).

———. 1995. "Quantifying Credit Risk in CMBS." In *The Handbook of Mortgage-Backed Securities,* Frank J. Fabozzi, ed. Chicago, IL: Probus Publishing Co.

Duff & Phelps Rating Co. 1994 "The Rating of Commercial Mortgage-Backed Securities." October.

Fisher, Jeffrey D. 1995. "Cash Flow versus NOI: An Analysis of Capital Expenditures for Malls." *Real Estate Finance* (Summer).

Fons, Jerome S.. 1987. "The Default Premium and Corporate Bond Experience." *Journal of Finance* (March): 81–97.

———. 1994. "Using Default Rates to Model the Term Structure of Credit Risk." *Financial Analysts Journal* (September/October).

Gichon, Galia. 1995. "The Role of the Servicer." *Commercial Real Estate Quarterly* (Nomura Securities International, Inc.) (January).

Graff, Richard A., and Michael S. Young. 1995. "Real Estate Return Correlations: Real World Limitations on Relationships Inferred from NCREIF Data." *Journal of Real Estate Finance and Economics*.

Ho, Thomas S. Y. 1990. *Strategic Fixed Income Investment*. Homewood, IL: Dow Jones-Irwin.

Jacob, David P., and Kimbell R. Duncan. 1995. "Commercial Mortgage-Backed Securities." In *The Handbook of Mortgage-Backed Securities,* Frank J. Fabozzi, ed. Chicago, IL: Probus Publishing Co.

Kao, Duen-Li. 1993. "Valuation: Fair Trading." *Balance Sheet* (Winter): 15–19.

Moody's Investors Service. 1994. *Corporate Bond Defaults and Default Rates: 1970–1993*. Special report.

Vandell, Kerry D. 1992. "Predicting Commercial Mortgage Foreclosure Experience." *Journal of the American Real Estate and Urban Economics Association* 20(1): 55–88.

———. 1993. "Handing Over the Keys: A Perspective on Mortgage Default Research." *Journal of the American Real Estate and Urban Economics Association* 21(3): 211–246.

Young, Michael S., David M. Geltner, Willard McIntosh, and Douglas M. Poutasse. 1995. "Defining Commercial Property Income and Appreciation Returns for Comparability to Stock Market-Based Measures." *Real Estate Finance* (Summer).

Wurtzebach, Charles, David Hartzell, and David Shulman. 1987. "Refining the Analysis of Regional Diversification for Income Producing Real Estate." *The Journal of Real Estate Research* (Winter): 89–95.

CHAPTER 9

An Investor's Guide to Floating-Rate Notes: Conventions, Mathematics, and Relative Valuation

Raymond J. Iwanowski
Vice President of Fixed Income Research
Salomon Brothers

INTRODUCTION

Practically every sector of the fixed-income market contains bonds with floating-rate coupons. The popularity of these types of securities arises from the reluctance of many investors to accept a long-maturity fixed bond, particularly in periods of fears of rising interest rates. Indeed, consider a bond which is issued at a price of 100, accrues a coupon of some easily observed index plus some prespecified spread, has no credit risk, no embedded options, certainty with respect to the timing of the payment of principal, and the coupon accrual resets to the new index level whenever the index level changes (instantaneous reset). In this case, the intuition that floating-rate notes have no price sensitivity and should always trade at or near 100 is valid.

Of course, such bonds do not exist in today's markets and, therefore, all floating-rate notes (FRN) do have some degree of price sensitivity. In reality, no floating-rate securities reset instantaneously and there typically is a lag before the index rate used in coupon accrual resets to the market index rate. Corporate and emerging market floaters have exposure to changes in credit spreads. Floating-rate mortgage-backed securities and many products in the structured note market usually have embedded options such as caps and floors. Mortgage-backed FRNs have the additional feature of the prepayment option which affects the amortization of principal. In addition to the usual effect that faster or slower prepayments have on the performance of a mortgage bond, unexpected prepayment speeds will affect the value of the embedded caps and floors.

Investors who purchase FRNs are usually aware of these issues. However, it is not always easy to evaluate the implied risks and the appropriate compensation for taking on these risks. In fact, given the nature of floating-rate securities, it is not trivial to *measure* the compensation that the investor is receiving for taking risks. A framework by which to measure risk-return trade-offs are particularly important for investors who have the flexibility to invest in FRNs across several different sectors.

The purpose of this research is twofold. First, we provide a reference which describes in detail the various conventions and tools which are used in FRN markets. We explicitly define pricing relationships and commonly used terms such as *discount margin* and *reset margin*. We also describe various sensitivity measures such as *effective duration, partial duration* and *spread duration* and compare these measures to those of fixed coupon bonds. Next, we discuss the relative valuation of different types of FRNs and provide some frameworks by which to assess their risk/return trade-offs.

FLOATING-RATE NOTE PRICING: EQUATIONS AND DEFINITIONS

In this section, we explicitly define the various pricing equations and market conventions used in floating-rate security markets. This section is designed to serve as a reference although we also provide examples to make the exposition more lucid.

Consider the following bullet corporate floating-rate note (FRN) which matures at the end of period T and pays a coupon which resets every period to a particular rate, I^A_t, plus a specified spread called the reset margin (RM^A). The note is noncallable and nonputable. Principal amount is $100. For ease of explanation, we assume the pricing date is the reset date.

If $I^A_1, \ldots, I^A_{T-1}$ were known at time 0, the pricing relationship of the floater would be:

$$P^A(0,T) = 100 * \left[\frac{I^A_0 + RM^A}{(1+d(1)+S^A)} + \frac{I^A_1 + RM^A}{(1+d(2)+S^A)^2} + \ldots + \frac{I^A_{T-1} + RM^A + 1}{(1+d(T)+S^A)^T} \right]$$

$$= 100 * \left[\sum_{i=1}^{T} \frac{I^A_{i-1} + RM^A}{(1+d(i)+S^A)^i} + \frac{1}{(1+d(T)+S^A)^T} \right] \quad (1)$$

where $P^A(t,T)$ = price of floater A with T periods until maturity observed at period t.

RM^A = reset margin of bond A. This margin is fixed at issuance.
$d(t)$ = discount rate of a risk free $1 paid at time t.
S^A = discount spread of corporation A.

Floating-rate notes are typically "set in advance," which means the index level that is applied to the coupon at time t is the observed index at time $t-1$ (I^A_{t-1}).

Since $I^A_1 \ldots I^A_{T-1}$ are not observable at time 0, a projected coupon must be substituted. We denote the series of projected coupons as $X^A_1 \ldots X^A_{T-1}$ (we will discuss the determinants of the X^A's later).

The pricing equation is then modified to:

$$P^A(0,T) = 100 * \left[\sum_{i=1}^{T} \frac{X_{i-1}^A + RM^A}{(1+d(i)+S^A)^i} + \frac{1}{(1+d(T)+S^A)^T} \right] \quad (2)$$

where $X_0^A = I_0^A$ if pricing date is a reset date. For ease of explanation, we make this assumption henceforth.

The trading convention is to quote FRN prices in terms of a *discount margin* (DM), which is analogous to the yield spreads on fixed corporate bonds. Discount margin is defined as the spread over the appropriate index which equates the price of the FRN to the present value of the projected cash flows. In other words, the DM is defined such that:

$$(1+d(i)+S^A)^i = (1+I_0^A+DM)(1+X_1^A+DM)\ldots \quad (3)$$
$$(1+X_{i-1}^A+DM), \text{ for all } i$$

Therefore, equation (2) can be rewritten in terms of discount margin as follows:

$$P^A(0,T) = 100 * \left[\frac{I_0^A + RM^A}{(1+I_0^A+DM^A)} + \frac{X_1^A + RM^A}{(1+I_0^A+DM^A)(1+X_1^A+DM^A)} + \ldots + \right.$$

$$\left. \frac{1 + X_{T-1}^A + RM^A}{(1+I_0^A+DM^A)(1+X_1^A+DM^A)\ldots(1+X_{T-1}^A+DM^A)} \right] \quad (4)$$

The transformation from equation **(2)** to equation **(4)** is a restatement of the appropriate discount rate for the issuer $(d(i) + S^A)$ in terms of the projected coupon indices $(I_0^A, X_1^A, \ldots, X_{T-1}^A)$.

Example: Consider a new-issue FRN which is indexed to three-month LIBOR $(LIB3)_A$ + 20 basis points, has a maturity of 2 years, pays and resets quarterly, and is priced at par at time 0 $(P^A(0,T) = 100)$. Suppose that on the pricing date, LIB3 = 6.06 percent and, for now, we make the assumption that $LIB3_1 = LIB3_2 = \ldots = LIB3_{T-1} = 6.06$

An Investor's Guide to Floating-Rate Notes

percent.[1] LIB3 FRNs typically pay on an actual/360 basis and, for simplicity of this example, we assume each quarter has 91 days. Therefore, the quarterly coupon in our example is:

$$X_{t-1} = (\text{LIB3}_{t-1} + 20 \text{ bp})*(91/360) = (0.0606 + 0.0020)(91/360)$$

Note that the index and discount margin in the denominator are accrued on the same basis as the coupon. We can now rewrite equation (4) as:

$$100 = 100 * \left[\frac{(.0606 + .0020)*(91/360)}{(1 + ((.0606 + DM^A)*(91/360)))} \right.$$

$$+ \frac{(.0606 + .0020)*(91/360)}{(1 + ((.0606 + DM^A)(1 + .0606 + DM^A)(91/360)(91/360)))}$$

$$+ \ldots + \frac{1 + ((.0606 + .0020)*(91/360))}{(1 + ((.0606 + DM^A)*(91/360)))(1 + ((.0606 + DM^A)*(91/360)))\ldots}$$

$$\left. (1 + ((.0606 + DM^A)*(91/360))) \right]$$

(5)

The discount margin is the value of *DM*, which solves equation (5). In this example, since the bond is priced at par, it is clear that the solution is *DM* = .0020 = 20 b.p. In fact, whenever a floater is priced at par, *RM* = *DM*. However, if the price were to drop instantaneously to 99.75, then substituting by 99.75 into the left-hand side of equation (5), we obtain *DM* = 33 b.p. The following rule applies to FRNs:

If *RM* > *DM*, then Price > 100
RM < *DM*, then P < 100
RM = *DM*, then P = 100

Equation (4) motivates the following questions:

- We assumed that future levels of LIB3 are equal to today's level. This is currently the convention in corporate, mortgage, and asset-backed markets. For

---

[1]. We will discuss the use of alternative assumptions later.

a given DM, how does the calculated price change under different assumed coupon levels? What is the appropriate assumption to use?

- What is the sensitivity of the FRN's price to changes in the Treasury yield curve (effective and partial durations)? What is the price sensitivity of the FRN with respect to changes in DM (spread duration)?
- How are the reset margins of new issue or discount margins of secondary market issues determined? How should the RMs and DMs differ across indices (e.g., prime versus LIB3) for the same issue?

The subsequent analysis provides some answers to these questions. In evaluating these issues, it is useful to rewrite equation (4) in the following way:

$$P^A(0,T) = 100 * \left[\frac{I_0^A + RM^A + (DM - DM)}{(1 + I_0^A + DM^A)} + \frac{X_1^A + RM^A + (DM - DM)}{(1 + I_0^A + DM^A)(1 + X_1^A + DM^A)} \right.$$

$$\left. + \ldots + \frac{1 + X_{T-1}^A + RM^A + (DM - DM)}{(1 + I_0^A + DM^A)(1 + X_1^A + DM^A)\ldots(1 + X_{T-1}^A + DM^A)} \right] \quad (6)$$

Rewriting equation (6) by recombining terms yields the following equation:

$$P^A(0,T) = 100 * \left[\left[\frac{I_0^A + DM}{(1 + I_0^A + DM^A)} + \frac{X_1^A + DM}{(1 + I_0^A + DM^A)(1 + X_1^A + DM^A)} \right. \right.$$

$$\left. + \ldots + \frac{1 + X_{T-1}^A + DM}{(1 + I_0^A + DM^A)(1 + X_1^A + DM^A)\ldots(1 + X_{T-1}^A + DM^A)} \right] +$$

$$\left[\frac{RM - DM}{(1 + I_0^A + DM^A)} + \frac{RM - DM}{(1 + I_0^A + DM^A)(1 + X_1^A + DM^A)} \right.$$

$$\left. \left. + \ldots + \frac{RM - DM}{(1 + I_0^A + DM^A)(1 + X_1^A + DM^A)\ldots(1 + X_{T-1}^A + DM^A)} \right] \right] \quad (7)$$

Although at first glance equation **(7)** may appear to be an unnecessarily long restatement of the pricing relationship, it actually provides some valuable intuition in understanding FRNs. The first term in the brackets represents a FRN whose reset margin is equal to its discount margin. Therefore, the value of this quantity is par. The second term is the present value of an annuity which pays the difference between the reset margin and the discount margin. Equation **(7)** can be summarized as:

$$P^A(0,T) = 100 + \text{Present Value of Annuity which pays } (RM - DM) \quad (8)$$

The first payoff of viewing the floater pricing equation in this framework is to confirm the rules of premiums and discounts set forth above. If $RM = DM$, the second term of equation **(8)** is zero and the bond is priced at par. If RM is greater than DM, the second term is positive and the price of the floater is greater than par (premium). If RM is less than DM, the second term is negative and the price of the floater is less than par (discount).

Equations **(7)** and **(8)** also provide a framework in which to evaluate the questions posed earlier. Recall that the first question was: *For a given DM, how does the calculated price change under different assumed index levels?*

Example: Consider the following corporate FRN:

Index: LIB3
Reset margin: 100 basis points
Reset/pay frequency: quarterly/quarterly
Maturity: 5 years
For simplicity, assume that the settlement date is a coupon date.

Suppose we were to consider two sets of index projections:

(a) $LIB3_0 = LIB3_1 = \ldots = LIB3_{T-1} = 6.31\%$
(b) $LIB3_t = LIB3_{t-1} + 25$ basis points.
(i.e., $LIB3_0 = 6.31\%$, $LIB3_1 = 6.56\%$, ... $LIB3_{t-1} = 10.81\%$)

TABLE 9-1

Prices under Various Discount Margins and Assumed Index Levels (basis points)

Discount Margin	Assumed Index Projection	
	(a) All LIB3 remain at current level (6.31%)	(b) LIB3 increase 25bp each quarter
200	95.87	96.02
100	100.00	100.00
0	104.34	104.18

Case (b) was chosen arbitrarily to illustrate the differences across assumptions, but these projections resemble using the forward LIB3 rates implied by the swap curve in a sharply upward sloping yield curve environment.

We substitute the projections, parameters, and various discount margins into equation **(7)** and solve for price. The results are shown in Table 9–1.

The calculated price is:

- The same under either assumption when the discount margin is equal to the reset margin,
- *Greater* under the rising index assumption when the discount margin exceeds the reset margin (discount); and
- *Lower* under the rising index assumption when the reset margin exceeds the discount margin (premium).

The terms under the first set of brackets in equation **(7)** will equal 100 **regardless of the assumed index level.** This is true because the discount rates in the denominator of each term will exactly offset any increased or decreased assumed coupon. On the other hand, the values of the terms under the second bracket will change under various assumptions of the index level. Specifically, a higher assumed level of the index will increase the rate at which the fixed annuity is discounted. We can use equation **(8)** to define:

Premium = $P^A(0,T) - 100$ = Present Value of Annuity which pays $(RM - DM)$

$$100 * \left[\frac{RM - DM}{(1 + I_0^A + DM^A)} + \frac{RM - DM}{(1 + I_0^A + DM^A)(1 + X_1^A + DM^A)} \right.$$
$$\left. + ... + \frac{RM - DM}{(1 + I_0^A + DM^A)(1 + X_1^A + DM^A)...(1 + X_{T-1}^A + DM^A)} \right] \quad (9)$$

As the projected index levels increase, the value of the premium decreases. Since a discount can be viewed as a negative premium, increasing the projected indices results in a lower discount and a higher price. This example demonstrates that the price of the bond for a given DM is clearly sensitive to the projected index level except in the special case where $RM = DM$. The longer the maturity of the bond and the greater the difference between RM and DM, the more pronounced this differential between coupon projection methods. This example illustrates that the discount margin, although a convenient tool by which to quote prices on FRNs, is a flawed measure of relative value.

PRICE SENSITIVITIES

Equations **(7)** and **(8)** also provide insight into our second question: *What is the sensitivity of the FRN's price to changes in the Treasury yield curve?*

Effective Duration

The usual definition of *effective duration* is the sensitivity of a bond's price to a parallel shift of the Treasury yield curve, keeping yield spreads constant. By keeping the spread between the index rate and Treasury constant, this definition is equivalent to saying that *effective duration measures the sensitivity of the price of the FRN to changes in the level of its index.* Henceforth, we use these two definitions interchangeably.

Consider two cases:

Case 1: Suppose $P(0,T) = 100$. Then $RM = DM$ and the annuity shown in equation **(7)** is equal to zero. Now, suppose I^A_0 instantaneously increased by a small amount to $I^A_0 + \Delta I$. After the next reset, coupons are increased to reflect the higher level of I^A. Equation **(7)** will now be written as:

New P^A =

$$100 * \left[\frac{I^A_0 + DM}{1 + I^A_0 + \Delta I + DM} + \sum_{i=2}^{T} \frac{X^A_{i-1} + \Delta I + DM^A}{(1 + I^A_0 + \Delta I + DM^A)...(1 + X^A_{i-1} + \Delta I + DM)} + \right.$$

$$\left. ... + \frac{1}{(1 + I^A_0 + \Delta I + DM^A)...(1 + X^A_T + \Delta I + DM)} \right] = 100 * \left[\frac{1 + I^A_0 + DM}{(1 + I^A_0 + \Delta I + DM)} \right]$$

(10)

The terms sum in this manner because the value at time 1 of all subsequent projected cash flows is equal to par. Therefore, *the effective duration of a noncallable, nonputable bullet FRN is the modified duration of a bond which matures at the next reset date.*

Example: Recall the example from the previous section:

Index: LIB3 (current level = 6.31%)
Reset margin: 100 basis points
Reset/pay frequency: quarterly/quarterly
Maturity: 5 years
Settlement date: Reset date.

Suppose that this FRN is priced at par. If the index level increases 10 basis points instantaneously (ΔI=.0010), the new price is given by equation **(10)** as:

$$\text{New } P^A = 100 * \left[\frac{1 + ((.0631 + .01)(91/360))}{(1 + ((.0631 + .001 + .01)(91/360)))} \right] = 99.9752 \tag{11}$$

Similarly, a decrease of the index of 10 basis points (ΔI= −.0010) gives us a new price of 1.000243. Therefore, the average price change for a 10 basis point shift in the index level is equal to (100.0243 − 99.9752)/2 = 0.0248 = .0248%. Since effective duration is defined to be the price change for a 100 basis point change in yields,

Effective Duration = .0248% × 10 = 0.248%

Note that this is exactly the modified duration of a zero coupon bond which matures in 91 days and has a yield of (.0631)(91/360).

Case 2: $RM \neq DM$ (i.e., the FRN is trading at a discount or a premium).

From equation **(7),** we can view this bond as a "portfolio" of a long position in a par floater and a long position in an annuity paying $RM - DM$ (or a short position in an annuity paying $DM - RM$ if a discount). As shown in Case 1, the long floater will have an effective duration equal to the modified duration of a bond which matures at its next reset. The annuity position will have a longer duration. In the case of a discount, the annuity piece will reduce the effective duration of the portfolio. If the annuity is a significant enough portion of the portfolio, the effective duration of the discount floater may actually be negative. Unfortunately, in this case, the effective duration *will* be affected by the method used to project the coupons because the effective duration of the annuity piece will differ for different index levels.

Example: Suppose the LIB3 floater described above had a dollar price of 85. Using the portfolio approach, the floater can be decomposed into a long position in a FRN priced at 100 and a short position in an annuity worth 15. The present value of that annuity is given by the terms under the second set of brackets in equation **(7).** We assume all subsequent levels of LIB3 are equal to the current level of 6.31 percent and can solve for the *DM* which sets that annuity value equal to –15.[2] In this case, the *DM* equals 492 basis points. We have shown earlier that the effective duration of the par floater piece is equal to 0.248 years. The effective duration of an annuity which pays *DM – RM* (392 b.p.) for five years is equal to 2.367 years. Using the portfolio approach and the fact that the effective duration of a portfolio is equal to the market-value-weighted average of the components of the portfolio, we can obtain the effective duration of the discount FRN as follows:

Effective Duration = (100/85)*(0.25) – (15/85)*(2.37)
 = –0.12 years

Partial Durations

A careful, quantitative analysis of partial durations requires more detail than we care to get into here. However, several intuitive points can be made from our simple pricing equations:

- If the coupon of the FRN is indexed to a short rate and the bond is priced at par, then from equation **(10),** the price will only be sensitive to movements in the index, and other partial durations will be zero.
- If the bond is at a premium or a discount, we can take the "portfolio" approach discussed above. Shifts

---

2. A short position in a portfolio is indicated by a negative present value.

of intermediate rates will affect the price of the bond to the extent that the annuity in the portfolio is affected.
- Some FRNs are indexed to a longer maturity rate such as the two-year constant maturity Treasury (CMT2). Even if they are priced at par, such floaters are sensitive to shifts of various portions of the curve because their prices are sensitive to shifts in the longer forward rates.

Spread Duration

We define *spread duration* as the price sensitivity of a FRN with respect to changes in its DM. To derive some intuition of the spread duration, it is easiest to consider equation (4):

$$P^A(0,T) = 100 * \left[\frac{I_0^A + RM^A}{(1 + I_0^A + DM^A)} + \frac{X_1^A + RM^A}{(1 + I_0^A + DM^A)(1 + X_1^A + DM^A)} + \right.$$

$$\left. \cdots + \frac{1 + X_{T-1}^A + RM^A}{(1 + I_0^A + DM^A)(1 + X_1^A + DM^A)\ldots(1 + X_{T-1}^A + DM^A)} \right] \quad (4)$$

It is clear that any increase in DM affects the denominator of equation (4) but is not accompanied by an increase in the numerator. In fact, increasing the DM of a floater will have the same price effect as increasing the yield on a fixed bond which pays the projected coupons out to the maturity of the floater. Therefore, a longer-maturity FRN will have a spread duration equal to the modified duration of a fixed bond paying the projected coupons out to the maturity of the floater. This measure will also be affected by the method used to project the coupons.

TABLE 9-2

Corporate Floating-Rate Note Indication Levels
(as of March 10,1995)

Quality: A2/A Maturity	Discount Margin (b.p.) Index					
	LIB3	TB3	Prime	Fed Funds	CMT2	CP1
One year	+13	+23	−255	+25	+10	+5
Two year	+20	+33	−250	+28	+18	+8
Five year	+35	+55	−240	+30	+25	+15

Index	Level
Federal funds	5.93%
Three-month T-bill (TB3)	5.93
One-month commercial paper (CP1)	6.08
Three-month LIBOR (LIB3)	6.31
Two-year constant maturity Treasury (CMT2)	6.82
Prime rate	9.00

All rates quoted in CD equivalent except CMT2 which is quoted in bond equivalent.

Example: The five-year LIB3 floater used in our previous examples has a spread duration of 4.15 years when priced at par, and the future levels of LIB3 are assumed to be the current level (6.31 percent). This is the modified duration of a bond which pays a quarterly coupon of 7.31 percent for five years.

RELATIONSHIP BETWEEN DISCOUNT MARGINS ON FLOATERS AND FIXED CORPORATE SPREADS

Table 9–2 shows the discount margins of various types of corporate FRNs observed on March 10, 1995. One immediate observation from the table is that discount margins increase as the maturity of the FRN increases (term structure). In the previous section, we showed that, for a given reset frequency, FRNs will have the same effective duration regardless of their maturity. However, longer-maturity floaters have longer spread durations. Therefore, the term structure of DMs for a given issuer represents the compensation for taking on spread duration risk. We now discuss how this term structure of DM is determined by focusing on FRNs indexed to LIB3.

Three-Month LIBOR (LIB3)-indexed Floating-Rate Notes

Consider the following transaction:
- Purchase a newly issued fixed bond with a maturity of five years which is priced at 100 with a coupon of the five-year Treasury ($TSY5_0$) plus spread (CS).
- Enter into a five-year interest rate swap where the investor pays a fixed rate plus a swap spread (SS) and receives the three-month LIBOR observed at reset date ($LIB3_{t-1}$).[3] Table 9–3 shows the market levels of swap spreads observed on March 10, 1995.[4] Table 9–4 shows the net cash flows of this transaction.
- The net cash flow approximates the cash flow on a LIBOR floater where:

Reset Margin (RM) = spread on fixed corporate bond
    − swap spread = $CS - SS$

---

3. Swaps are conventionally set in advance, which means that the time t floating-rate payment is LIB3 observed at time $t-1$.
4. Actual swap rates may deviate from the indication levels shown in Table 9–3 due to differential credit risk of counterparties. See Eric H. Sorenson and Thierry F. Bollier, *Pricing of Interest Rate Swap Default Risk,* Salomon Brothers Inc., October 1993, for a discussion on the determinants of this adjustment.

TABLE 9-3

Swap Spread Indication Levels, Fixed Rate versus Three-Month LIBOR (as of March 10, 1995)

	Spreads to Treasury (b.p.)	
Maturity	Receive Fixed	Pay Fixed
One year	+30	+33
Two year	+26	+29
Three year	+26	+29
Four year	+26	+29
Five year	+25	+28

TABLE 9-4

Net Cash Flow of Swapped Corporate Bond

Transaction	Cash flow at Quarter t=1	Cash flow at Quarter 4=2
Buy fixed bond		$(TSY5_0+CS)/2$

Interest rate swap
  Receive float
  Pay fixed
	$+LIB3_0*Act/360$	$+LIB3_1*(Act/360)$
		$-(TSY5_0+SS)/2$

Net cash flow	$+LIB3_0*Act/360$	$(LIB3_1*Act/360)+(CS-SS)/2$

The swapped fixed bond differs from a FRN only by slight differences in timing of cash flows since the synthetic will receive its "reset margin" semiannually and the FRN will receive the reset margin quarterly.

Therefore, the fixed corporate bond and swap markets provide a good rule of thumb as to where LIB3 floaters should trade. For corporate issuers with similar credit quality to that implied by the swap market, this rule of thumb should hold fairly closely. There should be some deviation when the credit quality of the corporate issuer differs substantially from the credit quality of the swap counterparty.[5] Some theoretical models of credit spreads provide analytic solutions for the price of a FRN, thereby quantifying the difference between swapped fixed bonds and corporate FRNs. However, a thorough discussion of these models is beyond the scope of this analysis.[6]

Does this hold in practice?

On March 10, 1995, the following sets of prices were observed in the market:

	Yield Spread (b.p.)
(a) GMAC (Baa1/BBB+) 6.35% of 6/28/98	= +68/actual
Swap spreads: Pay fixed - three year	= +29
four year	= +29
Corporate spread – swap spread	= 68 b.p. – 29 b.p. = 39 b.p.

A GMAC floating rate note with a coupon of LIB3 + 25 coupon and maturing on 2/2/98 was trading at a discount margin of LIB3 + 37.5 b.p.

	Yield Spread (b.p.)
(b) NationsBank (A2/A) 7.50% of 2/15/97	= +40/actual
Swap spreads: Pay fixed – two-year	= +29
Corporate spread – swap Spread	= 40 b.p. – 29 b.p. = 11 b.p.

NationsBank floating-rate note with a coupon = LIB3 + 6 b.p. and maturity in 11/96 was trading at a discount margin = 12 b.p.

In these two cases, the relationship between swapped fixed corporate bonds and floaters held quite closely.

---

5. For an extreme example, see Vincent J. Palermo, et al., "Brady Bond Fixed-Floating Spreads—Forget History," Salomon Brothers, Inc., December 15, 1993.
6. See Francis A. Longstaff and Eduardo S. Schwartz, "Valuing Risky Debt: A New Approach," Anderson Graduate School of Management, UCLA, October 1993, and Nicole El-Karoui and Helyette German, "A Probabilistic Approach to the Valuation of General Floating-Rate Notes with an Application to Interest Rate Swaps," *Advances in Futures and Options Research* 7, JAI Press Inc., 1994.

An Alternative Specification

Investors who are familiar with the swap market know that there is a close relationship between the fixed swap rate and the yield on a strip of Eurodollar futures contracts. In this analysis, we will not provide a detailed description of hedging swaps with Eurodollar futures contracts, but we will briefly discuss the relationship between corporate floaters and Eurodollar futures.[7]

Suppose we entered into the following transactions:

- Purchase a newly issued floating-rate note with a maturity of five years which is priced at 100 with a quarterly coupon of LIB3 plus a reset margin (RM).
- Buy the series of Eurodollar futures contracts maturing each quarter until the maturity of the FRN. The notional amount of the contracts equals the par amount of the bond.
- If a Eurodollar futures contract which matures at time t is held to maturity, the payoff at time t is:

$$F_{t,t} - F_{0,t} = 100 - \text{LIB3}_t - [100 - \text{FLIB3}_{0,t}] \quad (12)$$
$$= \text{FLIB3}_{0,t} - \text{LIB3}_t$$

where $F_{t,T}$ = the time t price of a Eurodollar futures contract which matures at time T.

$\text{FLIB3}_{t,T}$ = the yield on a T period Eurodollar futures contract observed at time t. This rate will be closely related to the forward LIB3_t but will differ slightly due to the mark-to-market feature of futures contracts. Henceforth, we will use the terms *futures yield* and *forward rate* interchangeably.

---

7. For a detailed discussion of hedging swaps with Eurodollar futures, see Galen Burghardt, et al. *Eurodollar Futures and Options*. (Chicago: Probus Publishing Company, 1991). For a discussion on the effect of convexity on the relative pricing between swaps and Eurodollar futures, see Galen Burghardt and Bill Hoskins, "A Question of Bias," *Risk*, March 1995.

TABLE 9-5

Net Cash Flow of Buying a Floater and a Series of Eurodollar Futures Contracts

Transaction	Cash Flow at Any Quarter t
Buy floater	$(LIB3_{t-1} + RM)*(Days/360)$
Buy futures contract	$(Forward\ LIB3_{t-1} - LIB3_{t-1})/4$
Net cash flow	$(Forward\ LIB3_{t-1} + RM + \varepsilon)/4$

ε = The difference in interest due to day count conventions.

- The net cash flows of these transactions can be approximated as shown in Table 9–5.
- The table shown above is slightly unrealistic because: (1) the maturity date on the contracts will not exactly match the coupon dates of the bond, (2) the bond coupon is set in advance to $LIB3_{t-1}$ but the cash flow of the futures contract would have taken place at $t-1$, and (3) the mark-to-market feature of futures contracts has a slight effect.
- We have now essentially created a synthetic fixed bond which pays the forward rates plus a reset margin using prices which are observed at time 0. Therefore, the synthetic should trade at a similar yield spread as actual fixed bonds of the same issuer. Note that the partial durations are not matched to those of a fixed coupon paying bond of the same maturity. If the Eurodollar curve is upward sloping, the synthetic will have lower coupons in the early quarters and higher coupons in later quarters.

Does this hold in practice?

- Recall from the earlier example that a secondary market GMAC FRN with approximately three years to maturity traded at a discount margin of 37.5 basis points. Three-year fixed GMAC bonds were trading at a yield spread of 68 basis points.

TABLE 9-6

Prices on Eurodollar Futures Contracts (March 10, 1995)

Maturity	Price	Yield
6/19/95	$93.43	6.57
9/18/95	93.20	6.80
12/18/95	92.98	7.02
3/18/96	92.91	7.09
6/17/96	92.84	7.16
9/16/96	92.80	7.20
12/16/96	92.72	7.28
3/17/97	92.76	7.24
6/16/97	92.72	7.28
9/15/97	92.70	7.30
12/15/97	92.63	7.37
3/16/98	92.64	7.36

ε = The difference in interest due to day count conventions.

- Suppose GMAC issued a new floating-rate note with a dated date of 3/13/95 priced at 100 with a reset margin of 37.5 basis points. We test how closely the theoretical relationship described above holds by substituting the futures rate as shown in Table 9–6 for the appropriate coupon each quarter and allowing the interest to accrue on an Actual/360 basis. The calculated yield on this synthetic fixed bond was 7.57%, which was equal to the three-year Treasury + 64 basis points.

Given the relationship between FRNs, swap markets, and futures contracts, one may argue that the appropriate method of projecting the coupons on FRN is to the forward rates because an investor can effectively fix his coupons to the forwards. Nevertheless, the convention in corporate, mortgage, and asset-backed markets has always been to use current LIBOR levels as the projected coupon in calculating DM. It is likely that this convention has persisted because of its simplicity and because of the difficulty in practice of creating arbitrage opportunities from the mispricings. If the market prices FRNs using a fixed index, then transactions like those of the previous two examples will occasionally allow the investor to synthetically create a "cheap" fixed corporate bond. However, it is extremely unlikely that there exists a fixed corporate bond of the same issuer, coupon. and maturity which an investor can costlessly short sell, thereby collecting arbitrage profits. Furthermore, as we saw in Table 9–1, in most cases, the differences in methodology will be small.

A CASE STUDY: EURODOLLAR PERPETUAL FLOATERS

One application which nicely demonstrates the points made in the previous two sections is the case of *perpetual* FRNs which are common in the Eurobond market. A typical perpetual FRN will represent a promise to pay the level of an index plus a prespecified spread (RM) forever. These securities usually reset and pay frequently (e.g., every three months). Many of these securities were issued at par by banks in the mid-1980s in the Eurobond market. A magazine article published in 1984 which discussed the popularity of FRNs states, "Since an FRN coupon is reset to market levels every three or six months, Eurodollar FRN investments are similar to rolling over funds in the certificate of deposits market."[8] A portfolio manager who was quoted in the same article considered a floater portfolio as "sort of an insurance policy against rising rates."[9]

---

8. "The FRN Dilemma," *Institutional Investor—International Edition,* April 1984, pp. 215–18.
9. Ibid.

One typical A2/A-rated perpetual issue has a coupon of six-month LIBOR + 12.5 basis points, reset and paid quarterly. Most of the perpetual issues are callable and some have floors but, for the purpose of this example, we assume that these securities do not contain these embedded options. Like most bonds in this market, this issue currently trades at a substantial discount. In this case, the bond has an offer price of 80.5.[10] If floaters are indeed an "insurance policy" or a similar investment to rolling CDs, what caused such drastic price depreciation?

For the purpose of this example, suppose that this security was issued at par on August 1, 1985. LIB6 on this date was 8.25 percent. We can rewrite the pricing equation (4) for a perpetual as follows:

$$P^A = 100 * \left[\sum_{i=1}^{\infty} \frac{X_{i-1}^A + RM^A}{(1 + I_0^A + DM^A)...(1 + X_{i-1}^A + DM^A)} \right] \quad (13)$$

Suppose we project the index to some constant level ($X_i = I$ for all i). Then, using the solution of an infinite geometric series, we obtain the following analytic solution for equation (13):

$$\text{Price of Perpetual} = 100 * \frac{I + RM^A}{I + DM^A} \quad (14)$$

Equation (14) is consistent with our previous pricing expressions in the sense that if $RM = DM$, then the price will equal 1 irrespective of the projected index.

Despite the extremely long maturity (infinite), equation (10) is still appropriate in evaluating the effective duration of a perpetual FRN priced at par. Therefore, the effective duration on August 1, 1985, was slightly less than 0.25 years. In this sense, the security is a similar investment to rolling certificates of deposit.

---

10. As of July 7, 1995.

But, now consider the spread duration of these bonds. By differentiating equation **(14)** with respect to DM and dividing by the price, we obtain the following expression:

$$\text{Spread Duration of Perpetual FRN} = \frac{1}{I + DM^A} \quad \textbf{(15)}$$

Using the August 1, 1985, LIB3 rate of 8.25% as the projected coupon, equation **(15)** becomes:

Spread Duration of Perpetual FRN

$$= \frac{1}{0.0825 + 0.00125} = 11.94 \text{ years} \quad \textbf{(16)}$$

The long spread duration is the major risk of the perpetual FRN relative to traditional short-term strategies such as rolling CDs or buying short-dated floaters. If LIB3 increased 100 basis points on August 1, 1985, the perpetual would have only experienced a price depreciation of approximately $0.25 since its effective duration is approximately 0.25 years. On the other hand, an increase in the market discount margin of 100 basis points due either to deteriorating credit or to technical would have resulted in a price depreciation of $11.94. In the case of perpetual floaters, spreads widened and, to the surprise of some investors, the price was quite sensitive to it.

The perpetual also provides a nice example of how an investor can use the swap market in assessing relative value in the floating-rate note market. On the date that the perpetual floater in our example was priced, the following Treasury and swap rates shown in Table 9–7 were observed.

Suppose an investor purchased the perpetual floater at $80.50 on August 1, 1995, and entered into a 30-year

TABLE 9-7

Treasury and Swap Rates (July 7, 1995)

Maturity	Treasury Yield	Swap Spreads	Fixed Swap Rate
10 years	6.08%	42%	6.50%
30 years	6.55	45	7.00

TABLE 9-8

Net Cash Flow of Swapped Perpetual Floater

Transaction	Cash Flow at time t
Buy perpetual floater	$+(LIB_{t-1}+0.125)*(Act/360)$

Interest rate swap
  Pay float
  Receive fixed
	$-LIB_{t-1}*(Act/360)$
	$(TSY30_0+SS)/2$

Net cash flow	$(TSY30_0+SS)/2+(0.125*(Act/360))$

swap where he pays LIB and receives the fixed swap rate.[11] His net cash flows for 30 years is then as shown in Table 9-8.

Therefore, the investor has locked in a fixed semiannual coupon of approximately 7.00% + 0.125% = 7.125% for 30 years at a dollar price of $80.50. The synthetic differs from a fixed corporate bond in the sense that, after 30 years, the bondholder does not receive principal but rather still owns a perpetual stream of floating-rate cash flows. In order to value the synthetic, we must value this stream today. This can be done by the following steps:

1. Assume a LIB (LIB*) for the coupons from year 30 onward.

---

11. Assume July 7, 1995, Treasury and swap rates are prevalent on that date. The floating rate on plain-vanilla swaps is usually LIB3. The difference on the fixed rate between a swap which receives either LIB3 and a swap which receives LIB6 is typically not more than a few basis points. For simplicity, we assume that these rates are the same.

An Investor's Guide to Floating-Rate Notes   211

2. Use the perpetual pricing formula (equation **(14)**) to obtain a value of these cash flows at the end of year 30.
3. Discount this value back to today.

This allows us to calculate the yield on the synthetic floater as follows:

$$Price = \sum_{i=1}^{60} \frac{(TSY30_0 + Swap\ Spread + RM_{perpetual\ FRN})/2}{(1 + yield/2)} \quad (17)$$

$$+ PV(perpetual\ which\ pays\ LIB6^* + RM)$$

$$= \sum_{i=1}^{60} \frac{(TSY30_0 + Swap\ Spread + RM_{perpetual\ FRN})/2}{(1 + yield/2)}$$

$$+ \frac{(LIB6^* + RM)/2}{(yield/2)(1 + yield/2)^i}$$

Of course, this calculation is dependent upon our assumption of LIB*, but the first cash flow for which the assumption is important is 30 years hence. Many investors are reluctant to enter into a 30-year swap because of credit and liquidity issues. We can also use equation **(17)** to calculate the yield of a synthetic which is swapped for 10 years by substituting a term of 20 semiannual periods rather than 60. In this case, the yield on the synthetic is more sensitive to the assumptions of LIB* because the assumed level enters the pricing relationship only 10 years hence.

Table 9–9 shows the spread over the "old"[12] 30-year Treasury of the perpetual floater swapped for 10 and 30 years under various assumptions for LIB in the "tail." The historical average over the past ten years of LIB6 was 6.55%.

---

12. Corporate bonds are conventionally not spread off the newest-issued 30-year, but the previous issue. In this case, we used the yield of the 7.50% of 11/24.

TABLE 9-9

Yield Spread of Swapped Perpetual over "Old" 30-year Treasury (basis points)

Assumed LIB after Maturity of Swap (%)	Yield Spread of Perpetual Swapped for 30 Years	Yield Spread of Perpetual Swapped for 10 Years
10.00%	252	330
7.00	226	191
6.50	221	164
5.75	214	121
3.00	184	−82

An investor can use Table 9–9 to compare the spreads of the swapped perpetual to the spreads of long corporate fixed bonds. For a perpetual which is swapped for 30 years, even after imposing extremely conservative assumptions to the unswapped cash flows, the spread does not change much. Of course, because of lesser liquidity, an investor should expect the synthetic to trade at wider spreads than a fixed issue. The table enables the investor to assess how much he is being compensated to accept the lower liquidity.

COMPARING FLOATING RATE NOTES OF DIFFERENT INDICES: BASIS RISK

Recall Table 9–2, which shows the indication discount margins of generic A-rated FRNs across various indices as of March 10, 1995. These levels also approximate where the reset margin on a generic new-issue FRN of A-rated credit quality would be set.

A quick addition of the various index levels to the appropriate new-issue reset margins show that, for the same credit quality, the current coupon on FRNs across indices and maturities is not the same. Table 9–10 shows a comparison of FRNs of the various indices to a LIB3 floater. The previous sections illustrate that the coupons typically

An Investor's Guide to Floating-Rate Notes   213

TABLE 9-10

Current Coupon Comparison of Corporate Floating-Rate Notes (as of March 10, 1995)

Quality: A2/A	Current Coupon versus Three-Month LIBOR Floater (b.p.) Index				
Maturity	TB3	Prime	Fed Funds	CMT2[a]	CP1[b]
One year	−28	+1	−26	+33	−28
Two year	−25	−1	−30	+34	−32
Five year	−18	−6	−43	+26	−40

Index	Reset Frequency
TB3	Weekly reset, quarterly pay
Prime	Daily reset, quarterly pay
Fed funds	Daily reset, quarterly pay
CMT2	Quarterly reset, quarterly pay
CP1	Monthly reset, monthly pay

a = Adjusted to reflect the difference in day count convention. b = Adjusted to reflect the difference in pay frequency.

increase across maturities to compensate the investor for taking on additional *spread duration risk*. It is important to understand the reasons why these FRNs may trade at different current coupons for the *same maturity* FRN.

Four reasons why an investor may purchase a floater with a lower initial coupon are:

1. Avoid the risk of deviating from benchmark. Many short-term investors such as money market funds and securities lending accounts by short-maturity floaters and hold them to maturity. As long as the bond does not default, these funds earn a return of the index plus the reset margin. The objective of such funds is to earn a modest excess return over some benchmark, which is often some rate such as LIB3 with a very low tolerance for substantive underperformance over any period of time.

Given their extreme risk aversion, the natural choice of managers of such funds is to purchase floaters which match their benchmarks unless the current coupon advantage is sufficiently enticing.

2. Institutional restrictions. Some investors are constrained against buying floaters of certain indices.

3. More-frequent reset. In the previous section, we showed that the effective duration of a FRN without options prices at par is approximated by the time to the next reset. Therefore, a short-term investor who has an outlook of immediate Fed tightening may prefer a daily-reset Fed Funds FRN or a weekly-reset TB3 FRN, rather than one indexed to LIB3 that resets quarterly, even if the current coupon is lower.

4. Speculation on relative movements between rates. Many investors may accept a lower coupon on an FRN to benefit from an expected change in the relationship between two rates (basis). For the various FRN shown in Tables 9–9 and 9–10, this basis arises for a number of reasons:

a. LIB3 - TB3: This is the spread between two indices with the same maturity, but LIB3 will always be the higher rate since it reflects the rate on Eurodollar deposits which are subject to credit risk and have less liquidity than Treasury bills. This spread, which is variable through time, is often known as the "TED spread."[13]

b. CMT2 - LIB3, LIB3 - Fed Funds: There are two components of these bases, since the spread comprises the difference between a longer-maturity Treasury rate and a

---

13. The common usage of the term "TED spread" refers to the spread between prices on the Treasury bill futures contract and the Eurodollar futures contract. This distinction is irrelevent for the purpose of this discussion, and henceforth we will "misuse" the term as the difference between the spot rates.

An Investor's Guide to Floating-Rate Notes   215

shorter-maturity credit-risky asset. Thus, in addition, to the TED spread, the CMT2 − LIB3 spread reflects the term structure of Treasury yields from the two-year to three-month part of the curve. We must emphasize that the decision between choosing a CMT2 quarterly reset floater rather than a LIB3 quarterly reset floater *does not* constitute a decision to extend effective duration, as the effective duration is driven by the reset frequency. In fact, as we shall discuss in more detail later, the decision of which of these two indices to invest in reflects a view on the *slope* of the Treasury curve rather than the level. Similarly, the LIB3 − Fed Funds basis reflects the slope of the Treasury curve on the very short end (overnight to three months) as well as the TED spread.

c. CP1 - LIB3, Prime − LIB3: These bases are similar to CMT2 − LIB3 spreads in that they are comprised of both the term structure of Treasury yields and some credit spread (although not necessarily the same credit component as that which drives the TED spread). These spreads differ from the Treasury − LIBOR spreads shown above by their statistical properties and because there is not a futures market by which to hedge them.

Earlier, we showed that a strong relationship exists between the fixed corporate bond, swap, and FRN markets. There is also an active-basis swap market which links the LIBOR-indexed FRN market to FRNs of the same issuer but indexed to alternative rates.

Consider the following transactions (shown in Table 9–11):

- Purchase a newly issued LIB3 floater with two years to maturity which is priced at 100 and pays a quarterly coupon of LIB3 + a reset margin (RM).

TABLE 9-11

Net Cash Flows of a LIB3 FRN and a LIB3-Fed Funds Basis Swap

Transaction	Cash Flow at Quarter t
Buy LIB3 floater	+(LIB3 +RM$^{\text{LIB3}}$)*Act/360
Basis swap:	
Receive Federal funds + basis swap spread	+(Avg. daily fed funds+BSS)*Act/360
Pay LIB3	−LIB3 *Act/360
Net cash flow	+(Avg. daily Fed funds+RM$^{\text{LIB3}}$+BSS)*Act/360

- Enter into a two-year basis swap where the investor pays LIB3 receives the average daily Federal Funds rate + a basis swap spread (BSS).
- This net cash flow approximates the cash flow on a Fed Funds floater where:

$$\text{Reset Margin } (RM^{\text{FF}}) = RM^{\text{LIB3}} + BSS \qquad (18)$$

Understanding the Current Coupon Differential between CMT2 and LIB3

Because there is an actively traded and liquid market for Eurodollar futures, we can look to those markets to help determine the current coupon differential between a FRN indexed to a longer Treasury rate and one indexed to LIB3. Consider a FRN which promises to pay CMT2 plus a reset margin (RM$^{\text{CMT2}}$) for five years. The issuer could conceivably hedge his exposure by selling the two-year Treasury rate forward each quarter over the five-year life of the bond. Since there is not an active market in futures on the two-year Treasury yield, the hedge wold involve a complicated position of long and short Treasuries.

A more popular alternative is to hedge the exposure in the liquid Eurodollar futures market. Although CMT2 is a two-year par rate and LIB3 is a three-month spot rate, the two-year forward rate can be expressed as a function of a series of three-month forward rates. The number of contracts needed to hedge this position can be determined by calculating the partial duration of the CMT2 floater with respect to each of the three-month forward rates.

Although the determination of the number of contracts needed to hedge the CMT2 exposure is beyond the scope of this discussion, the following observations are important in understanding the determinants of relative coupon differentials between CMT2 FRNs and LIB3 FRNs.

- The typical hedge amounts for a five-year maturity CMT2 floater consists of a short position in Eurodollar futures contract from quarters 0–7, long position in contracts from quarters 8–27. The long positions become much larger from quarters 20–27. Intuitively, the last promised cash flow is a two-year rate 4.75 years forward. Therefore, this bond will be sensitive to forward rates all the way out to the 6.75-year portion of the curve.

- Although the Eurodollar futures curve is comprised of both the Treasury forward rates and a forward TED spread, the issuer will be exposed to changes in the TED spread since the hedge is designed assuming constant spreads.

- The main implication with respect to floaters is that, since the CMT2 floater can be hedged by futures contracts, the current coupon differential between

CMT2 and LIB3 floaters will reflect differences in **forward** CMT2–LIB3 spread. More specifically, ignoring the effect of convexity on the optimal hedge ratios and differential option-adjusted spreads due to liquidity, the reset margin of a CMT2 floater is priced such that its present value equals that of a LIB3 floater of the same maturity *if the forward rates are realized.*[14]

Table 9–12 shows the spreads between forward CMT2 and forward LIB3 observed on March 10, 1995. This table represents a good starting point for an investor to assess the yield curve view which is embedded in the relative coupons of these floaters. If the investor believes that future yield curves will be steeper than those implied by the forwards shown in Table 9–12, then he should consider buying a CMT2 floater.[15] Of course, other factors such as liquidity should also enter into the decision.

Because the reset frequencies are equal and a parallel shift of the yield curve will have approximately the same effect on all of the forwards, the FRNs have equal sensitivity to small, parallel shifts of the yield curve in either direction. However, the bonds have different sensitivities to reshapings of the curve (partial durations). On March 10, 1995, substantial flattening from the two-year to three-month part of the curve was priced into the CMT2 floater, and this is why it receives a higher coupon at the pricing date.

---

14. The pricing coupons of the CMT2 floater will differ from the forwards because of convexity This error will increase with the term of the index. We can account for the liquidity differentials by obtaining the present value after discounting at the appropriate option-adjusted spread.
15. In assessing the relative coupons through time, one must account for the fact that LIB3 FRNs typically pay on an actual/360 basis, and the CMT2 pay on a 30/360 basis. On March 10, 1995, this differential was worth 10 basis points per annum.

TABLE 9-12

Comparison of Forward CMT2 to Forward LIB3
(March 10, 1995)

Years Forward	Forward CMT2	Forward LIB3	Difference
0.00	6.82%	6.31%	0.51%
0.25	6.95	6.48	0.47
0.50	7.06	6.77	0.29
0.75	7.13	6.99	0.14
1.00	7.17	7.08	0.09
1.25	7.23	7.15	0.08
1.50	7.24	7.19	0.05
1.75	7.26	7.27	−0.01
2.00	7.26	7.24	0.02
2.25	7.29	7.27	0.02
2.50	7.28	7.29	−0.01
2.75	7.29	7.35	−0.06
3.00	7.27	7.34	−0.07
3.25	7.28	7.37	−0.09
3.50	7.27	7.40	−0.13
3.75	7.28	7.43	−0.15
4.00	7.28	7.44	−0.16
4.25	7.31	7.45	−0.14
4.50	7.33	7.46	−0.13
4.75	7.38	7.48	−0.10

CMT2 forwards are calculated from the Salomon Brothers Treasury Model Curve. LIB3 forwards are calculated from the swap curve.

The Use of Historical Data in Assessing Basis Risk

In comparing indices such as Fed funds, TB3, and Prime to LIB3, the term structure of interest rates is not as important because the maturities embedded in these rates are near the maturity of LIB3. Furthermore, for Fed funds and Prime, there is not a futures market by which an issuer can hedge the financing rates by buying the indices forward. Therefore, there are not arbitrage relationships which dictate how these FRNs should trade relative to each other.

For example, consider an investor who is benchmarked to Fed funds and fears an imminent Fed tightening. He makes the decision to purchase a two-year floater on March 10, 1995, and compares a daily reset Fed funds floater to one of the same credit quality indexed to LIB3. We define the relative coupon at any quarterly payment date t as:

Relative Coupon$_t$
$$= ([\text{LBI3}_{t-1} + RM^{\text{LIB3}}] - [\text{average daily fed funds observed over period } t + RM^{\text{FF}}])(\text{days}/360)$$
$$= ([\text{LIB3}_{t-1} - \text{avg. daily fed funds observed over period } t]$$
$$+ [RM^{\text{LIB3}} - RM^{\text{FF}}]) * (\text{days}/360) \qquad (19)$$

If the Fed funds rate does not change over the first quarter,

Relative Coupon$_1$
$$= [(6.31\% - 5.93\%) + (0.20\% - 0.28\%)] * (\text{days}/360) \qquad (20)$$
$$= 8 \text{ basis points}$$

Should the investor accept the eight basis point advantage and take on the basis risk and the longer time to reset, given his views on Fed tightening? If the Fed tightens, how long does it take for LIB3 to adjust?

One way to assess such risk-reward trade-offs is to use historical data to: (a) compare current spreads between the indices to historical average spreads to determine whether the basis is at historical wide or tight levels, and (b) measure the propensity of these rates to move together. Estimates of historical volatilities and correlations between the indices allow the derivation of an expected change in one index *conditional* on a specified change in the other index.

There is enough data available on these rates to provide good estimates of the average levels of these spreads and their propensity to move together. However, in practice, there are many statistical issues and problems which must be addressed. They include:

- What frequency of data should be used to estimate the parameters?
- Over what time period should the estimate be calculated? In other words, over what time period is the assumption of stationarity of parameters a good one?
- Does the data warrant a more complicated time-varying parameter model such as ARCH or GARCH?[16]
- In comparing changes in rates, are only contemporaneous correlations important or should we account for various lags?

Table 9–13 shows a comparison of the average spreads between various indices. These tables illustrate that the estimates can differ significantly across measurement frequency and across subperiods.

Spreads of LIB1, LIB3, and CP1 over TB3 have clearly gotten tighter through time. Regardless of the subperiod or frequency of measurement, one might have concluded on March 10, 1995, that prime spreads are historically wide and TSY2 spreads are historically tight. Other spreads are near their averages, at least over the last five years.

If spreads between indices tend to be mean reverting, then one may conclude that prime floaters are "rich" relative to LIB3, since Table 9–10 shows that the two securities were essentially receiving the same coupon. As we discussed in detail earlier, the CMT2 floaters receive a high current coupon because some flattening of the yield curve is priced into the bond. However, historical spreads indi-

---
16. ARCH stands for autoregressive conditional heteroscedasticity; GARCH stands for generalized autoregressive conditional heteroscedasticity.

TABLE 9-13

Comparison of Average Spreads of Various Indices

Average Rates (%), Mar. 82 to Jan. 95	Prime	CP1	FEDF	LIB3	LIB1	TSY2	TB3
Quarterly	9.35	7.40	7.59	7.65	7.52	7.98	6.80
Monthly	9.29	7.16	7.34	7.54	7.42	7.91	6.74
Weekly	9.32	7.13	7.14	7.56	7.36	7.92	6.76
Daily	9.32	7.16	7.19	7.56	7.37	7.93	6.78
March 10, 1995	9.00	6.08	5.93	6.31	6.13	6.82	5.93

Average Spreads to 3-month T-Bill (%)							
Quarterly	2.55	0.60	0.79	0.85	0.72	1.18	x
Monthly	2.55	0.42	0.60	0.80	0.68	1.17	x
Weekly	2.56	0.37	0.38	0.80	0.60	1.16	x
Daily	2.54	0.38	0.41	0.78	0.59	1.15	x
March 10, 1995	3.07	0.15	0.00	0.38	0.20	0.89	x

Average Daily Spreads to Three-Month T-Bill for Various Time Periods

	Prime	CP1	FEDF	LIB3	LIB1	TSY2
Full Sample	2.54	0.38	0.41	0.78	0.59	1.15
3/82–6/86	2.50	0.29	0.55	1.07	0.83	1.49
6/86–9/90	2.30	0.62	0.65	0.90	0.72	0.83
9/90–1/95	2.85	0.23	0.06	0.39	0.24	1.14
March 10, 1995	3.07	0.15	0.00	0.38	0.20	0.89

cate that the CMT2–LIB3 spreads are tighter-than-average historical levels, which may suggest that CMT2 floaters offer value.[17]

Using historical average spreads between indices does not address the issue of how we incorporate the view of imminent Fed tightening into the decision process. Correlations provide a measure of the propensity of two random variables to move together. Table 9–14 shows estimated correlations and standard deviations between various indices for our full sample and the most recent one-third of the sample. We will show how these estimates can be used to incorporate an investor's views on Fed funds into the choice of FRNs.

Several observations emerge from Table 9–14:

- Across nearly all of the frequencies and subperiods, the Fed funds index is the most volatile (highest standard deviation) index.
- n general, the correlations are smaller the more frequently the data are sampled.
- Some of the estimated parameters change substantially over time. One of the most difficult issues to resolve in the use of statistical measures to assess financial risk is to determine which set of data is appropriate in estimating parameters. On one hand, one would prefer the longest time series of data possible in order to obtain more precise estimates.[18] On the other hand, if the true relationship between the variables has changed over time, then some of the earlier observations will not be relevant in estimating the new parameter.

---

17. Of course, even if an investor believe historical spreads are applicable today, he may prefer to hold prime floaters because of the frequent reset, or to not hold CMT2 floaters for reasons such as liquidity.
18. Precision refers to the degree of error in estimating the parameters.

TABLE 9-14
Correlations Between One-Period Changes in Various Indices (March 1982–January

Monthly Frequency	Prime	CP1	FEDF	LIB3	LIB1	TSY2	TB3
Prime	1.00						
CP1	0.59	1.00					
FEDF	0.34	0.50	1.00				
LIB3	0.64	0.79	0.51	1.00			
LIB1	0.60	0.76	0.54	0.93	1.00		
TSY2	0.57	0.62	0.35	0.86	0.72	1.00	
TB3	0.47	0.70	0.40	0.80	0.75	0.74	1.00
Standard Deviation	0.36	0.56	0.81	0.50	0.53	0.45	0.66
Weekly Frequency							
Prime	1.00						
CP1	0.10	1.00					
FEDF	0.09	0.17	1.00				
LIB3	0.27	0.27	0.33	1.00			
LIB1	0.23	0.28	0.35	0.84	1.00		
TSY2	0.12	0.19	0.26	0.66	0.52	1.00	
TB3	0.09	0.19	0.32	0.61	0.49	0.71	1.00
Standard Deviation	0.16	0.70	0.39	0.23	0.24	0.18	0.22

TABLE 9-14
Continued

Daily Frequency	Prime	CP1	FEDF	LIB3	LIB1	TSY2	TB3
Prime	1.00						
CP1	0.06	1.00					
FEDF	0.02	0.26	1.00				
LIB3	0.04	0.52	0.16	1.00			
LIB1	0.04	0.47	0.13	0.56	1.00		
TSY2	0.03	0.18	0.07	0.27	0.20	1.00	
TB3	0.04	0.19	0.08	0.24	0.17	0.60	1.00
Standard Deviation	0.07	0.09	0.30	0.11	0.12	0.08	0.10

(September 1990–January 1995)

Monthly Frequency	Prime	CP1	FEDF	LIB3	LIB1	TSY2	TB3
Prime	1.00						
CP1	0.55	1.00					
FEDF	0.20	−0.19	1.00				
LIB3	0.57	0.55	0.31	1.00			
LIB1	0.49	0.39	0.33	0.88	1.00		
TSY2	0.52	0.40	0.20	0.79	0.58	1.00	
TB3	0.64	0.48	0.30	0.86	0.75	0.79	1.00
Standard Deviation	0.28	0.32	0.69	0.31	0.42	0.32	0.25

TABLE 9-14

Continued

Weekly Frequency	Prime	CP1	FEDF	LIB3	LIB1	TSY2	TB3
Prime	1.00						
CP1	0.23	1.00					
FEDF	0.15	0.23	1.00				
LIB3	0.24	0.37	0.01	1.00			
LIB1	0.12	0.40	0.04	0.74	1.00		
TSY2	0.09	0.29	0.11	0.53	0.38	1.00	
TB3	0.15	0.28	0.18	0.46	0.40	0.68	1.00
Standard Deviation	0.14	0.19	0.34	0.13	0.18	0.13	0.08

Daily Frequency	Prime	CP1	FEDF	LIB3	LIB1	TSY2	TB3
Prime	1.00						
CP1	0.14	1.00					
FEDF	−0.02	0.08	1.00				
LIB3	0.08	0.37	0.00	1.00			
LIB1	0.04	0.25	0.04	0.48	1.00		
TSY2	0.02	0.19	0.06	0.21	0.12	1.00	
TB3	0.07	0.21	0.10	0.21	0.11	0.59	1.00
Standard Deviation	0.06	0.07	0.31	0.06	0.10	0.06	0.04

Tables 9–13 and 9–14 show that the estimated distributions of LIB1 and LIB3 have changed through time, with the average spreads and volatilities decreasing substantially since the late 1980s. Most market participants would argue that there has been a fundamental shift in the relationship between LIBOR rates and Treasury rates. If this is true, then the estimated parameters derived from the most recent subperiod would be the most applicable in measuring the current basis risk.

Table 9–14 also presents an example whereby it may be more appropriate to use the full sample of data. For the last subperiod (September 1990–January 1995) and monthly frequency, the estimated correlation between CP1 and Fed funds is –0.19. However, this estimate was driven by a large negative correlation in late 1990 and 1991. This period had a large impact on the subperiod estimates since there were a small number of observations. The estimated correlation between CP1 and Fed funds over the entire time period (March 1982–January 1995) was 0.50. The 1991 period makes a much smaller contribution to the estimate for the full sample. Most market participants would argue that the full sample estimate appears more reasonable in this case.

Prime–Treasury Spreads

One bit of conventional wisdom is that banks react quickly to raise their prime lending rate as Treasury rates increase, but react much more slowly when interest rates drop. This phenomenon would have positive implications for prime floaters since the coupon would reset quickly to higher rates but slower to lower rates, thereby improving performance relative to other FRNs, keeping everything else equal. Our simple statistics shown in Table 9–14 do not tell whether this conventional wisdom is substantiated since our estimates represent an "average" of rising and falling interest rate environments. Table 9–15 gives average changes in rates for prime and Fed funds, and correlations in different environments. The environments are determined by whether the Fed funds rate rises ($\Delta FF > 0$) or falls ($\Delta FF <= 0$) for the given period.

The evidence in Table 9–15 does not support the conventional wisdom. If prime rates moved with Treasury rates in rising rate environments but remained "sticky" in falling rate environments, then we should see higher correlations and substantially positive changes in the prime rate in rising rate environments. This is not supported by the data, except possibly in the June 1986–September 1990 subperiod. In fact, Table 9–15 provides more support to the conjecture that the prime rate falls with decreases in Treasury rates but is "sticky" in rising rate environments.

Using the Statistics to Assess the Basis Risk

The average one-period change of each of these indices was close to zero for all frequencies and time periods. We can say that our *unconditional* expectation of the change in any particular index over any frequency equals zero. Given the appropriate frequency and time period has been chosen, the estimated correlations allow an estimate of an expectation *conditional* on a particular view. For example, if the investor believes that the Fed will raise the Fed funds rate by 50 basis points within the next week, what should be his expected increase in LIB3?

The link between conditional expectations and correlations can be seen in the standard regression equation:

$$y = a + \beta x \qquad (21)$$

TABLE 9-15
Comparison of Changes in the Prime Rate to Changes in Fed Funds in Different Interest Rate Environments

	ΔFF > 0				ΔFF < 0		
March 1982–Jan. 1995	Corr. (ΔFF, ΔPrime)	Ave. ΔPrime	Ave. ΔFF	Corr. (ΔFF, ΔPrime)	Ave. ΔPrime	Ave. ΔFF
Monthly	−0.06	0.05	0.48	0.30	−0.60	−1.10
Weekly	−0.08	0.01	0.21	0.37	−0.15	−0.62
Daily	−0.04	0.00	0.21	0.15	−0.03	−0.23
March 1982–June 1996	Corr. (ΔFF, ΔPrime)	Ave. ΔPrime	Ave. ΔFF	Corr. (ΔFF, ΔPrime)	Ave. ΔPrime	Ave. ΔFF
Monthly	−0.12	−0.01	0.66	0.39	−0.29	−0.92
Weekly	−0.19	−0.03	0.34	0.13	−0.04	−0.36
Daily	−0.01	0.00	0.25	0.05	−0.01	−0.20
June 1986–Sept. 1990	Corr. (ΔFF, ΔPrime)	Ave. ΔPrime	Ave. ΔFF	Corr. (ΔFF, ΔPrime)	Ave. ΔPrime	Ave. ΔFF
Monthly	0.27	0.09	0.38	0.06	−0.04	−0.44
Weekly	0.33	0.03	0.13	0.09	−0.02	−0.12
Daily	0.02	0.00	0.16	0.01	0.00	−0.12
Sept. 1990–Jan. 1995	Corr. (ΔFF, ΔPrime)	Ave. ΔPrime	Ave. ΔFF	Corr. (ΔFF, ΔPrime)	Ave. ΔPrime	Ave. ΔFF
Monthly	−0.22	0.06	0.40	0.22	−0.12	−0.46
Weekly	0.04	0.01	0.18	0.19	−0.02	−0.20
Daily	−0.08	0.00	0.22	0.07	0.00	−0.15

ΔFF = one period change in Fed funds rate, ΔPrime = one period change in prime rate

$$\beta \text{ is defined as } \frac{\text{covariance }(x, y)}{\text{std}(x)^2} \qquad (22)$$

$$\text{correlation }(x, y) = \frac{\text{covariance }(x, y)}{\text{std }(x) \text{ std }(y)} \qquad (23)$$

where std (x) std = standard deviation of x.

Also, taking expectations of the standard regression equation shows that:

$$a = E(y) - \beta E(x) = \bar{y} - \beta \bar{x} \qquad (24)$$

where $\bar{x}$ = expected value of x, $\bar{y}$ = expected value of y

Substituting these equations into the standard regression equation yields the following relationship:

$$E(y \text{ conditional on } x)$$
$$= \bar{y} + \left(\frac{\text{correlation }(x, y) * \text{std }(y)}{\text{std }(x)}\right)(x - \bar{x}) \qquad (25)$$

We can substitute the estimated values from the table for weekly frequency into equation **(25)**, to get the following relationship:

$$E[\text{change in LIB3}] = 0 + \left(\frac{0.328)(0.226)}{0.390}\right) \qquad (26)$$

$$(\text{changeFEDF} - 0) = 0.19 * \text{change FEDF}$$

Suppose, as stated earlier, we want to investigate the case where change in FEDF equals 50 basis points over the next week. Then, to get the updated or "conditional" expectation, we substitute 0.50 percent for change FEDF in equation **(26)**, which yields the following result:

$E[\text{change LIB3} \mid \text{conditional on change in FEDF}$
$= 0.5\%] = 0.19*0.50\% = 0.095\% = 9.5 \text{ b.p.}$

The statistic R^2 provides a measure of the "goodness of fit" of the regression model. For a univariate regression (one variable), R^2 equals correlation$(x,y)^2$. Therefore, in our case, $R^2 = (.328)^2 = 10.8\%$. This implies that the change in Fed funds only "explains" 10.8 percent of the total variation in LIB3.

In this example, we only considered contemporaneous correlations. To better quantify basis risk, we should also consider lagged changes of indices. A *vector autoregression model*[19] estimates the effects of shocks to a particular index and on its expected future levels and those of other indices. An investor could use such a model to estimate relative cash flows between two FRNs over time, conditional on a particular change of one of the indices.

OPTIONALITY

So far, we have only discussed FRNs which do not contain embedded options. However, some corporate and asset-backed floaters are subject to maximum or minimum coupons. Many structured notes are comprised of fairly complicated option positions. Floating-rate mortgage securities such as adjustable-rate mortgages (ARMs) or floating-rate CMOs have maximum and minimum coupons and are subject to prepayment options. In comparing these securities to non-call securities of the same issuer or to each other, an investor must: (a) identify the option position embedded in the bond; and (b) value the option position.

For some FRNs with embedded options, it is relatively straightforward to decompose the security into a portfolio of a long position in a non-call FRN and a position in some commonly traded option.

---

19. For a technical definition and discussion of vector autoregression models, see James D. Hamilton, *Time Series Analysis* (Princeton, NJ: Princeton University Press, 1994).

TABLE 9-16

Cash Flow of Portfolio Consisting of an Unfloored FRN and a Long Floor

Portfolio	Cash Flow at Time t
Long unfloored floater	$LIB3_{t-1} + 0.125\%$
Long floor with a 4.20% strike	$Max[4.20\% - LIB3_{t-1}, 0]$
Net cash flow	$Max[4.35\%, LIB3_{t-1} + 0.125\%]$

Floored Corporate FRNs

Consider a FRN with the following characteristics:

Rating:	A3/A–
Maturity:	7/15/03
Coupon:	LIB3 + 12.5 b.p.
Minimum coupon:	4.35%
Reset/pay frequency:	Quarterly/quarterly

This security can be decomposed into a portfolio of a long position in an unfloored FRN with a coupon of LIB3 + 12.5 basis points and a long position in a LIBOR floor maturing on the same date with a strike equal to 4.20 percent. The cash flows of this portfolio at any coupon date are given by Table 9–16. This table illustrates that the portfolio replicates the cash flows of the floored floater.

This approach is extremely useful in relative valuation. Suppose that, on 7/15/95 (exactly eight years from maturity), the market price of the floored floater was $98.00. On this date, a fixed bond of the same issuer maturing on 2/1/03 was trading at a yield spread of 92 basis points over the seven-year Treasury. For simplicity, assume that this is also the fair yield of a fixed bond which matures on 7/15/03. On 7/15/95, the fixed rate on an eight-year swap was 6.45 percent. Therefore, the floored floater could be swapped into a fixed coupon of 6.575%

(6.45% + 0.125% reset margin). Using a yield spread of 92 basis points, the present value of the swapped floater (ignoring the value of the floor) is $97.85. Therefore, the implied price of the embedded floor is equal to $0.15 ($98.00 − $97.85). Using an arbitrage-free term structure model, for an eight-year floor with a strike equal to 4.20 percent and a dollar price of $0.15, we obtain an implied volatility of 12.7 percent. Since the implied volatility of offered floors of similar maturity and strikes on 7/15/95 was 23 percent, the floored floater appears "cheap."

Several caveats apply to this type of analysis. One practical issue is that if the floored FRN is less liquid than the portfolio of an unfloored floaters and an OTC floor, then we should expect it to be slightly cheaper to reflect higher transactions cost of unwinding the position. Another issue is whether an investor can extract the "cheapness" of the floored floater. Suppose an investor agreed with our analysis but wants to purchase an FRN because he has a view that interest rates will rise in the near term. He asks, "Even though the embedded floor appears cheap at a premium of $0.15, why should I even pay that premium when I have such strong views that rates will rise?"

One answer which is often given is that the investor can extract the cheapness today by writing an OTC 4.20 percent strike floor with the same coupon dates and maturity as the FRN. Assuming the bid volatility of the OTC floor was 21 percent, such a floor would provide the investor with an upfront premium of $0.94. Therefore, he now created a synthetic unfloored FRN at approximately 25/32 of a point "cheap" ($0.94 − $0.15). This is a completely valid argument if the investor's intention is to keep the long and short position until maturity and does not have to mark this position to market. If the floors were to come into the money at any time over the life of the bond, any cash flow that the investor would have to pay on the short floor would be exactly offset by the difference between the floored floater coupon and that of an unfloored floater.

However, suppose the investor had an investment horizon shorter than the eight-year maturity of the FRN and either had to mark the combination to market or trade out of the position at the short horizon. Suppose the implied volatility on the OTC floors increased to 30 percent. There is no mechanism to ensure that the embedded option in the FRN will increase to reflect the higher market volatility. Therefore, the investor may have a marked-to-market loss on the short floor position and no marked-to-market gain on the FRN. Alternatively, suppose LIB3 decreased 50 basis points from its 7/15 level of 5.81 percent. If the implied volatilities on the OTC floors remained constant, then they would appreciate because the option would be closer to the money. Once again, the FRNs may not necessarily increase in price accordingly; they may just trade at even lower implied volatilities.

These caveats do not invalidate the analysis as a measure of richness or cheapness. Purchasing this FRN under the market conditions given in the example still appears to be a cheap way of adding convexity since the FRN should eventually experience price appreciation due to changing option value if rates decrease. This example simply illustrates that the mispricing does not represent arbitrage opportunities.

Other types of FRNs contain much more complicated embedded option positions. Many structured notes are bonds that pay a coupon that is some function of LIB3. Although the component parts may not be as obvious as in the previous example, these securities can often be decomposed into a replicating portfolio in a similar manner.[20]

---

20. For some examples, see Raymond J. Iwanowski, *Floating-Rate Securities: Current Markets and Risk/Return Trade-Offs in Rising Interest Rate Environments* (New York: Salomon Brothers Inc.), April 6, 1994.

However, mortgage-backed FRNs do not lend themselves to such a clean decomposition because of the existence of the prepayment option.

Mortgage FRNs

A complete discussion of all of the relevant factors which influence the ARM and floating-rate CMO markets would require much more detail and analysis than we intend to devote in this chapter. However, we will broadly outline some of the main issues which an investor should consider in comparing a mortgage-backed FRN to those of other asset classes, particularly in the context of our discussion of optionality.

Like all mortgage-backed securities (MBS), floating-rate CMOs and ARMs differ from corporate and government bonds in that the securities amortize through time. Furthermore, although the securities are priced with respect to some scheduled amortization, this schedule is based on projected prepayments. Actual prepayments which deviate from scheduled prepayments will cause the amortization schedule to change over time.

Actual prepayment speeds which are faster (slower) than pricing prepayment speeds positively affect the total return performance of fixed mortgage-backed securities when the bond is purchased at a discount (premium), and negatively affect performance when the bond is purchased at a premium (discount). This intuition also holds for floating-rate MBS. However, suppose the floating-rate mortgage is priced at or near 100. Why should prepayment variability affect this bond? As long as spreads remain the same, shouldn't you be able to reinvest fast prepayments back into another floater with the same spread to current LIB3?

The main reason why prepayment variability affects the price of a floating-rate MBS is the effect prepayments have on the embedded options. Specifically, both ARMs and floating-rate CMOs have maximum and minimum[21] coupons. ARMs also have *periodic caps* which are the maximum amount the coupon could change at any particular reset.

Some investors attempt to "uncap" floating-rate CMOs by decomposing the floating-rate MBS into an uncapped floater and a short position in LIBOR caps with maturities equal to the average life of the CMO. A more sophisticated approach to the same idea is to value a short position in an *amortizing* cap where the amortization schedule is set to the amortization schedule of the MBS at the pricing date. However, this "replicating portfolio" idea misses the effect of prepayment variability. Although actual prepayments are difficult to predict and the best forecasting models will always have some error, it is quite predictable that, all other factors constant, prepayments speed up when interest rates fall and slow when interest rates rise. This phenomenon increases the value of the caps because the "maturity" of the caps increase as they become nearer the money. This effect decreases the value of the bond since the bond has an embedded *short* position in the caps.

For example, suppose a floating-rate CMO with a reset margin of 40 basis points and a 9.40 percent cap is priced on 7/15/95 and had a weighted average life of five years. The market-implied volatility for five-year 9 percent OTC caps of 24.5 percent, which results in the "value" of the cap, ignoring extension risk, of $1.06.[22] Now, suppose

---

21. The floors are typically struck at very low levels, in some cases at 0%. For the ensuing discussion and without loss of generality, we assume that the securities have caps but no floors.
22. Floating-rate CMOs typically are indexed to one-month LIBOR and pay monthly.

the LIBOR yield curve experiences an instantaneous parallel increase in rates of 50 basis points. Because the cap is 50 basis points closer to becoming "in the money," a five-year cap would now be worth $1.45. However, suppose that the CMO extends such that, at the new yield curve levels, the market would be pricing the CMO to a seven year average life. Now, the price of a seven-year cap under the same volatility and the new yield curve is $2.87.[23] This example illustrates that "uncapping" the floating-rate MBS in this manner overvalues the security since the method ignores the extension risk.

One method of comparing floating-rate MBS to FRNs of other asset classes is through the use of option-adjusted spread (OAS) methodology. Standard OAS methodology takes a term structure of interest rates and a volatility assumption and values the security over a distribution of possible interest rate paths. The parameters of the distribution are calibrated such that the current term structure is correctly priced and arbitrage opportunities are precluded. For mortgages, a prepayment function is applied at each path and, therefore, the OAS calculation will incorporate the effect of extension on the value of the caps. However, it must be emphasized that the calculated OAS is a function of the assumed term structure and prepayment models. Even the most accurate models will capture the true distributions with some error. Therefore, a comparison of the OAS of a complex optionable security like floating-rate MBS to a FRN without options should incorporate some additional spread due to "model risk."

Alternatively, the canonical decomposition methodology[24] extends the replicating portfolio idea to account for

---

23. This value is slightly overstated because longer caps typically get priced at lower volatility. At 22% volatility, the value of the cap is $2.36.

24. See Thomas S. Y. Ho, "Arbitrage-Free Bond Canonical Decomposition," *Global Advanced Technology* and this volume, April 1995.

the negative convexity implied by the extension risk of the caps. Specifically, this approach uses an arbitrage-free term structure model to determine a portfolio of Treasury bonds, caps, and floors which replicate the cash flows of the floating-rate MBS across all possible paths. The decomposition allows an investor to evaluate the risks embedded in a complex security in the context of a portfolio of very liquid instruments. Additionally, this portfolio does not require continuous rebalancing. Of course, like the OAS methodology, the accuracy by which the cash flows of the portfolio replicate the cash flows of the FRN along all paths is subject to the accuracy of the term structure and prepayment model.

The mortgage example illustrates another important intuition in the valuation of embedded options in FRN. The spot LIB1 observed on 7/15/95 was 5.88 percent. Given the 9.00 percent strike on the embedded caps, these options are currently over 300 basis points "out of the money." An investor who is familiar with option pricing theory may be surprised that options so far "out of the money" would be valued so highly. In reality, caps are comprised of a set of options on *forward rates*. Therefore, one should look at the implied forward rates over the life of the cap to determine "in the moneyness." In an upward sloping yield curve environment, the options may be much nearer to the money than what is implied by the difference between strike and spot LIB1.

CONCLUSION

Floating-rate securities have been, and will continue to be, popular in practically all asset classes of fixed-income markets, particularly for investors who are bearish on interest rates. Many of the features of these markets make comparisons of the risks, and even the compensations for taking risks, difficult to quantify. We presented many of the measures and conventions that are currently used in the various FRN markets. We hope that these discussions will be useful as a reference that makes these commonly used measures more concrete. We then describe in detail the risks which the various instruments are subject to and offer frameworks by which an investor can assess these risks.

CHAPTER 10

Liquidity Risk: A First Look

Scott Y. Peng
Vice President
BlackRock Financial Management

and

Ravi E. Dattatreya
Senior Vice President
Sumitoma Bank Capital Markets

Liquidity risk is often discussed, yet rarely systematically quantified. The aim of this chapter is to define some of the issues surrounding liquidity risk and outline the analysis in a systematic manner.

The liquidity risk analysis will serve to illustrate and quantify the increased liquidity risks posed by a mismatch of the asset and liability risk profiles. Some simple, prudent measures such as cash buffering or disaster hedging can significantly reduce the liquidity risk of the portfolio. Readers should not infer that the liquidity risk of all portfolios will be as high as shown by the sample portfolio since many portfolio managers already practice some combination of the liquidity risk prevention methods that will be recommended. What readers should take away from the analysis is that an understanding of the asset/liability risk profiles, in combination with several prudent risk management measures, can dramatically lower the probability of the onset of liquidity risk and portfolio decimation.

In this chapter, the role of liquidity risk within the risk universe will be outlined. Then the definition of liquidity risk will be provided, followed by an analysis of

FIGURE 10-1

The Risk Universe

```
                    RISK UNIVERSE
                   /             \
           VISIBLE RISK      INVISIBLE RISK
```

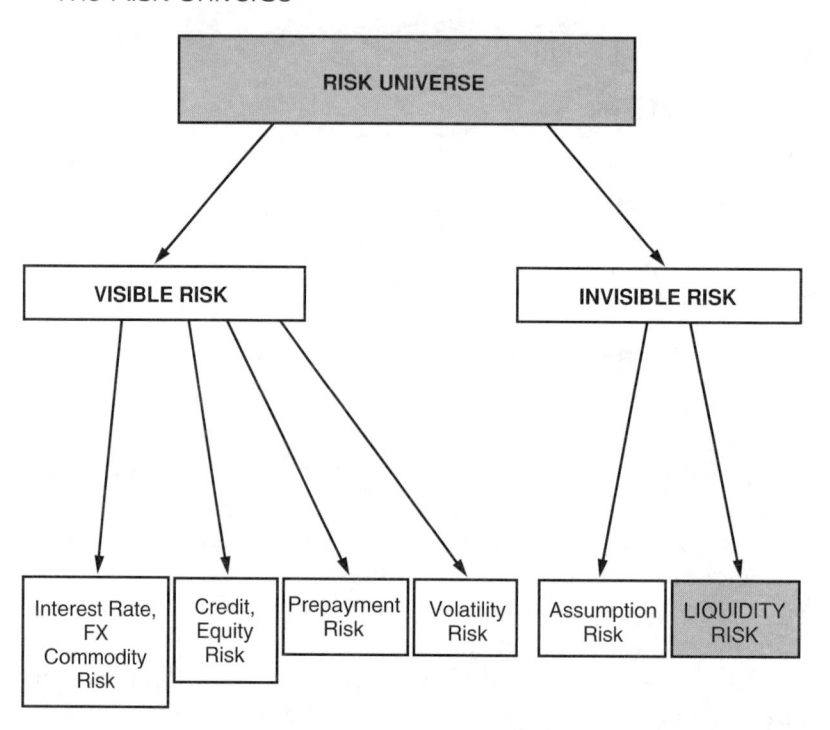

| Interest Rate, FX Commodity Risk | Credit, Equity Risk | Prepayment Risk | Volatility Risk | Assumption Risk | LIQUIDITY RISK |

liquidity risk using a physical model. After the results of the liquidity risk analysis are interpreted, several portfolio management techniques which can lower liquidity risk are presented, along with the associated risk simulation results.

THE RISK UNIVERSE

Like the real universe around us, the risk universe can be thought of as consisting of two distinct parts: a visible risk universe, encompassing risks which are evident, and an invisible risk universe encompassing risks which are not obvious. As Figure 10–1 illustrates, the visible risk universe includes many of the risks which are routinely monitored,

FIGURE 10-2

Flow of Liquidity Created by Organizational Structure

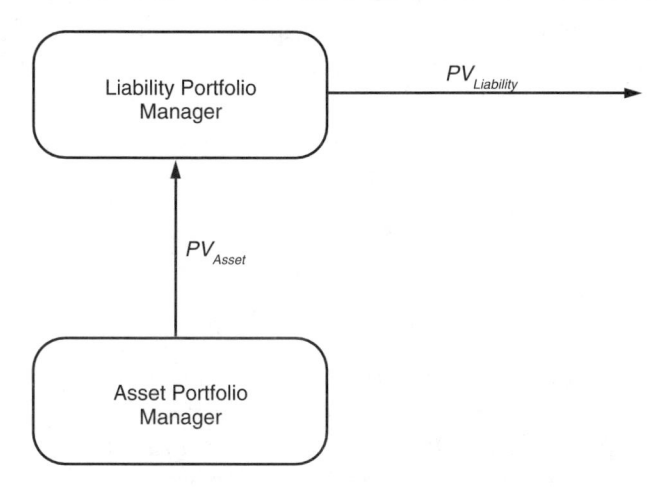

```
        ┌──────────────────┐
        │ Liability Portfolio │ ──── PV_Liability ───▶
        │     Manager      │
        └──────────────────┘
                 ▲
                 │  PV_Asset
                 │
        ┌──────────────────┐
        │  Asset Portfolio │
        │     Manager      │
        └──────────────────┘
```

understood, and quantified. The invisible risk universe, on the other hand, includes risks which are often discussed, and sometimes considered, yet rarely quantified.

LIQUIDITY RISK

Liquidity risk is defined as the risk in a portfolio that is attributable to investor or shareholder redemption behavior. Specifically, it is the crisis brought on as a result of insufficient cash to adequately satisfy redemption requirements.

Within a financial institution such as an insurance company, liability management and asset management are, for the most part, separate functions. While this separation of functions may have served in the past, the explosion in the variety of asset classes and new liability products of the 1990s can pose severe risks to financial institutions that do not coordinate the risk management of their asset and liability portfolios.

Figure 10–2 shows how such "separate but equal" organizational structures can result in liquidity problems.

The example is that of an insurance company which is represented by an asset portfolio and a liability portfolio, each with its own manager. The liability portfolio manager is obligated to pay to the policyholders, upon demand, some previously agreed-upon amount, $PV_{LIABILITY}$, which reflects the benefits guaranteed by the contract. The cash with which to make this payment must come from the liquidation of the asset portfolio which is managed by the asset manager. However, the cash that is available can only be the liquidation value of the assets which are associated with the liability product. If the cash value is less than the guaranteed benefit, a net deficit will occur. This mismatch of liability portfolio risk to asset portfolio risk is one of the primary causes of liquidity risk.

Liquidity risk often increases when any one of the following conditions occur. Often these conditions occur in tandem, which would further deepen the liquidity crisis.

1. *The asset or liability portfolio is not adequately marked to market.* This is the most common source of liquidity crisis. Upon redemption by shareholders, the portfolio manager discovers that the liquidation value of the assets is significantly different from the mark-to-market value.

2. *The asset portfolio contains assets which are illiquid or have become illiquid.* Illiquid assets carry very large bid-offer spreads which can adversely affect the amount of cash available after liquidation to pay shareholders.

3. *Asset risk does not match liability risk.* This risk arises when the asset portfolio must be liquidated to pay liabilities at a guaranteed level, but the asset portfolio has decreased in value. When the asset risk profiles do not match the liability risk profiles, liquidation by the liability policyholders will result in the liquidation of the asset portfolio, which will prove insufficient to provide the required cash.

4. *The herd effect may cause shareholders to redeem shares in unison.* When adverse news concerning a portfolio, its manager, or the overall market is made available to the public, shareholders may rush in a herd-like manner to redeem shares before a perceived collapse occurs. This behavior can result in significant reduction in the capital base of the portfolio, and will exacerbate the liquidity problem generated by any of the previous three situations.

MODELING OF LIQUIDITY RISK

The methodology that will be used to analyze and model liquidity risk is that of a physical model analysis, which attempts to analogize the portfolio analysis to a physical problem. The analysis of the portfolio is then transformed into understanding and applying known methodologies to the physical problem. The steps of the analysis are:

1. *Selection of a physical model.* This is the most important step in the analysis. The selection of an appropriate model results in a good framework upon which to base the liquidity risk analysis.

2. *Analogize physical traits in the model to the various portfolio characteristics.* The various physical traits must be related to the relevant portfolio attributes.

3. *Analyze the physical model via simulations or analytical techniques.* Once the physical attributes have been linked to the appropriate portfolio characteristics, the analysis of the physical model can proceed based on analysis techniques which are appropriate for the model. The analysis must make accommodations for any shortcomings in the physical-portfolio analogy.

4. *Interpret and understand results.*

FIGURE 10-3

Physical Model: The River

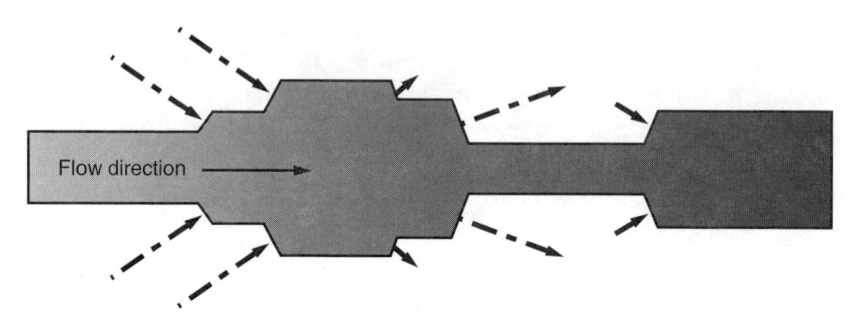

Physical Model: The River

The physical model that will be selected to analyze the issue of liquidity risk is, appropriately enough, the fluid flow of a river. The river is constrained to flow in a straight linear manner at a constant depth. In Figure 10–3, the river is observed from a top-down perspective. The river can encounter tributaries in the course of its path. These tributaries can either bring in additional water or remove water from the river. Since the river is constrained to flow at a constant depth, the width of the river must expand to accommodate any inflow, and must decrease if there is outflow.

In addition to the width of the river, a second characteristic which will be useful in the analysis of liquidity risk is the temperature of the fluid within the river. It will be assumed that various heat sources and heat sinks exist under the riverbed which can change the temperature of the fluid flow. This temperature profile is reflected in Figure 10–3 by various shades, with lighter shades representing flows at colder temperatures, and darker shades indicating hotter temperatures.

Analogy: Physical Model to Portfolio

With the basic physical model selected, an analogy of the characteristics of the river model can be made with those of a portfolio.

The index of liquidity risk will be referred to as the *quality*. Quality is a term taken from multiphase fluid mechanics. In the context of this chapter, quality will refer to the overall energy of the river at each cross section. The energy content of the fluid flow is calculated by multiplying the flow mass by the flow temperature. In the portfolio universe, quality refers to the liquidation value of the portfolio, and is calculated by multiplying the number of shares outstanding by the asset value per share. In other words:

$$q_{flow} = m_{flow} * T_{flow} \quad (1)$$

$$q_{flow} = m_{port}[\# shares] * T_{port}\left[\frac{\$}{share}\right]$$

Figure 10–4 describes the relevant features that will be used in the analysis of the river flow, and their corresponding features in the portfolio universe.

DEFINITION OF LIQUIDITY CRISIS

Given the river analogy, the next question that must be answered is the definition of a liquidity crisis. This can be best illustrated by examining the flow in Figure 10–5.

In the illustration, the fluid flow progresses from left to right. During the course of the flow, tributaries (not shown) drain away the amount of fluid remaining within the system. At the same time, heat sinks lower the temperature of the fluid. The result is less fluid remaining within the river, and the remaining fluid is flowing at a lower temperature.

FIGURE 10-4

Analogies of Physical Model to Portfolio

	River Characteristics	Portfolio Characteristics	Comments
m	Width of River (reflects volume or mass flow)	Number of shares	Width of river reflects the number of liability policies in force.
T	Flow temperature	Price per share	This is the cash value per policy that is available from the asset portfolio.
q	Quality (mass * Temp)	Total cash in portfolio (# shares)* (price/share)	Total cash reflects amount available to meet liquidity demands. Low quality indicates high liquidity risk.
x	Flow location	Time	Location reflects distance in time from initial analysis date.
q_{IN}	Heat source	Events which result in increases of asset portfolio value	Market changes such as shifts in interest rates can result in increased asset values (temperature) without altering the number of policies in force (mass).
q_{OUT}	Heat sink	Events which result in decreases of asset portfolio value	

The analogy of this situation to the portfolio is as follows: first, policyholders are redeeming shares (removing mass flow), and secondly, market events cause the assets remaining in the portfolio to lose value (lower temperature). The net result is that there is less cash (quality) remaining within the system.

Given this analogy, the occurrence of a liquidity crisis is easy to visualize. At some point in the course of the flow, the amount of cash remaining within the system will drop

FIGURE 10-5

Liquidity Crisis in River Flow

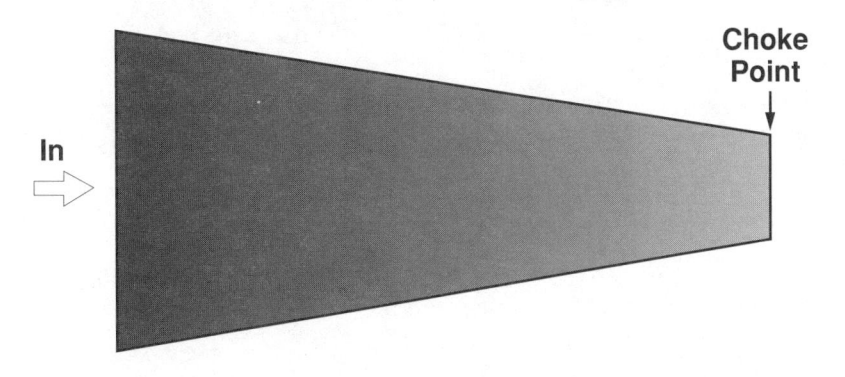

to such a low point that the portfolio loses viability. The analogy to the physical model is that, at some point in the flow, the river will become so narrow and the temperature so cold that the flow will freeze. The freezing point is referred to as the *choke point* and defines the onset of liquidity crisis. Note that the choke point may be different for each portfolio manager and should be defined beforehand. For the analysis performed in this chapter, the choke point occurs when the flow quality decreases to 15 percent of the original quality of the portfolio q_0.

LIQUIDITY ANALYSIS

In the analysis of liquidity risk within the context of the river model, first, conservation laws must be defined. Secondly, three different analysis regimes will be defined which address the different couplings, or correlations, between various fluid flow characteristics. Next, the analysis of a simple one-asset portfolio will be made within the context of the three regimes.

Conservation Laws

Two conservation laws employed in the analysis of the river model are the *conservation of mass* and the *conservation of energy*.

Conservation of mass. Conservation of mass can be stated as follows:

$$\text{Retained mass} = \sum m_{in} - \sum m_{out} \qquad (2)$$

If we break the flow into infinitesimal segments, conservation of mass is expressed as:

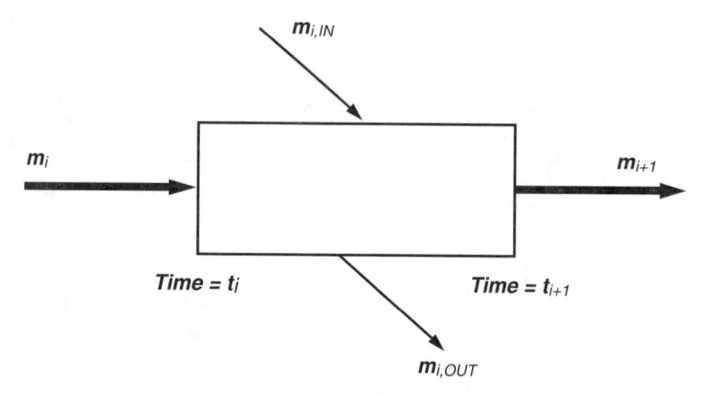

Conservation of mass can thus be rewritten as:

$$m_{i+1} = m_i + m_{i,IN} - m_{i,OUT} \qquad (3)$$

Conservation of energy. The second conservation law that will be useful in the analysis of our river model is the conservation of energy.

$$\text{Retained energy} = \sum E_{in} - \sum E_{out} \qquad (4)$$

Energy in the river flow model is defined as the product of mass times the temperature, i.e.,

$$E_i = m_i * T_i \qquad (5)$$

Liquidity Risk: A First Look

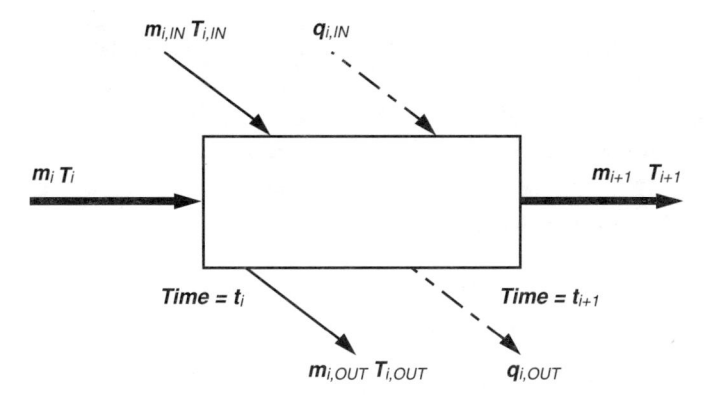

For the above element, the conservation of energy is:

$$E_{i+1} = E_i + E_{i,IN} - E_{i,OUT} + q_{i,IN}\ q_{i,OUT} \qquad (6)$$

or, expressed in terms of the two fluid flow characteristics,

$$(m * T)_{i+1} = (m * T)_i + (m * T)_{i,IN} \\ - (m * T)_{i,OUT} - q_{i,IN}\ q_{i,OUT} \qquad (7)$$

where $q_{i,IN}$ and $q_{i,OUT}$ are heat-sink and heat-source events which add or remove heat directly from the flow without altering the mass. These injections of quality correspond in the portfolio universe to market events which can result in a higher or lower value of the asset portfolio (quality) without changing the number of liability policies (mass) in force.

Coupling Investor Behavior to Portfolio Performance

Now that the two sets of conservation conditions have been imposed, the problem can be constructed. As mentioned previously, liquidity crisis is a result of rational investor behavior. Thus, the connection between investor behavior and portfolio performance should prove to be a vital link in the causal analysis of liquidity risk.

The three cases to be examined are:

   1. *No coupling occurs between mass outflow and fluid temperature.* This corresponds to situations where investor

investments and redemptions have no correlation with the actual performance of the portfolio itself. The two timelines below illustrate the evolution of the temperature and mass flows and the separate processes $T(t)$ and $M(t)$ which govern each. Note that the two processes are not coupled in any way.

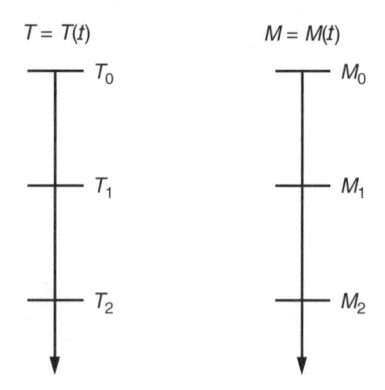

$T = T(t)$ $M = M(t)$

T_0 M_0

T_1 M_1

T_2 M_2

2. *Mass inflow/outflow is linked to temperature.* This corresponds to the situation in which investors will be more likely to withdraw when a portfolio underperforms.

The illustration below clearly shows that the temperature process is still evolving independently, but the mass flow process now has a component which is related to the temperature evolution.

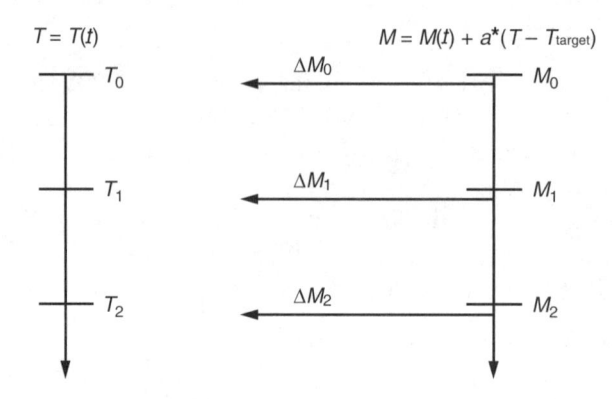

$T = T(t)$ $M = M(t) + a^*(T - T_{\text{target}})$

T_0 ΔM_0 M_0

T_1 ΔM_1 M_1

T_2 ΔM_2 M_2

Liquidity Risk: A First Look

3. *Mass and temperature are co-coupled.* This corresponds to the most realistic and complicated situation, in which investor behaviors are influenced by the portfolio performance, and the portfolio performance is influenced by investor withdrawals at some guaranteed price which may be different from the portfolio's net asset value.

The two processes are now intertwined. A change in the temperature process will have an effect on the mass flow process, which in turn will affect the temperature of the flow.

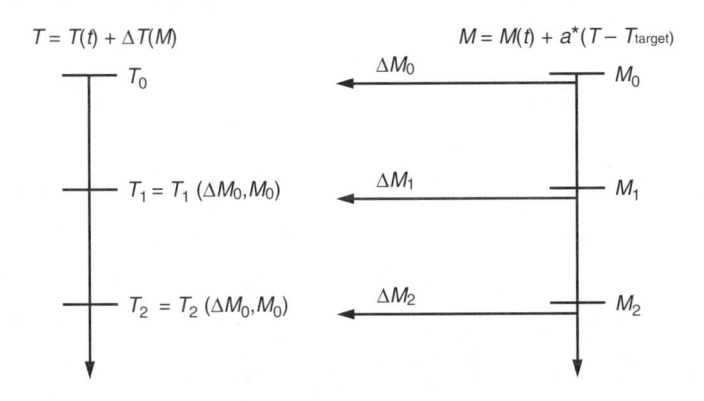

$T = T(t) + \Delta T(M)$ $\qquad\qquad\qquad\qquad M = M(t) + a^*(T - T_{\text{target}})$

- T_0 $\qquad\qquad\qquad \Delta M_0 \qquad\qquad\qquad M_0$
- $T_1 = T_1(\Delta M_0, M_0)$ $\qquad \Delta M_1 \qquad\qquad\qquad M_1$
- $T_2 = T_2(\Delta M_0, M_0)$ $\qquad \Delta M_2 \qquad\qquad\qquad M_2$

It is the third case which can introduce what is termed the *feedback effect,* also known as the *vicious circle.* Feedback effect refers to the dual coupling from the temperature to the mass flow and back to the temperature again. This can result in a cascading effect which can be visualized by examining Figure 10–6.

The figure clearly shows what can occur when mass outflow happens at a guaranteed temperature. In the figure, an initiating event results in the lowering of the portfolio temperature. Since the mass outflow is coupled to the portfolio temperature, this event will result in higher mass outflow. This mass outflow can occur at the guaranteed temperature, which is higher than the current portfolio

FIGURE 10-6

The Vicious Circle
The diagram clearly shows the effect of the coupling from flow temperature to mass outflow back to flow temperature.

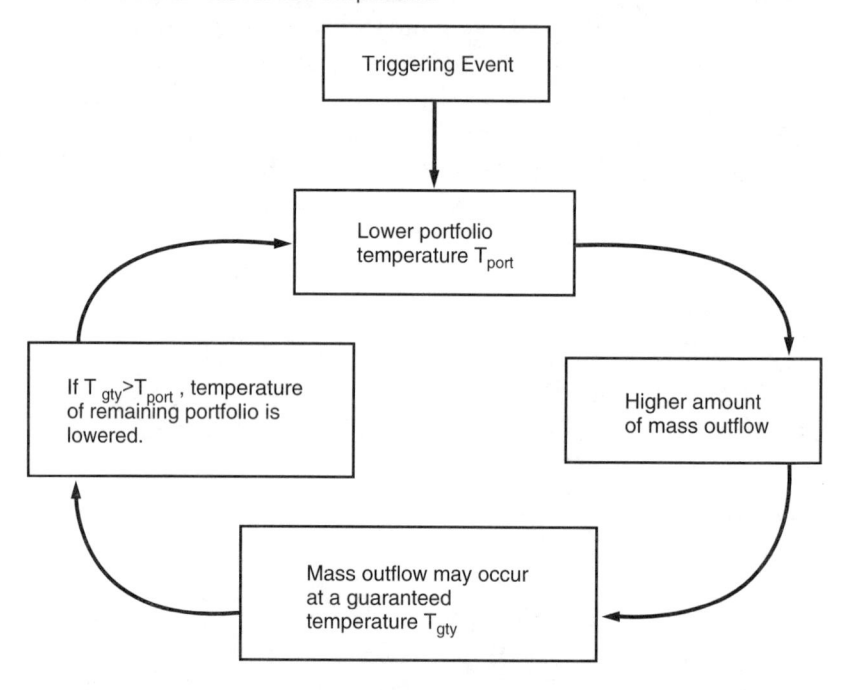

```
                    ┌─────────────────┐
                    │ Triggering Event│
                    └────────┬────────┘
                             │
                             ▼
        ┌───────────────────────────────────┐
    ┌──▶│ Lower portfolio temperature T_port │──┐
    │   └───────────────────────────────────┘  │
    │                                          ▼
┌───┴──────────────────┐              ┌──────────────────┐
│ If T_gty > T_port,   │              │ Higher amount    │
│ temperature of       │              │ of mass outflow  │
│ remaining portfolio  │              └────────┬─────────┘
│ is lowered.          │                       │
└───────▲──────────────┘                       │
        │                                      ▼
        │         ┌──────────────────────────────┐
        └─────────│ Mass outflow may occur at a  │
                  │ guaranteed temperature T_gty │
                  └──────────────────────────────┘
```

temperature. As mass is withdrawn at the higher temperature, conservation laws dictate that the remaining portfolio temperature be reduced, such that the net energy of the system is conserved. This additional lower portfolio temperature, in turn, drives more mass outflow. Although the feedback is incremental, it is expected that the feedback will have a negative effect on the portfolio's liquidity risk profile. This will shortly be evident in the simulation analysis.

Sample Portfolio

For the analysis, a simple portfolio will consist of one bond.

Portfolio Characteristics

Bond:	One fixed-coupon bond
Coupon:	7.00%
Initial 10-yr. Discount Rate:	7.00%
Maturity:	10 years
Credit:	Constant credit spread is assumed
Simulation length:	5 years
Investor response factor:	a = 2. This means that for every 1% drop in the price/share, the base case share redemption effect will be 2%.

The simulation will be based on the to-maturity discount rate. For this exercise, it will be assumed that the yield curve is flat, i.e., the forward discount rate for all maturities at simulation inception are identical to each other.

Based on the above conditions, the conditions of the river model can be set as follows:

River Conditions

Initial mass:	100 MU (mass units)
Initial temperature:	100 degrees
Initial quality:	10,000
Heat sink/source:	Change in interest rate which could result in shifting temperatures.
Effect of interest rate change:	A variation in interest rate will result in a change in temperature of: $\Delta T(\Delta r_i) = T_i D_i \Delta r_i$ where D_i, T_i, and Δr_i, are the duration, temperature, and change in interest rate of the portfolio for the ith period.

LIQUIDITY ANALYSIS RESULTS

The results of the analysis will show, first, the flow quality of a single simulation run for the three different levels of coupling. Then, the result of a 3000 simulation run showing the probability of achieving a minimum quality below a certain target is presented. Finally, some conclusions are drawn from the results of the simulation analysis.

Flow Simulation: One Simulation Run

The quality of the three different levels of correlation over one simulation run is shown on Figure 10–7. The qualities of each correlation case originate at time 0 at a value of 100. The exhibit clearly shows the effect of the feedback between temperature and mass. The case with dual correlation between flow temperature and mass exhibits similar quality behavior with the other two lesser levels of coupling over the first few periods. As flow quality begins to deteriorate under certain heat outflow situations, the dual correlated flow begins to deteriorate faster than the other two, until the dual correlation flow quality reaches zero.

The analogy of the single simulation run to portfolio management is this: in cases where investor redemption behavior is linked to the portfolio performance (mass to temperature coupling), and where the portfolio performance is adversely affected by investor redemption due to some guaranteed redemption (temperature to mass coupling), the total amount of cash (quality) in a portfolio can be significantly deteriorated versus other cases. Both the linkages are caused by rational behavior: investors who see adverse performance tend to pull their money out, and certain liability policies guarantee a withdraw value. Thus, for the single simulation run case, the dual coupling posed by rational investor behavior results in a significant deterioration in the liquidity position of the asset portfolio.

Quality Simulation: Liquidity Risk

The true effect of the *mass–temperature* or *performance-redemption-guarantee* coupling can be viewed by examining

FIGURE 10-7

Simulation of Uncoupled and Coupled Mass and Temperature Flow Quality

The flow quality of uncorrelated, single correlation, and dual correlation flows for a single simulation run is shown. For this particular simulation, the effect of single and dual correlation on the flow quality is quite evident: correlation reduces the quality of the flow.

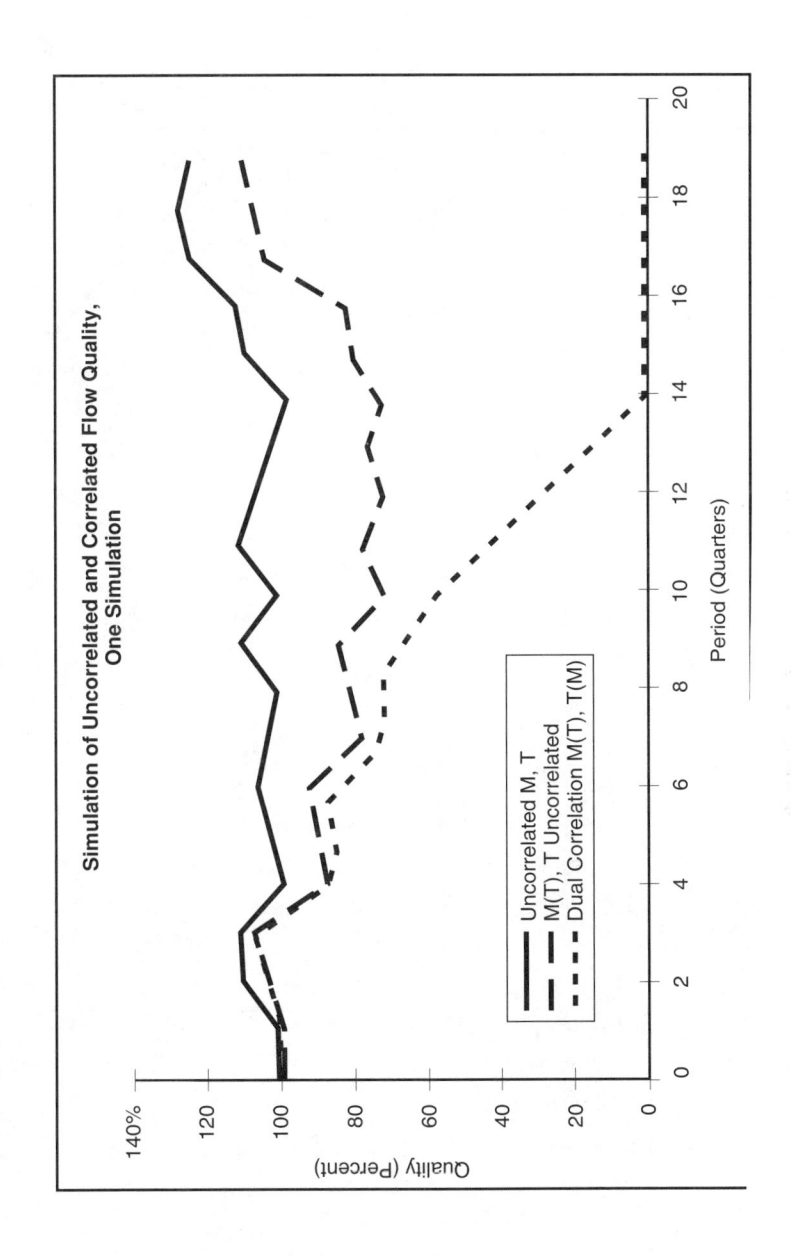

FIGURE 10-8

Liquidity Risk Simulation of Uncoupled and Coupled Mass and Temperature Flow

The y-axis displays the probability that the sample portfolio can attain a *minimum quality* below that indicated on the x-axis. This 3000 simulation analysis illustrates the effect of mass–temperature coupling on the liquidity risk of the portfolio: coupling increases the risk of attaining a lower minimum quality. Point A shows the dual coupling case having a 10 percent probability of achieving a minimum portfolio quality below 15 percent.

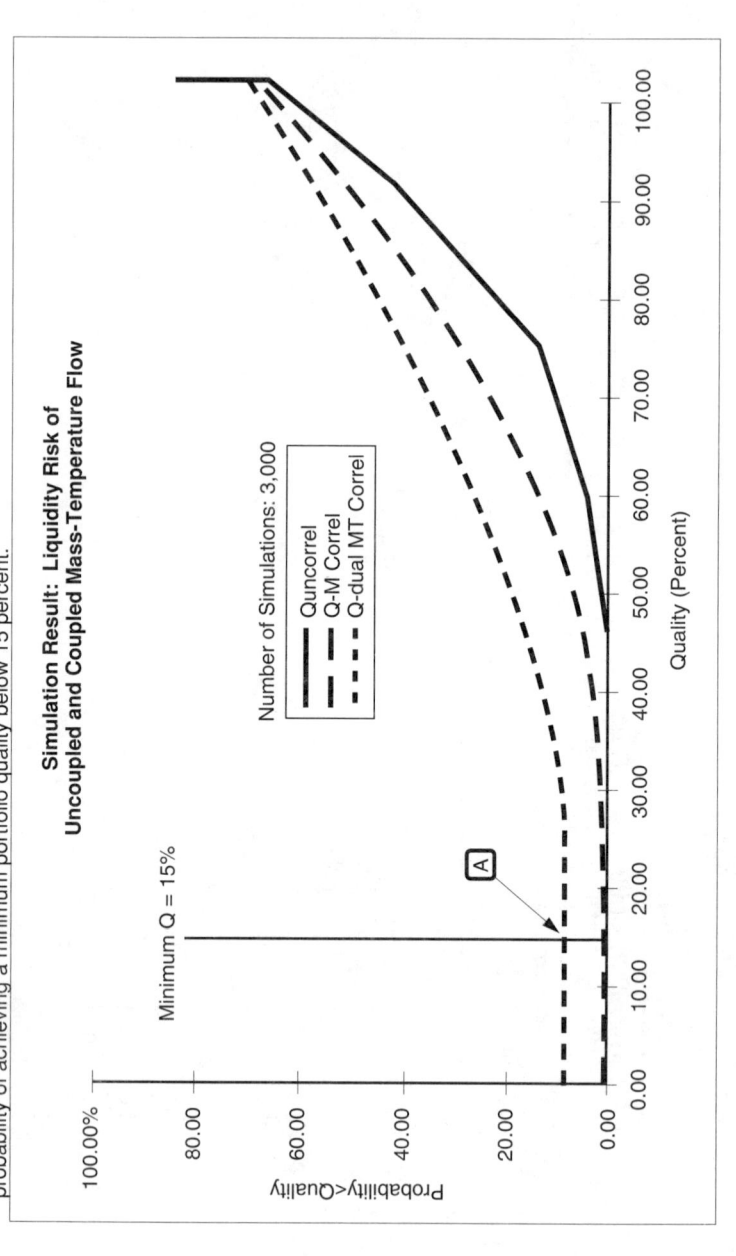

Simulation Result: Liquidity Risk of Uncoupled and Coupled Mass-Temperature Flow

Number of Simulations: 3,000

258

the result of a 3000 run simulation. Figure 10–8 shows the compilation of the *minimum quality* that is attained over each run. The probability that a portfolio will possess a minimum quality lower than various quality bogeys (on the x-axis) is plotted on the y-axis.

The analysis can be understood by viewing the dual coupling data in the figure. A portfolio manager has defined liquidity crisis to be when the portfolio's cash value drops to 15 percent of the initial cash value (shown by the minimum-Q line). The probability that a portfolio will attain a minimum cash value *below* 15 percent is found from the intercept of the minimum-Q line with the liquidity risk line (point A) on the y-axis. Point A shows that, over the 5-year time horizon of the analysis, there is a 10 percent probability that the minimum quality of the sample portfolio will fall below the 15 percent liquidity crisis point. For the sake of comparison, the cases where there is either no coupling or a single coupling between share redemption and portfolio performance show a minimal probability (< 1 percent) of the portfolio reaching the liquidity crisis point.

Simulation Analysis Conclusions

What insights can be drawn from this analysis? The results show that liquidity risk can be driven by several fairly common factors: high investor responsiveness, a guaranteed withdraw price, and a mismatch of asset/liability risk profiles. A combination of these factors corresponds to the dual coupling flow scenario, which exhibits a much larger probability of attaining the point of liquidity crisis.

Given that these factors are relatively common occurrences in insurance company products, are there measures that can be taken to reduce this risk? We will begin to address that question in the next section.

MANAGEMENT OF LIQUIDITY RISK

The previous section ended on the following question: If rational investor behavior, in combination with a guaranteed surrender price, can result in a relatively high probability of a portfolio reaching the liquidity crisis point, what can be done to reduce the liquidity risk of a portfolio?

This section demonstrates the effect of certain risk management techniques on the liquidity risk profile of a portfolio. It will be evident that several easily implemented prudent measures can drastically lower the liquidity risk of a portfolio.

The liquidity risk management measures to be discussed are:

1. Correctly marking assets and liabilities to market.
2. Maintaining a liquid cash reserve.
3. Hedging a portion of the asset/liability risk gap via catastrophe hedging.
4. Return shares at then-prevailing market price.
5. Bailout by a rich parent.

Correctly Marking Assets and Liabilities

Although the technique of correctly marking assets and liabilities may appear to be simple, it is by no means easy to implement. The lessons learned from the collapse of the Granite funds show that marking assets to market can be extremely difficult, given illiquid securities, inadequate risk measurement and control systems, proprietary in-house marks, and a market in crisis. However, managers can lessen the risks of incorrect marks by taking into consideration some of the following measures:

1. *Mid-market mark versus bid-side mark.* Many securities, even if marked to market, will be based on a mid-market price. The liquidation of securities, however, occurs on the bid side of the market. Thus, a manager should either obtain bid-side marks or have a firm grasp of the bid-mid spreads of the most illiquid securities within the portfolio.

    2. *Mark-to-market versus mark-to-model.* As much as possible, managers should use both an external mark provided by dealers as well as an internal mark. The use of both marks will minimize errors on both sides.

    3. *Frequent calibration of in-house models.* In-house models must be frequently calibrated. The manager should perform periodic reality checks to compare model marks to market marks. If the gap is large, the manager should re-tune the internal models to reflect current market conditions. This would minimize the potential for mismarking the value of securities.

Maintaining a Liquid Cash Reserve

The second liquidity risk management technique is one whose effect can be quantified. This simple technique sets aside a fraction of the portfolio as a cash buffer, i.e., not invested in longer-maturity fixed income assets. Cash and equivalent instruments such as Treasury bills can serve as the cash buffer. The cash reserve acts as a buffer against redemptions. In the analysis performed in this section, it will be assumed that any redemption will impact the buffer until the buffer is exhausted. Only after the exhaustion of the buffer will redemptions affect the portfolio itself. The redemptions are still driven by the performance of the portfolio.

    Figures 10–9 and 10–10 show the effect of the buffer on liquidity risk. Over the course of one scenario, it appears that the presence of the buffer was able to delay the onset of liquidity risk. The results of the simulation analysis agree with this assessment. The risk of the portfolio

FIGURE 10-9

Single-Scenario Simulation of Buffered and Unbuffered Portfolio

The buffer consists of uninvested cash whose asset value does not change with the rest of the portfolio. Only after the buffer is depleted does the outflow begin to affect the invested portfolio. This scenario shows that the buffer was able to protect the portfolio from the onset of liquidity risk for a longer period of time.

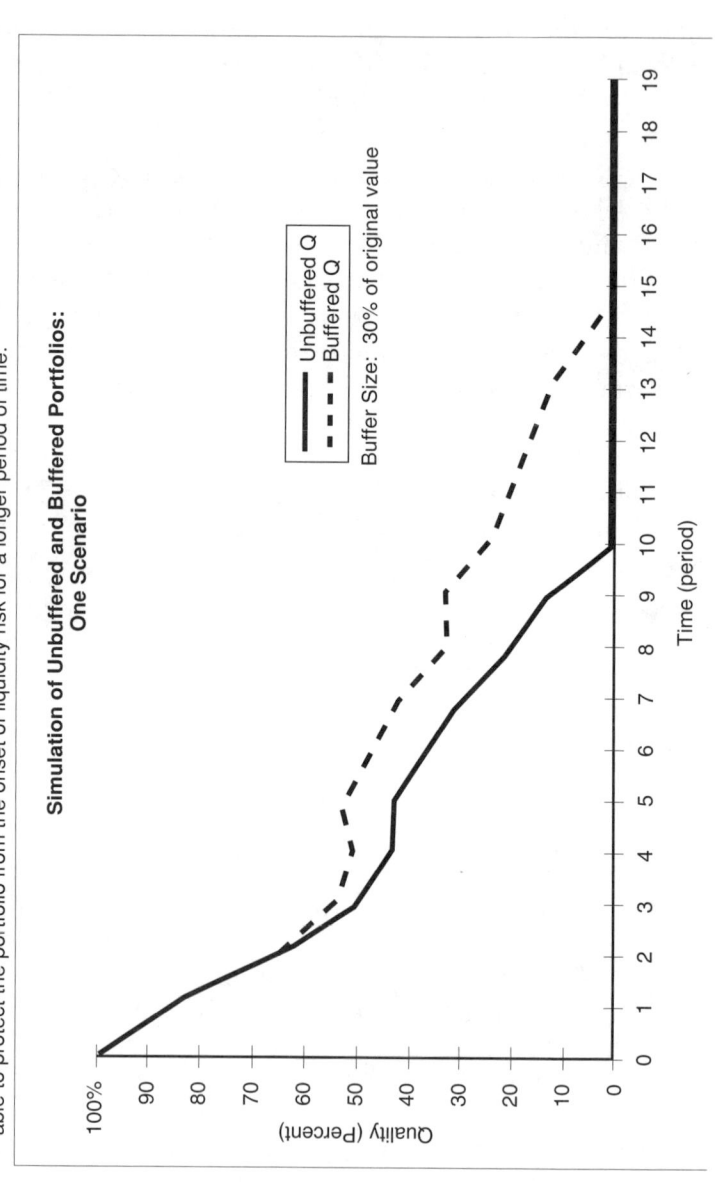

Simulation of Unbuffered and Buffered Portfolios: One Scenario

Buffer Size: 30% of original value

Liquidity Risk: A First Look

FIGURE 10-10

Simulation of Buffered and Unbuffered Portfolios

The buffer consists of uninvested cash. Thirty percent of the initial portfolio quality was earmarked for the buffer. Although the buffer shows promise as a liquidity risk management technique, the amount of improvement over an unbuffered portfolio is not large. The probability of the buffered portfolio's minimum quality falling below the 15 percent liquidity crisis point has been reduced from 12 percent to 8 percent.

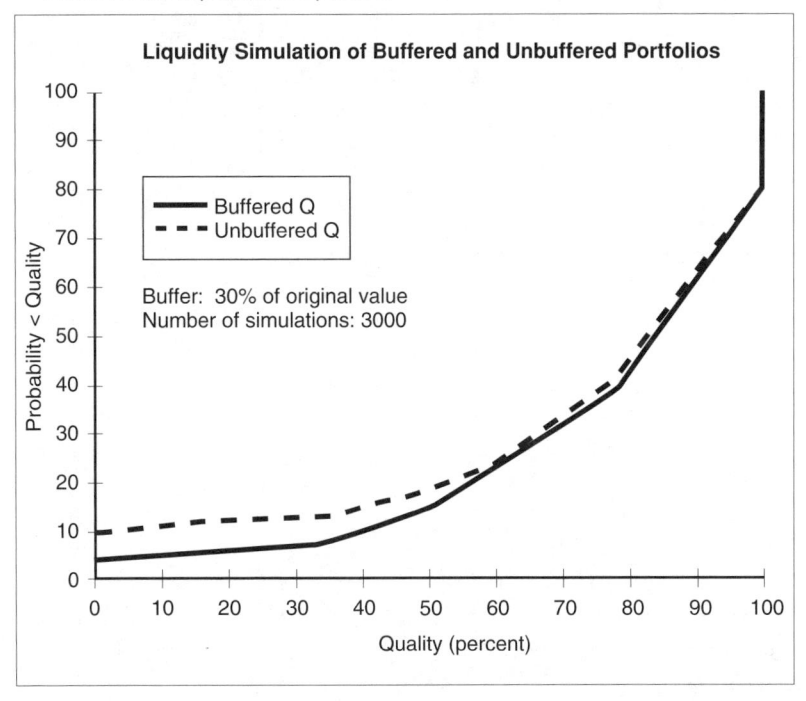

Liquidity Simulation of Buffered and Unbuffered Portfolios

Buffer: 30% of original value
Number of simulations: 3000

falling below the liquidity crisis point of 15 percent of initial quality has been reduced from 12 percent to 8 percent with the aid of the buffer.

Although liquidity risk was reduced by 30 percent with the buffer, the reduction is mild when compared with the results of a catastrophe hedge, as seen in the next section. The buffer also has the downside of tying up capital which would otherwise be invested. The buffered portfolio thus behaves better in adverse conditions, but underperforms the unbuffered portfolio when market conditions boost the prices of assets under management.

Partial Hedging of the Asset/Liability Risk Gap: The Catastrophe Hedge

Although many asset/liability managers consider catastrophe hedges, only a small fraction of them actually implement such a program. To examine the effect of catastrophe hedging on liquidity risk, the following hedge is used.

Maturity:	5 years.
Hedge payoff freq.:	Quarterly.
Hedge strike:	90% of initial portfolio price.
Hedge cost:	5% of initial amount.
Hedge payoff:	30% of portfolio downside after strike has been reached.

Figure 10–11 clearly shows that this catastrophe hedge results in a dramatic reduction in the liquidity risk of the sample portfolio. Whereas the unhedged case has a 12 percent probability of falling below 15 percent of its initial quality, the hedged flow has only a 10 percent probability of falling below 70 percent of its initial quality—a drastic reduction. The cost of the catastrophe hedge is 5 percent, which accounts for the hedged portfolio's quality curve topping out at 95 percent.

A quick comparison of the catastrophe hedge technique with the buffer technique shows that the catastrophe hedge is the superior one. The probability of falling below the liquidity crisis point was almost completely eliminated with the catastrophe hedge, whereas the buffer was only able to reduce 30 percent of the risk. It can thus be concluded that, although the catastrophe hedge carries a significant cost, its effectiveness as a liquidity risk management tool is significantly higher than that of a buffer.

FIGURE 10-11

Catastrophe Hedging and Effect on Liquidity Risk
Although the hedge only covers 30 percent of the downside below 90 percent of the initial quality, the effect on liquidity risk is quite dramatic. The probability of falling below the liquidity crisis point of 15 percent of initial quality has been lowered from the unhedged portfolio's 12 percent to almost none for the hedged case.

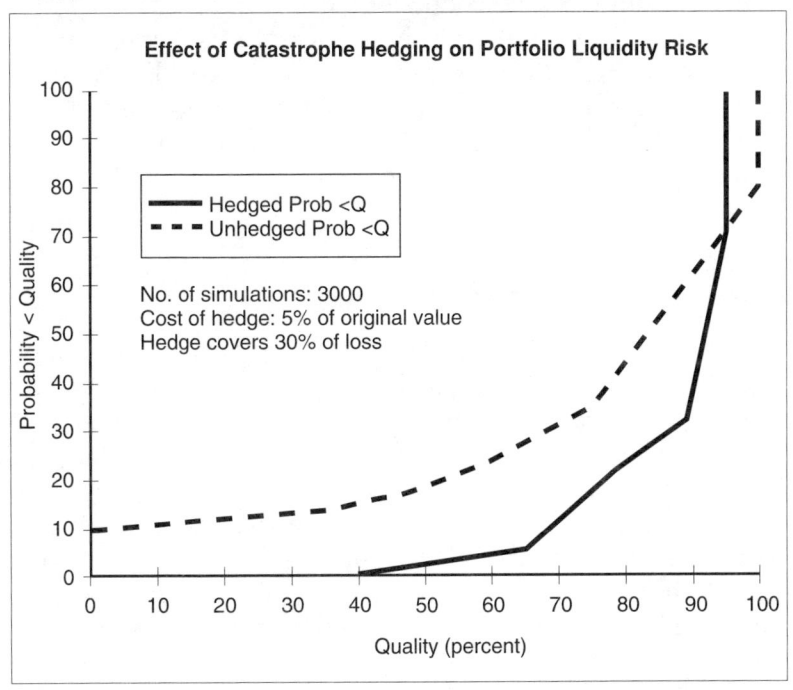

Effect of Catastrophe Hedging on Portfolio Liquidity Risk

— Hedged Prob <Q
- - - Unhedged Prob <Q

No. of simulations: 3000
Cost of hedge: 5% of original value
Hedge covers 30% of loss

Returning Shares at Their Market Values

Many types of liability products, such as the life policies (in non-mortality surrenders), variable annuities (VA), and market-value annuities (MVA), already contain a market-value feature. Returning market-valued shares can reduce liquidity risk by cutting the dual coupling between investor behavior and portfolio value. Although investors will still be driven to redeem by the performance of the portfolio, the shares they will receive will be at the same value as the rest of the portfolio. There will thus be no additional feedback from the redemption back to the remaining portfolio's NAV/share. This corresponds to our single coupling mass flow situation, which has been demonstrated in Figure 10–8 as having significantly less liquidity risk than the dual coupled case.

Returning shares at their correct asset value is the most straight forward way to close the asset/liability risk gap. It is obvious that if investors simply receive the market value of their shares, the fund manager retains little liquidity risk. This insight agrees with the results of the liquidity analysis.

Bailout by a Rich Parent

Given the bear market of 1994, many seasoned investment managers resorted to this final liquidity crisis prevention measure. Although being bailed out by one's parent company may seem like a painless risk management technique, in reality the consequences of such a move can be severe. In most cases, a bailout move is often followed by a swift change in the identity of the portfolio manager. Thus, this measure, although tempting, has a real possibility of introducing another risk—job risk—to the portfolio manager.

CONCLUSION

As we discussed at the beginning of this chapter, liquidity risk is an issue which is often discussed, yet rarely systematically quantified. It is hoped that the reader has now attained a better understanding of the causes of liquidity risk, the methods by which liquidity risk can be quantified, and some of the risk management techniques that can be used to reduce this risk.

Although the sample portfolio used in the analysis was a single 10-year fixed-coupon bond, the insights gained from the risk analysis are valid across all asset and liability classes. The results of the liquidity risk analysis in this chapter show that a portfolio whose asset and liability risks are not matched will incur a larger liquidity risk. This enlarged risk manifests itself in the form of an enhanced probability, over the analysis time horizon, of achieving a minimum portfolio quality (cash) which falls below a choke point where liquidity crisis can occur. It was also shown that some simple, prudent measures such as cash buffering or disaster hedging can significantly reduce the liquidity risk of the portfolio.

How can one lower liquidity risk? All the risk management techniques discussed in this chapter can be summarized as attempts to close the asset/liability risk gap. Liquidity risk largely occurs from the mismatch of the risk between the asset and liability sides. At the present time, many financial institutions still maintain the practice of running the two components of the institution, asset management and liability products, as separate business units. Although some leading companies are taking active steps to integrate or at least foster enhanced communications between the two units, the majority unfortunately do not. It is hoped that liquidity risk will be one of the arguments that can help close this asset/liability risk gap.

CHAPTER 11

Effective Duration and Convexity: Back to the Basics

Robert M. Lally
AEGIS Insurance Services
Chief Investment Officer and Treasurer

From a statistician's point of view, the interest rate shifts that took place in 1993 and 1994, were second or even third deviation events. One of the worst bear markets in history followed one of the strongest bull markets. Fixed-income investor concerns changed from evaporating durations in 1993 to extension risk in 1994. Many investors were whipsawed in the process.

What did investment professionals learn from this experience? It became clear that our prepayment models—and possibly our OAS models—do not work very well. For many organizations, it also became evident that their understanding of effective duration and effective convexity was not very strong, particularly as it relates to detecting, monitoring, and correcting 'model error.' [Note: Model error is responsible for producing spurious effective duration and effective convexity coefficients]. While this chapter makes no attempt to identify the sources of model error (e.g., inappropriate volatility assumptions, problematic splining techniques, etc.), it does offer practical advice on how to detect model error.

The goal is to improve one's understanding of effective duration and effective convexity, two cornerstones in the foundation of fixed-income portfolio management. In addition, duration management suggestions are provided within a portfolio management context.

BASIC NO. 1: DEFINITIONS

The clearest definitions for effective duration and effective convexity are based upon how these measures are literally calculated. Frequently used definitions for effective duration include: the percentage change in price for an instantaneous 100 b.p. parallel shift in the yield curve, the slope of the price-yield curve tangent, and the first term of the Taylor expansion formula. Frequently used definitions for effective convexity include: the change in duration with respect to changes in the interest rates, the curvature of the price-yield curve, and the second term of the Taylor expansion formula. For some, these definitions sound like quantitative double-talk. Nevertheless, the investment professional has an important responsibility to translate and clearly communicate these quantitative concepts to clients, management, and staff. By using calculation-based definitions that employ terminology most meaningful to the investor (i.e., total return), a clearer picture of the effective duration and effective convexity concepts appear, as demonstrated below.

BASIC NO. 2: EFFECTIVE DURATION

Effective duration represents the average of the difference in total return for the up and down parallel yield curve shift. There are only three numbers needed to derive effective duration (as well as effective convexity). In addition to the current market price, two theoretical prices are required: a projected price after a 100 b.p. parallel decline in interest rates, and another projected price after a 100 b.p. parallel rise in interest rates. From this information, the total rate of return (TROR) for the decline and rise in rates can be calculated.

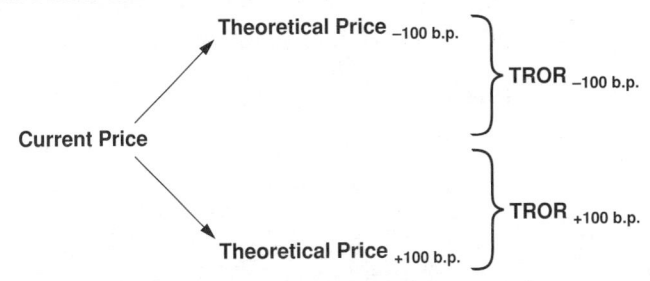

```
                  Theoretical Price _-100 b.p.
                 ↗                              ⎫
                                                ⎬  TROR _-100 b.p.
                                                ⎭
    Current Price
                 ↘                              ⎫
                                                ⎬  TROR _+100 b.p.
                  Theoretical Price _+100 b.p.  ⎭
```

$$\text{Effective Duration} = \text{Average TROR difference}$$
$$= [(\text{TROR}_{-100\ b.p.} - \text{TROR}_{+100\ b.p.}) \div 2] \times 100$$
$$= \frac{\text{Price}_{-100\ b.p.} - \text{Price}_{+100\ b.p.}}{2 * \Delta i * \text{Price}_{\text{Current}}}$$

The theoretical prices can be products of an OAS model, current price spreads for contiguous MBS coupons, a trader's intuition of expected spreads after these shifts took place, etc. The total rate of return (TROR) for the two shifts is simply the percentage price change. To calculate the effective duration, take the average TROR difference between an up and down shift, divide by two, and multiply by 100. (Note that total returns are scaled in terms of 100 b.p. shifts, e.g., total returns based upon 50 b.p. shifts are doubled.)

BASIC NO. 3: EFFECTIVE CONVEXITY

Effective convexity measures the allocation of the difference in the total return between the up and down parallel yield curve shift and, therefore, is inextricably linked to effective duration.

Example:

−100 b.p. TROR	Price	Current Price	+100 b.p. Price	TROR	TROR Difference	Duration	Convexity
5.00%	$105	$100	$95	−5.00%	10.00%	5.00	0.00
7.00	107	100	97	−3.00	10.00	5.00	0.40
3.00	103	100	93	−7.00	10.00	5.00	−0.40
10.00	110	100	100	-	10.00	5.00	1.00
0.00	100	100	90	−10.00	10.00	5.00	−1.00

where

Effective Convexity

$$= \frac{\text{Price}_{-100 \text{ b.p.}} + \text{Price}_{+100 \text{ b.p.}} - (2 * \text{Price}_{\text{Current}})}{\Delta i^2 * \text{Price}_{\text{Current}}}$$

While the bonds in the above example have the same duration, the convexity coefficients and the return profiles are very different. A zero convexity coefficient indicates that the return difference of 10 percent in this example is equally allocated between the up and down shift. A positive coefficient indicates that the return difference of 10 percent, or a duration of 5 [(10 percent ÷ 2) × 100], in this example is *unequally allocated in favor of* the down shift (i.e., the bond has more upside potential than downside potential). The larger the positive coefficient, the greater the relative upside potential. The exact opposite can be said of those bonds with negative convexity coefficients. These examples with identical durations but disparate return patterns and convexity coefficients highlight the need to view duration and convexity as different sides of the same coin, not apart from one another as is frequently the case.

Virtually all participants in the fixed-income markets have seen the "Convexity 101" chart shown in Figure 11–1 where noncallable and callable corporate prices are modeled over various interest rate environments. The callable bond is currently callable at $103.50. Negative convexity begins kicking in as the price approaches the call price. It

Effective Duration and Convexity: Back to the Basics 273

FIGURE 11-1

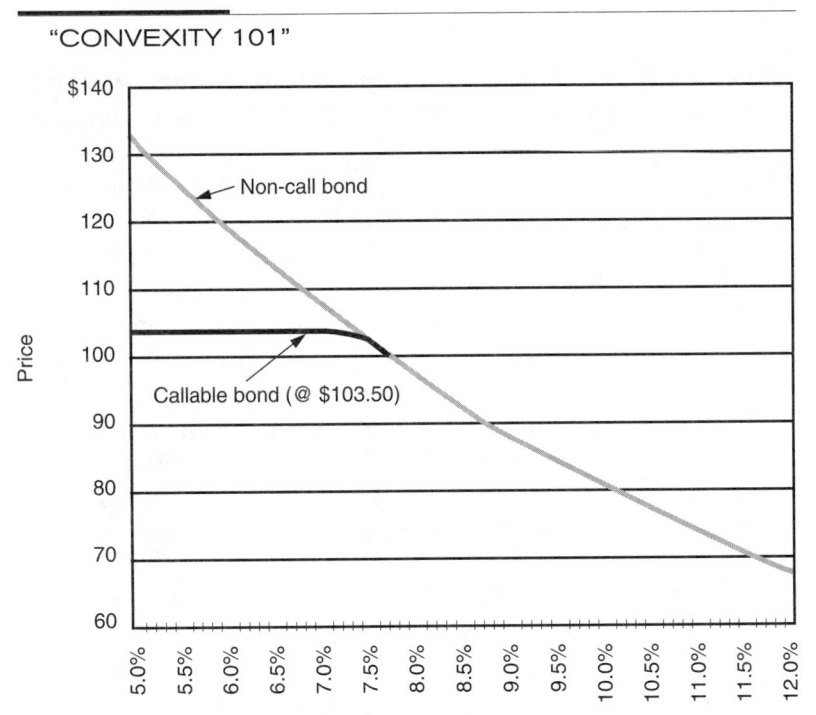

"CONVEXITY 101"

[Chart: Price vs. yield from 5.0% to 12.0%, showing a Non-call bond curve declining from ~$133 to ~$68, and a Callable bond (@ $103.50) curve that flattens near $103.50 at lower yields.]

is unfortunate that many of the participants in the fixed-income market have not taken the prerequisite course for Convexity 101; that is, they have not learned how the numbers are calculated, what assumptions have the greatest sensitivity upon results, and what the results *really* mean.

For instance, the selection of the shift size (e.g., ±1 b.p., ±10 b.p., ±100 b.p., ±200 b.p., etc.) has a significant impact on the resulting effective duration and effective convexity coefficients. [Please note again that that total returns are scaled in terms of 100 b.p. shifts for purposes of calculating duration and convexity.] In the case of the callable bond, the impact can be significant if the three price points are on the same side or straddle the $103.50 inflection point.

BASIC NO. 4: MODEL ERROR

Monitor model error by understanding the sensitivity of effective duration and effective convexity to implied nominal spread changes. Model error occurs when spurious theoretical nominal prices, or, conversely, spreads, are generated for a specified interest rate change. As a result of their dependency on theoretical prices, spurious effective duration and effective convexity coefficients are produced. The most effective method for identifying spurious prices is to analyze theoretical prices in nominal spread terms, the preferred lexicon for trading securities.

The chart in Figure 11–2 illustrates the sensitivity of effective duration to implied nominal duration spread changes. The graph also identifies the duration-neutral Treasuries for the 30-year corporate bond under various assumptions.

The bonds with the longest duration are naturally non-callable. The effective duration for a par-priced 30-year Treasury in this example is 12.1 years. The duration of the second bond, a par priced non-callable corporate, is 11.2 years, or almost a year shorter than the Treasury, simply due to the 80 b.p. higher coupon. [Note: For purposes of this chart, the spreads for the non-callable corporate did not change after the ±100 b.p. shift. In reality, spreads would widen after a significant interest rate rally because investors want a price concession for a super-premium bond (i.e., a bond with a price > $115) due to its reduced liquidity. This spread widening shortens the bond's duration.] The maturity for a par-priced duration-neutral Treasury is 2019, or 6 years shorter than the 30-year 'pricing' Treasury.

Finally, there are three versions of 30-year callable corporates, all noted in terms of changes in nominal spreads and initially priced at 80 b.p. over the 30-year Treasury.

Effective Duration and Convexity: Back to the Basics **275**

FIGURE 11-2

Maturity of Duration-Neutral Treasury

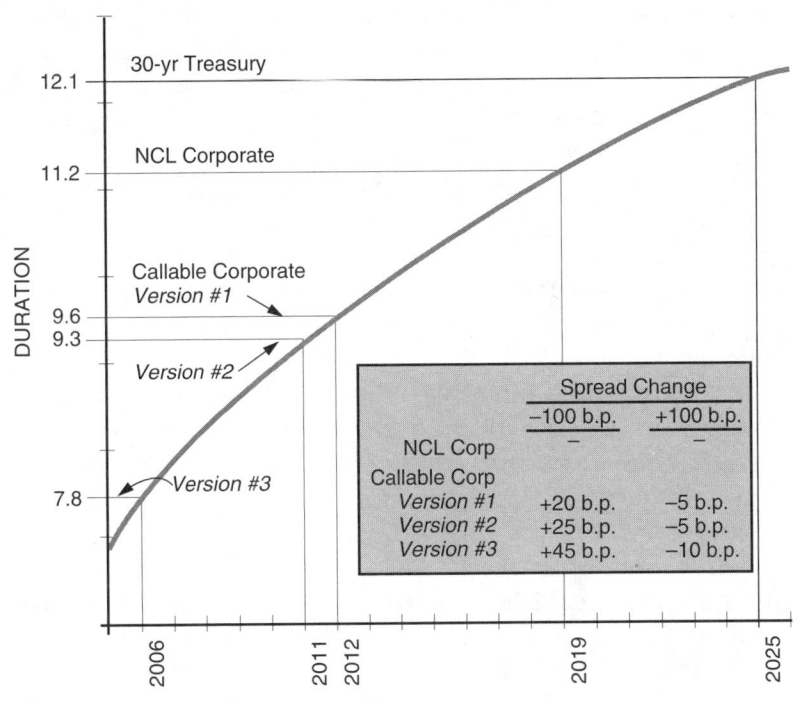

	Spread Change	
	−100 b.p.	+100 b.p.
NCL Corp	—	—
Callable Corp		
Version #1	+20 b.p.	−5 b.p.
Version #2	+25 b.p.	−5 b.p.
Version #3	+45 b.p.	−10 b.p.

The Corporate in this example is a 30-year par coupon issue priced at T30 + 80 b.p.

For the first version, a 100 b.p. downward shift produces a 20 b.p. spread widening, for a total spread of 100 b.p. The 20 b.p. widening is the result of the increased value of the call option. Further, there would be more issuance and investors would demand more spread/price concessions. This widening is consistent with observed market behavior. With a 100 b.p. rise in rates, the option becomes less valuable and the bond would probably be trading a little bit tighter to the curve (i.e., −5 b.p. tighter, or +75 b.p. net). These plausible spread changes generate a 9.6 effective duration. The maturity for a par-priced duration neutral Treasury is 2012, or 13 years shorter than the 30-year 'pricing' Treasury.

In Version 2, the bond is exactly the same as in Version 1 except that the bond would widen to 25 b.p. instead of 20 b.p. with a fall in rates. This 5 b.p. change shortens the bond's effective duration by three months, to 9.3 years. The maturity for a par-priced duration-neutral Treasury is 2011, or 14 years shorter than the 30-year 'pricing' Treasury.

Version 3 assumes that the spreads widen by 45 b.p. overall, for a total spread of 125 b.p. over the 30-year 'pricing' Treasury. Effective duration shortens to 7.8 years. The maturity for a par priced duration-neutral Treasury is 2006, or 19 years shorter than the 30-year 'pricing' Treasury.

Whereas the effective duration calculation is based upon using prices as inputs, investors are well advised to convert the prices into nominal spreads to check for the reasonableness of the theoretical prices (i.e., model error). As demonstrated above, effective duration of callable bonds is very sensitive to the implied changes in nominal spreads. Further, the maturity for a par-priced duration-neutral Treasury is very different than the 30-year maturity of the callable corporate.

BASIC NO. 5: BREAKEVEN ANALYSIS

Make extensive use of breakeven analysis to understand the downside risk associated with model error and convexity mismatches in general. A breakeven analysis identifies the amount of time for which an investor is indifferent between holding an underperforming corporate bond with a higher yield and a better-performing, but lower yielding, duration-neutral Treasury. In the case of Version 1, a 100 b.p. decline in rates results in the corporate bond underperforming the duration-neutral Treasury by 69 b.p. It requires 8.3 months [(69 b.p. · (100 b.p. extra yield/year ÷ 12 months/yr.)] for the callable corporate's extra yield to compensate the investor for its negative convexity.

	30-year Callable Corporate					Duration-Neutral Treasury			
	-100 b.p.		+100 b.p.			-100 b.p.		+100 b.p.	
Duration	Spread	TROR	Spread	TROR	Maturity	TROR	Diff.	TROR	Diff.
9.62	100 b.p.	9.58%	75 b.p.	(9.67%)	2012	10.27%	(0.69%)	(8.97%)	(0.70%)
9.30	105 b.p.	8.94	75 b.p.	(9.67)	2011	9.93	(0.99)	(8.72)	(0.95)
0.32		0.64		0.00		0.34		(0.25)	

A breakeven analysis is a powerful tool for performing reasonability checks as well as for portfolio management purposes. A breakeven analysis typically begs the following questions

Reasonability checking related:
- Are the theoretical nominal spreads credible (i.e., are they consistent with recent market behavior)?
- If not, is there a problem with the modeling assumptions or systematic model error? What steps can be taken to correct it?
- How sensitive is effective duration to changes in nominal spreads?

Key issues related to spread assets with embedded options:
- What duration are the spread assets carried at in the portfolio?
- How do the duration-neutral Treasuries compare with the pricing Treasury in terms of maturity?
- Is this bond going to outperform its duration-neutral Treasury?

Portfolio management related:
- Is holding the spread asset worth the risk (including model error-related risk)?

FIGURE 11-3

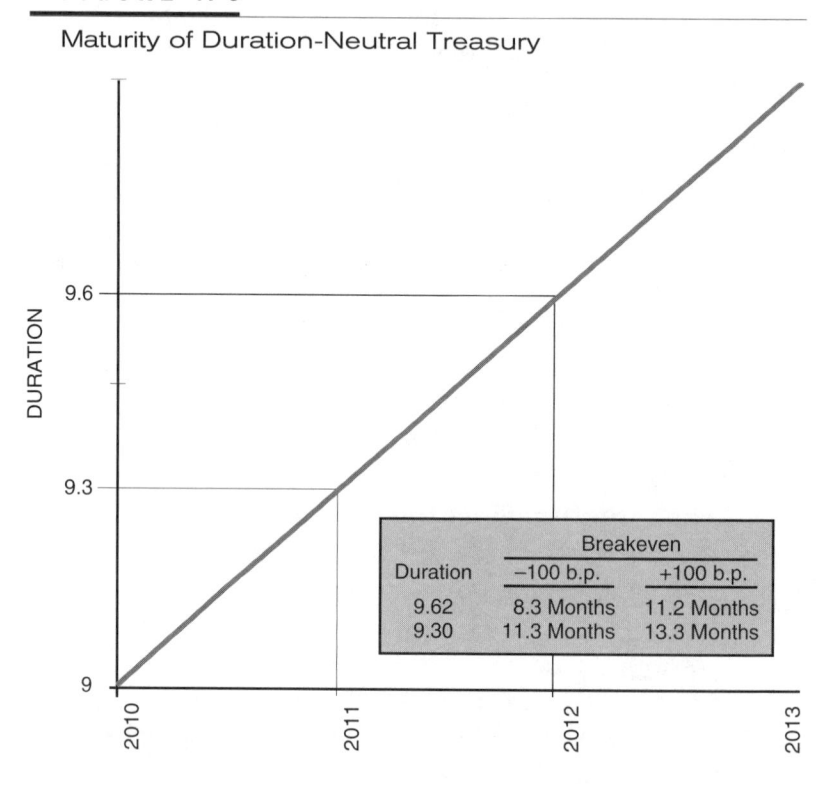

Maturity of Duration-Neutral Treasury

Duration	Breakeven −100 b.p.	+100 b.p.
9.62	8.3 Months	11.2 Months
9.30	11.3 Months	13.3 Months

- If I did not own this asset now, would I buy it today? If the answer is no, an immediate sale is not necessarily recommended, but the portfolio manager should ask What is my exit strategy? Under what conditions would I sell it?

BASIC NO. 6: COMPARISON TO MUNICIPAL BONDS

The effective duration and effective convexity of municipal bonds are significantly different than their taxable counterparts. The theoretical prices used in effective duration and effective convexity calculations are based upon parallel shifts in *Treasury rates*. This is true for all domestic fixed-income markets including the corporate bond, mortgage-backed securities, *and* municipal bond markets.

The effective duration and effective convexity of municipal bonds is very different than Treasuries, even Treasuries with the same coupon and maturity. The reason is simple. Munis trade on a yield ratio to Treasuries (e.g., 5.6 percent muni bond yield ÷ 7 percent Treasury yield = 80 percent yield ratio). A comparison of the effective durations and effective convexities for a 30-year comparable coupon municipal and Treasury with an 80 percent municipal/Treasury yield ratio shows:

	Effective Duration	Effective Convexity
Treasury	11.88	2.29
Municipal @ 80 percent muni/Treasury yield ratio	10.60	1.74

This difference in effective duration and effective convexity for municipals with identical coupons, maturity and structural features is the result of the impact of the muni/Treasury yield ratio. When the Muni-Treasury yield ratio is 80% and there is a 100 b.p. shift in Treasury yields, municipal yields only change 80 b.p. as seen below:

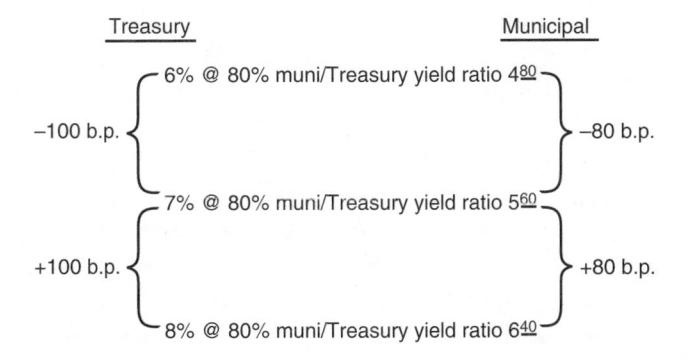

	Treasury		Municipal
−100 b.p.	6% @ 80% muni/Treasury yield ratio 4.80		−80 b.p.
	7% @ 80% muni/Treasury yield ratio 5.60		
+100 b.p.	8% @ 80% muni/Treasury yield ratio 6.40		+80 b.p.

There are other complications to calculating muni durations and convexities. Being a retail-dominated market, muni prices historically lag the institutionally dominated Treasury market both on the downside and the upside as rates change. A similar observation could be made about the mortgage-backed securities (i.e., MBS) market. Unlike the MBS market, however, this lagging can be unrelated to embedded options.

Whereas it is possible to quantitatively capture MBS lagging effect with an OAS model, empirical analysis is the only tool available to reasonably capture the muni lagging effect. For instance, some institutions adjust the traditionally calculated effective duration by 80 percent. The adjustment is based upon the historical volatility of the muni/Treasury bond yield ratio and the volatility of Treasury yields in general. Using an 80 percent volatility adjustment factor, municipal adjusted duration (MAD) equals 4 years when the effective duration is 5 (5 years * 80 percent).

BASIC NO. 7: MANAGING "SPREAD" FIXED-INCOME ASSETS

When managing "spread" fixed-income assets having embedded options, the investor should have clearly defined goals and strategies. "Spread" has been placed in quotations because fixed-income assets having embedded options may underperform Treasuries as rates change. Many investment professionals work for institutions who are in the "spread banking," or "arbitrage," business. The investment professional buys mortgage-backed securities, callable bonds, and other instruments with embedded options on the expectation that these instruments will produce a suitable spread over Treasuries, or their cost of funds (i.e., liabilities). For a variety of reasons, not the least of which is the change in the cost of option values, history has many times shown that these assets have not produced the advertised spread, or any positive spread for that matter.

In general, there are two basic goals to keep in mind when managing fixed-income assets with embedded options. The first goal is to attempt to match or exceed the total return of duration-neutral Treasuries over the short term while earning a growing risk premium over the intermediate to long term. If the spread asset downside performance is limited to matching duration-neutral Treasury performance over the short term, incremental value will assuredly be added to the portfolio. Although limiting downside performance in this way is difficult to achieve, the long-term goal is to obtain a reasonable risk premium as compensation for the negative convexity risk.

The second goal for managing fixed-income assets with embedded options is that they should be applied on a "ground up," or a bond-by-bond basis. If every bond is cost-justified versus a duration-neutral Treasury, then the maximum value is added to the portfolio.

CONCLUSION

This chapter sought to improve the reader's understanding of effective duration and effective convexity, with an emphasis on detecting model error. In addition, duration management suggestions were provided for portfolio managers.

Calculation-based definitions were recommended to describe effective duration and effective convexity. Specifically, effective *duration* can be thought of as the *average total return difference* between the up and down shift in interest rates. *Convexity* is a measure of the *allocation of this total return difference* between the two shifts and, thus, is a relative measure of the upside potential versus the downside risk.

This chapter also recommended that extensive use of breakeven analysis be applied for purposes of understanding the risk associated with model error and convexity mismatches in general. Model error occurs when spurious theoretical prices are produced upon which effective duration and effective convexity coefficients are generated. Spurious corporate prices are identified by checking the credibility of the implied nominal spread (in b.p.) associated with the theoretical prices for the up and down shift. Spurious MBS prices are identified by checking the credibility of the implied *contiguous coupon price spreads* associated with the theoretical prices for the up and down shift.

As a result of the municipal/Treasury yield ratio, municipal prices lag the price changes for comparable Treasuries for a given change in rates. Consequently, municipals have a shorter duration than comparable coupon and maturity Treasuries.

Finally, two suggestions were offered to portfolio managers who manage portfolios with embedded options. The first portfolio management goal is to attempt to match or exceed the total return of duration-neutral Treasuries over the short term while earning a growing risk premium over the intermediate to long term. The second goal for managing fixed-income assets with embedded options is that they should be applied on a "ground up," or a bond-by-bond basis. If every bond is cost-justified versus a duration-neutral Treasury, then the maximum value is added to the portfolio.

CHAPTER 12

Arbitrage-Free Bond Canonical Decomposition

Thomas S. Y. Ho
President

and

Michael Z. H. Chen
Research Analyst
Global Advanced Technology Corporation

The development of bond valuation models in the past 20 years has had a dramatic impact on the bond market. Pricing models provide market participants the necessary tools to measure relative values and manage risks. For example, we use arbitrage-free models to develop an option-adjusted spread (OAS) approach for measuring the bond value relative to other bonds. We also use these models to calculate the duration measures in formulating hedging strategies. As a result, traders, portfolio managers, risk managers, asset/liability strategists, and research analysts find applications for these pricing models. For details, Ho (1995) provides an overview of the use of bond models.

As fixed-income securities become more complex and bond markets become more volatile, the applicability of both the OAS approach and duration methodologies becomes questionable. OAS is the additional spread (or yield) the bond offers above the Treasury yields, net of the cost of the embedded options. However, the OAS approach does

The authors thank Pamela Hyder, Freddy Eng, and Sanjay Mazumdar for their comments, suggestions and assistance.

not offer any description of the embedded options. Indeed, any uncertainty of cashflows is often referred to as embedded options. If two bonds differ significantly in their embedded options, there is no simple interpretation of their relative values by their OASs. We cannot assert that the bond that offers a higher return has a better value, primarily because the bonds are incomparable. It follows we must precisely identify the embedded options before we can measure their relative values.

Duration measures (or key rate durations) are also limited in their applications for complex securities in risk management. Durations are price sensitivity measures for small movements of interest rates. Therefore, durations offer a dynamic hedging strategy for controlling interest rate risks. Hedgers need to continually revise the hedging portfolio. Further, they must respond to the market in that they must trade when rates rise or fall. Such dynamic hedging strategies can be costly, especially when the market is less liquid. Most bond markets are not perfectly liquid. As a result, a more static hedging strategy is needed for managing interest rate risks when the market is illiquid.

This chapter proposes a new methodology in determining relative values of bonds and in managing interest rate risks. The methodology is called arbitrage-free bond canonical decomposition (ABCD). ABCD proposes a standardized (canonical) way of decomposing any bond into its basic parts. This decomposition is based on an objective relative valuation (arbitrage-free), and not on the investor's subjective views. Further, these basic parts are standard securities that are traded in the market. If we know the prices of these basic securities, we can determine the cost of the bond according to the decomposition.

We will prove theoretically that such a decomposition is possible. A practical procedure in decomposing a collateralized mortgage obligation (CMO) is then presented. As will be shown, ABCD can offer many applications in the bond market, avoiding the limitations of the OAS approach and the duration measures. More specifically, ABCD offers the following advantages:

1. A standardized and specific description of the bond risk, avoiding ambiguous terminologies such as "embedded option";

2. A more-precise hedging technique using caps and floors against changes in volatilities, comparable to the use of "vega";

3. A hedging methodology that avoids continual revision of the hedging positions in response to the changes in the market;

4. Since a bond value is determined by the observed prices of the basic securities that compose the bond, the bond value is less dependent on the choice of the pricing model (for example, the choice of a normal versus a lognormal model); and

5. A practical approach to cashflow matching strategies for option-embedded bond portfolios.

For these reasons, ABCD should provide broad applications from arbitrage operations to asset/liability management.

BASIC FRAMEWORK

The model assumptions are the same as those proposed in arbitrage-free valuation in Ho and Lee (1985), a perfect capital market over discrete time. The assumptions are:

1. The market is frictionless. There are no taxes and no transaction costs, and all securities are perfectly divisible.

2. The market clears at regular time intervals. There is unlimited riskless borrowing and lending at each interval.

FIGURE 12-1

Binomial Lattice

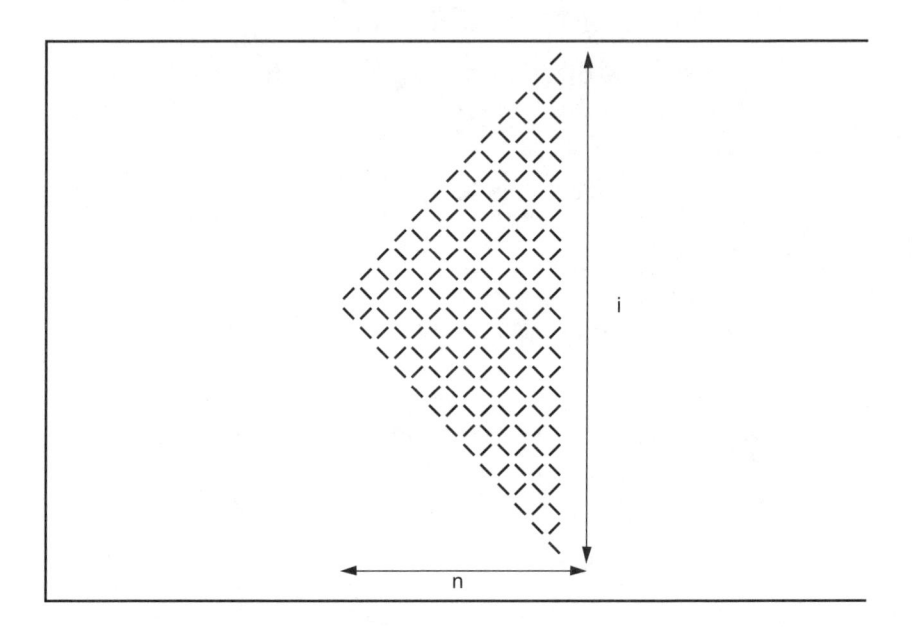

3. A discount bond of maturity T is defined to be a bond that pays $1 at the end of T years, with no other payments to its holders. The bond market is complete in that there exists a discount bond for all maturities. Let $P(T)$ denote the price of the discount bond with maturity T, with $P(.)$ being called the discount function.

4. There is no arbitrage opportunity at any time.

5. The discount function moves stochastically in a binomial lattice. A one-factor model where all interest rates are perfectly correlated is assumed. Denoting the i-th state, (i) is used, and (n) denotes the n-th period on the lattice. The binomial lattice is shown in Figure 12–1.

Given the initial discount function $P(T)$, an arbitrage-free movement of the discount function on the binomial lattice can be determined. Specifically, the one-period interest rate at each time n and state i can be determined. We denote this one-period rate by $r(i,n)$ and the discount factor $d(i,n)$ (= $1/(1 + r(i,n))$). An interest rate path $p(k)$ is a path taken from the binomial lattice. It follows that there are 2^N distinct paths in a binomial lattice with N intervals. The complete set of interest rate paths of a binomial lattice is called the path space.

Along each interest rate path, a cashflow can be assigned. A bond (or even a bond strategy) is an unambiguous assignment of cashflows to each of the possible paths. For example, a 10-year zero coupon bond assigns $100 at the end of the 10th year for all interest rate paths. In general, a bond is "option embedded" if the cashflows may differ depending on the interest rate path taken. We say that two bonds are the same when the bonds' cashflows are the same along each interest rate path. Ho (1993) describes the construction of bonds in more detail.

For a particular bond, option embedded or otherwise, select an interest rate path and the cashflows that are assigned to the path. The cashflow along the interest rate path can then be discounted. The resulting present value is called the pathwise value of that particular interest rate scenario of the bond. It is denoted by $pwv(k)$, where k is the index of the scenario.

Ho (1992) reported that the average of the pathwise values of all the interest rate paths of a bond is the arbitrage-free bond value. We now show that the pathwise values of a bond contain significant information about the bond. This information is, in fact, sufficient to decompose a bond.

DECOMPOSITION THEOREMS

ABCD is based on two analytical results. The first result applies to option-free bonds (bonds with no embedded options), and the second extends the previous result to the path-independent bonds.

Proposition 1.
Given an option-free bond, the bond cashflows are uniquely determined by the pathwise values. That is, given two option-free bonds, if their pathwise values are the same, then their cashflows are identical.[1]

This result shows that if we know the bond has no embedded option, and if we find a bond portfolio with no embedded option that can match the bond's pathwise values (hence implementing a pathwise immunization), we have in essence accomplished a cashflow matching. Pathwise values have complete information about an option-free bond. But what about an option-embedded bond? First, we must consider one significant option-embedded bond type: a path-independent bond.

A path-independent bond is a bond whose cashflows depend only on the time (n) and state (i) on the binomial lattice and not on the path that it has taken. For example, all option-free bonds and European options are path independent bonds.

Proposition 2.
Suppose there are two path-independent bonds having the same pathwise values. If their cashflows are identical along one interest rate scenario (any one scenario from the binomial lattice), then the two bonds are identical. Further, all path-independent bonds are a portfolio of option-free bonds, caps, and floors.[2]

This result shows that a path-independent bond using Treasury securities, caps, and floors which have liquidity

---

1. For a complete proof of Proposition 1, see Appendix A to this chapter.
2. Refer to Appendix B to this chapter for a complete proof of Proposition 2.

in the market, can be decomposed. Consequently, an inability to decompose the bond by the Treasuries, caps, and floors enables the measuring of the impact of the path dependency.

CANONICAL DECOMPOSITION

Using the above analytical results, ABCD follows a three-step procedure, referred to as the primary, secondary, and tertiary decompositions. Each step extracts the basic components of a given bond.

Primary Decomposition

Given a bond, the primary decomposition determines the bond cashflows along the forward curve. That is, the cashflows of the bond are determined if the interest rate volatility is zero. The cashflow is called the Treasury equivalent (TE).

Let T_n denote the zero coupon Treasury with maturity n years. The Treasury equivalent cashflows can then be represented by the following equation, where X_n represents the dollar value of position in the zero coupon Treasury bond with maturity n year.

$$TE = \sum (X_n T_n) \qquad (1)$$

It is important to note that the primary decomposition is, in general, not the total hedge position of a swap desk or other bond desks. Typically, these trading desks monitor their exposures to the changing shape of the yield curve by calculating their required Treasury positions to immunize their risks. These exposures are calculated by simulating the sensitivity of their portfolio value to the change of each key rate, and not using the forward curve. Treasury equivalent provides the correct hedging only in the case where there are no embedded options in the portfolio.

Secondary Decomposition

For the second step, the pathwise values of the Treasury equivalent are calculated and the difference between the pathwise values of the bond and those of the Treasury equivalent is considered.

$$Y_i = pwv_i(\text{bond}) - pwv_i(TE) \quad \text{for } i = 1 \ldots 2^N \quad (2)$$

According to Proposition 2, if the bond is path-independent, then Y uniquely determines the set of caps and floors which, together with the Treasury equivalent, have the same cashflows as the bonds for all the interest rate paths. The caps and the floors have their strikes above and below the forward rates effectively.

In bond analytics, option cost is often referred to as the difference between the bond value and the Treasury equivalent value. The option cost is the price change in the presence of interest rate volatility. Proposition 2 shows that this option cost can in fact be uniquely represented by caps and floors, if the scenario referred to in Proposition 2 is the forward curve. Therefore, secondary decomposition is the specification of the embedded options of a bond.

A forward cap with strike of $x\%$ and window between calendar years a and b is represented by $C_{x\%, a-b}$. For example, a forward cap of strike 8%, and with window 2000–2005 is denoted by $C_{8\%, 00-05}$. A forward floor is analogously denoted by $F_{x\%, a-b}$. Then a bond decomposition can be represented by the following equation where Y_i and Z_i are the market values of the caps and floors, respectively, in the decomposition.

$$B = TE + \Sigma(Y_i C_i) + \Sigma(Z_i F_i) \quad (3)$$

Proposition 2 asserts that equation (3) is unambiguously determined if the bond is path-independent.

Tertiary Decomposition

Equation (3) is correct only if the conditions of Proposition 2 are met. Generally, they are not met. In this case, the right side of equation (3) is the portfolio that provides the best fit of the bond pathwise values, and not the exact matching of the pathwise values. The standard minimization of mean squared errors without probability weighting may be used. The difference between the pathwise values of the bond and the pathwise values of the right side of equation (3) is the residual values. These residual values are then subject to further decomposition.

According to the analysis, the residual values arise from four possible sources: path dependency, model risk premium, liquidity premium, and arbitrage profit.

Path dependency.
The residuals of pathwise values can identify the impact of the path dependency of the bond. As a result of the fitting procedure, some residuals are positive and others negative. If the pathwise value of the bond exceeds that of the primary/secondary decomposition, then the bond outperforms in that scenario. Conversely, if the residual pathwise value is negative, then the bond underperforms in that scenario. Thus, it is found that the residuals of the decomposition provide an effective insight into the bond's performance across all the important scenarios.

Model risk premium.
The decomposition is based on the robustness of the model. However, the model may not capture all the risk sources such as credit risk for corporate issues and prepayment risks for mortgage-backed securities. As the pathwise values are calculated along the Treasury interest rate paths, it is not possible to capture the credit spread and the spread to compensate for the prepayment risks involved.

For this reason, the decomposition has to be applied to a sample of bonds with similar credit risks or prepayment risks to identify comparable premiums. These risks sources are beyond the model's specifications. However, the decomposition does isolate all the interest rate factors, enabling the comparison of the credit and prepayment premiums.

Liquidity Premiums.
Liquidity risk differs from credit and prepayment risks in that the liquidity risk depends not only on the bond but also on the market. For this reason, the class of bonds that is exposed to similar liquidity risks of the market must be identified before the premium for such risks can be isolated.

Arbitrage Profit.
Arbitrage profit is the value of the bond net of the primary/secondary decomposition and the risk/liquidity premiums. In essence, the ABCD approach translates the option-adjusted spread from yield measures in basis points to values in dollars. The arbitrage profits identify the discrepancy between the bond's quoted price and the cost of replicating the bond from the basic components.

A NUMERICAL EXAMPLE

This section applies ABCD to a collateralized mortgage obligation (CMO) to illustrate the use of the decomposition procedure. To implement the procedure, we need to make some simplifying assumptions. In practice, the binomial lattice of a pricing model is often based on a one-month step size, and the bond maturity may be up to 30 years. Therefore the number of paths (or the number of pathwise values) will be 2^{360}, which is astronomical.

Linear Path Space

One approach is to construct a set of paths that spans the path space. Here, linear path space (LPS) as described in Ho (1992) is used. LPS is a probability-weighted structured sampling technique to condense a binomial lattice with many periods into a lattice of manageable size.

Begin with the full binomial lattice with one-month time steps, and partition the path space into term segments at 1, 3, 5, 7, 10, 20, and 30 years. Then at each term, partition the full set of interest rate levels into much smaller sets of "gates."

A path can now be classified by the sequence of gates it travels through. Define an equivalence class. The number of paths in a given equivalence class as a proportion of the total number of paths is the "probability weight" for that class.

For each class, a representative path (the one going through the midpoints of each of its gates) is chosen. These representative paths are then used to determine the pathwise values of the decomposition.

Canonical Basis of Caps and Floors

In theory, the decomposition requires the basis of the caps and floors to have strikes at each node of the binomial lattice. In practice, we construct the basis that can sufficiently span the scenarios without requiring too many caps and floors.

Only the caps and floors with strikes above and below the forward rates are chosen. Their windows are determined by the term segments of the LPS. Therefore there are seven windows: 0–1 year, 1–3 years, 3–5 years, 5–7 years, 7–10 years, 10–20 years, and 20–30 years. The strikes of the forward caps and floors of a window are determined by the rate levels of the LPS representative paths at the beginning of each window. The reset rate of all the caps and floors is specified to be the six-month rate.[3]

Decomposition of FH1747:Q

The next procedure is to decompose a CMO. FH1747:Q is a fixed 8 percent coupon bond maturing on December 2003. The bond is a support tranche bearing much prepayment risk allocated from the PAC tranches. The collaterals are FHLMC 30-year with a net weighted average coupon of 8 percent. On the analysis date, January 9, 1995, the price is $92.09. The option cost is calculated to be 41 basis points and the option-adjusted spread is 64 basis points. Figure 12–2 depicts the unstable nature of the bond's cashflows.

At 100 PSA, the window of the bond's principal payments is 2015–2018. However, at PSA 200, the bond's window shortens to 1995–1998. This shortening of the weighted average life of the bond with the fall in interest rates (with the rise of prepayment speed) is referred to as the call risk. When the prepayment speed slows to PSA 75, Figure 12–2 shows that the window extends. The lengthening of the weighted average life with the rise in interest rate is called the extension risk. To explicitly model these call and extension risks, the decomposition is continued.

Figure 12–3 is the scattered plot graph of the pathwise values of the CMO against pathwise values of the bond's Treasury equivalent. If the bond has no call and extension risks, the scattered plots would assume the 45° line. Figure 12–3 clearly depicts the call risks when the Treasury equivalent pathwise values rise above $110, as the scattered points fall below the 45° line. The result shows that the loss under a worst-case scenario could exceed 20 percent.

---

3. The LPS representative paths and the canonical basis of the caps and floors are given in Appendix C to this chapter.

Arbitrage-Free Bond Canonical Decomposition 295

FIGURE 12-2

Dynamic Tranche Analyzer

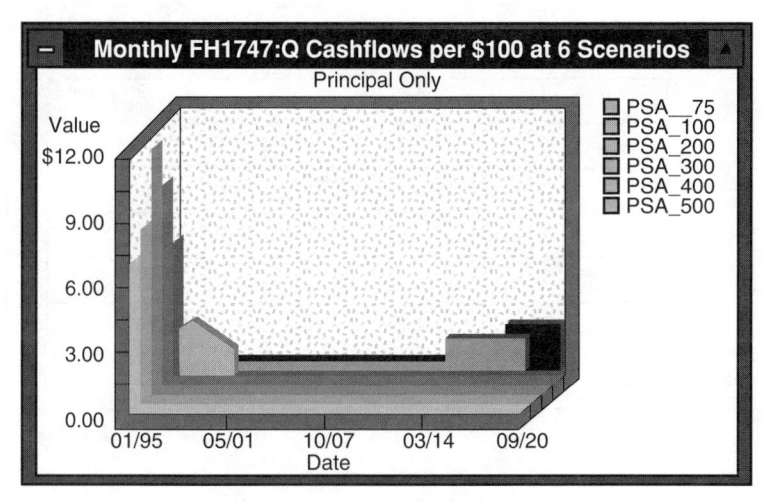

Monthly FH1747:Q Cashflows per $100 at 6 Scenarios
Principal Only

- PSA__75
- PSA_100
- PSA_200
- PSA_300
- PSA_400
- PSA_500

FHLMC 1747:Q 8.00% SUPfix 12/23 Collateral: 30 year, NWAC 8.00% Price: 92.09 Option Cost: 41 b.p. OAS: 64 b.p.

FIGURE 12-3

Pathwise Values, CMO: Treasury Equivalent

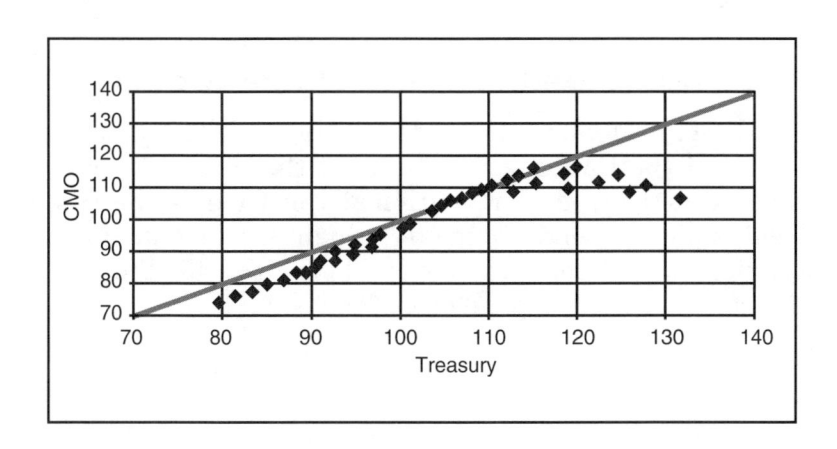

FIGURE 12-4

Pathwise Values, CMO: Treasury & Caps & Floors

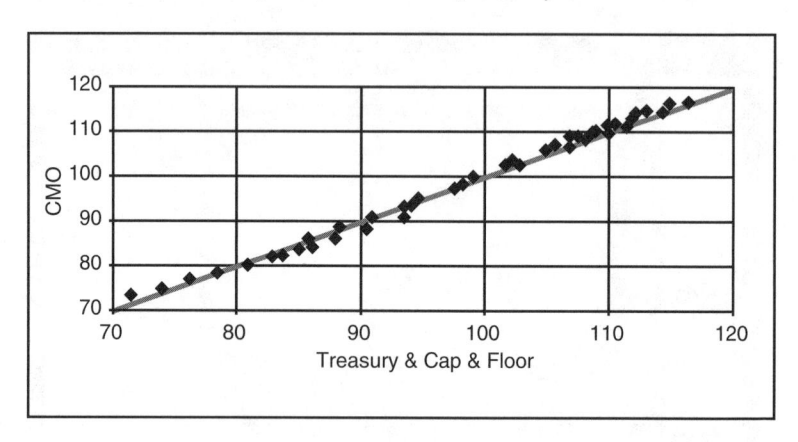

[Scatter plot: x-axis "Treasury & Cap & Floor" from 70 to 120; y-axis "CMO" from 70 to 120]

In contrast, since the bond has a long weighted average life along the forward curve, the extension risk is limited. Figure 12-3 shows that the cost of extension appears for those scenarios where the Treasury equivalent pathwise values fall below par. But the cost is limited, not exceeding 5 percent for all the scenarios.

Analytical Results of the Decomposition

Figure 12-4 depicts the scattered plots of the pathwise values of the CMO against those of the bond's Treasury, caps, and floors decomposition. Even though the CMO bond is path dependent, the fit is high, with $R^2 = .9688$. The positions of the points above and below the 45° line show the impact of path dependency of the bond.

$$
\begin{aligned}
CMO \quad = {} & -1.258 \text{ cash} + 110.343 \text{ Treasury} \quad (4)\\
& -1.485 \text{ cap} - 1.874 \text{ floor}\\
& -5.726 \text{ risk premium}\\
FHLMC\ 1747\ Q = {} & -1.258\ Ca + 9.815\ T_1 + 7.688\ T_2\\
& + 7.110\ T_3 + 6.574\ T_4 + 6.079\ T_5\\
= {} & + 5.619\ T_6 + 5.194\ T_7 + 4.801\ T_8\\
& + 4.436\ T_9 + 4.098\ T_{10} + 3.784\ T_{11}\\
= {} & + 10.298\ T_{12} + 9.412\ T_{13} + 8.903\ T_{14}\\
& + 7.114\ T_{15} + 5.774\ T_{16} + 3.642\ T_{17}\\
= {} & -1.485\ C_{95-10,\ 3.17\%} - 8.335\ F_{95-08,\ 6.54\%}\\
& + 6.461\ F_{95-10,\ 6.37\%}\\
= {} & -5.726\ RP
\end{aligned}
$$

where

Ca = cash
T = Treasury
C = cap
F = floor
RP = risk premium
R^2 = 0.9688

The ABCD equation (4) presents the exact decomposition of the bond of $100 value. The cashflow value of the bond is $109.08 ($110.343-$1.258). The cost of call risk is $1.874 and the cost of the extension risk is $1.485. The cost of extension risk is high because of the caps being close to "in the money," but the potential loss is limited, as discussed earlier. By way of contrast, the potential loss of call risk is much higher, but the floors are more "out of the money." The sum of the cost of the call risk and extension risk, amortized over the life of the bond, is the option cost.

According to the ABCD equation, the premium for the prepayment risk, the liquidity, and arbitrage profit is

$5.726 on the $100 bond value. This premium, amortized over the life of the bond, is the option-adjusted spread. Considering the unstable nature of the bond, it may be ambiguous in defining the amortization of the premium. For this reason, a measure of the premium in dollar terms can offer a more appropriate comparison of values. The ABCD equation shows the cashflow along the base case (the forward rate scenario) by the positions in Treasury securities. The embedded options are represented by the positions in forward caps and floors.

CONCLUSION

This chapter presents the analytical framework for decomposing a bond into its basic components, Treasuries, caps, and floors. Further, it provides an implementable procedure and illustrates the methodology with a numerical example. This decomposition methodology has broad applications in the bond market. The following are some of its applications:

1. *A standardized risk measure.* To date, we use bond sensitivities to describe bond risks. These sensitivities include duration, convexity, and option cost. When bonds become more complicated, these measures become less adequate in representing the bond risks. Further, they become inaccurate measures. For example, duration numbers become sensitive to model assumptions for some of the "risky" bonds. Or, option cost may be negligible because the cost of call risks cancels the cost of extension risks.

By way of contrast, if the bond is represented by its basic components, the description of the bond structure is relatively stable. From the decomposition, it can then be inferred whether or not the bond sensitivity measures are appropriate.

2. *Volatility hedging.* In hedging securities with significant embedded options, managing the change in volatility is important. Yet, to date, the use of vega is prevalent, though clearly inadequate. The decomposition shows exactly the caps and floors that the hedge requires in managing the volatility risks. In essence, the decomposition describes exactly where the embedded options are, and not just the volatility sensitivity.

3. *Static hedging versus dynamic hedging.* The decomposition enables us to implement a static hedging strategy versus a dynamic hedging strategy. Dynamic hedging requires us to continually rebalance the portfolio, responding to changes in the market. This hedging approach subjects the portfolio to high trading or liquidity risks. In contrast, static hedging is more stable. The hedging is constructed in such a way that the hedging portfolio anticipates the changes in duration, convexity, and other measures as the market changes. As a result, we do not need to be continually fine tuning. More importantly, the portfolio can be rebalanced at times to minimize the cost of trading.

4. *Valuation by observed prices.* Since the Treasuries, cap, and floor prices are observable, the bond price from these observed prices is determinable. The valuation model is used to determine the decomposition of the bond, specifying the sizes and types of the caps and floors. By using the observed prices of the basic components of the bond decomposition, inaccuracies of the pricing model can be avoided. For example, a lognormal interest rate model may overweigh the scenarios where interest rates are high. As a result, the model may overstate the cost of the extension risk.

Also such a model may overstate the cap values. However, by applying the observed cap prices, the misspecification of the model would not appear in the pricing of the bond. This decomposition approach is consistent with the pricing of bonds at the trading desks, where traders continually monitor the combination and recombination value of bonds. This decomposition procedure offers them a systematic way to implement this pricing operation.

5. *Cashflow matching by scenarios.* In asset/liability management, managers are concerned with the behavior of the surplus cashflows under different scenarios. When the assets and liabilities are significantly option embedded, the behavior of the surplus cashflows becomes very complicated to analyze.

We suggest that the manager can decompose the surplus and identify the embedded caps and floors in the surplus. This approach greatly simplifies asset/liability analysis. If there is success in eliminating the embedded caps and floors, the cashflows of the asset and liability may be quite well matched under all the scenarios.

Further, this decomposition approach suggests that optimal asset and liability management is not immunization of all risk exposures, but that decomposition should be used to depict the risk exposure.

There are many avenues to extend this research. This decomposition has more applications when used to compare a sample of bonds. While this chapter has analyzed one bond, the research can be extended to classify bonds according to the decomposition. Another important extension is to better understand the path-dependent nature of bonds. While analytical results for path-independent bonds has been furnished, it is possible to gain more insight into the tertiary decomposition if we have an analytical decomposition of path-dependent bonds.

REFERENCES

Ho, Thomas S. Y. 1992. "Managing Illiquid Bonds and the Linear Path Space." *Journal of Fixed-Income* 2, n. 1 (June).

_____. 1993. "Primitive Securities: Portfolio Building Blocks." *Journal of Derivatives* 1, n. 2 (Winter).

_____. 1996 "Evolution of Interest Rate Models: A Comparison." *Journal of Derivatives*.

Ho, Thomas S. Y., and Sang-bin Lee. 1986. "Term Structure Movements and Pricing of Interest Rate Contingent Claims." *Journal of Finance* 41.

APPENDIX A TO CHAPTER TWELVE PROOF OF PROPOSITION 1

Proposition 1: Given two option-free bonds, if their pathwise values are the same, then their cashflows are identical.

Proof:

The postulation is equivalent to proving that if a given option-free bond B has zero pathwise value along each path, then the bond B has zero cashflow along each path also.

Since the bond B is option free, its cashflow at time n is a function only of time (n), denoted by $B(n)$. The bond B is completely determined by the numbers $B(n)$, $n = 1, 2, \ldots, N$.

Assuming that the k-th scenario on the interest rate lattice $r(i,n)$ represented by the underlying interest rates $r(1), r(2), \ldots, r(N)$, discounting the cashflow of the bond B along the path, we have $pwv(k)$ as follows:

$$pwv(k) = B(1)e^{-r(1)} + B(2)e^{-r(1)-r(2)} \quad (5)$$
$$+ \ldots + B(N)e^{-r(1)- \ldots -r(N)}$$

Let path p and path q be two paths which are identical except for the last period. Path p ends at $r(i,N)$ and path q ends at $r(i+1,N)$. Following the assumption that bond B has zero pathwise value along each path, we have equations $pwv(p) = 0$ and $pwv(q) = 0$. Subtracting one equation from the other, we have equation $pwv(p)-pwv(q) = 0$, i.e.,

$$B(N)e^{-R-r(i,N)} - B(N)e^{-R-r(i+1,N)} = 0 \qquad (6)$$

where R is the summation of the interest rates along path p (or path q) from period 1 to period $N-1$. Equation (**6**) can be rewritten as:

$$B(N)(-r(i,N) - e^{-r(i+1,N)}) = 0 \qquad (7)$$

Since $r(i,N)$ is not equal to $r(i+1,N)$, we have $B(N) = 0$. Henceforth, bond B will be considered as a bond with maturity of $N-1$ periods. By the same argument it can be proved that B has zero cashflow at end of period $N-1$, i.e., $B(N-1) = 0$. Consequently from the same argument, we have $B(t) = 0$, for $t = 1,2, \ldots ,N$. Thus, bond B has zero cashflow along each path.

APPENDIX B TO CHAPTER TWELVE PROOF OF PROPOSITION 2

Proposition 2: Given two path-independent bonds having the same pathwise value, if their cashflows are identical along one interest rate scenario, then the two bonds are identical. Further, all path-independent bonds are a portfolio of option free bonds, caps, and floors.

Proof:

The proposition is equivalent to proving that if a given path-independent bond B has zero pathwise value along each path, and its cashflow is zero along one scenario, then bond B has zero cashflow along all the paths.

Since bond B is path-independent, its cashflow at time n depends only on time (n) and state (i), and not the historical interest rate paths it took to reach there. Its cashflow can be labeled on the nodes of the binomial interest rate lattice, denoted by $B(i,n)$, where $i = 1, \ldots ,n$, $n = 1, \ldots ,N$. Since there are total $N(N+1)/2$ nodes in the lattice, bond B is completely determined by the expression $B(i,n)$.

Let path p and path q be two paths which are identical except for the last period. Path p ends at $r(i,N)$ and path q ends at $r(i+1,N)$. By the assumption that bond B has zero pathwise value along each path, we have equations $pwv(p) = 0$ and $pwv(q) = 0$. Subtracting one equation from the other, we have equation $pwv(p)-pwv(q) = 0$.

$$B(i,N)e^{-R-r(i,N)} - B(i+1,N)e^{-R-r(i+1,N)} = 0 \qquad (8)$$

where R is the summation of interest rates along path p or path q from period 1 to period $N-1$)

Following our assumption that bond B has zero cashflow along one scenario, we can safely assert one of $B(1,N), \ldots ,B(N,N)$ is zero. Without loss of generality, let $B(1,N) = 0$. For the special case of Equation (8), $i = 1$, it follows that repeating our argument, $B(i,N)$ must be zero for $i = 1, 2, \ldots , N$.

$$B(2,N) - B(1,N)e^{r(2,N)-r(1,N)} = 0 \qquad (9)$$

Now, bond B can be considered as a bond with maturity of $N-1$ periods. By the same argument it can proved that B has zero cashflow at end of period $N-1$. Then, by induction, bond B has zero cashflow at every period and along every path.

Now it will be proven that all path-independent bonds are a portfolio of option free bonds, caps, and floors. At first, it is easy to see that a given path-independent bond is a portfolio of some simple bonds having zero cashflow at all lattice points except one node. Thus, it can be proved that these simple bonds are a portfolio of option free bonds, caps, and floors. Assume that at the N-th column of the interest rate lattice, we have $r(i,N)$ which satisfies the expression $r(N,N) > r(N-1,N) > \ldots > (1,N)$. Constructing a sequence of forward cap C_i which live in the N-th period with a strike rate of $(r(i,N) + r(i-1,N))/2$, $i = N, N-1, \ldots, 2$. The linear combination of C_i will give us all simple bonds in the column which have zero cashflow at all lattice points except for one node. For example, the bond C_N will strike at only the top node of the column. The bond $C_{N-1}-(2r(N,N)-r(N-1,N)-r(N-2,N))/(r(N,N)+r(N-1,N))C_N$ will only strike at the node $r(N-1,N)$. Similarly, we can construct all the other simple bonds from the linear combinations of C_i. However, it is desirable to choose a basis which makes sense in financial theory. Therefore, it is natural that the zero coupon Treasury with maturity N periods was chosen. Selection of the caps and floors was made by placing them above and below the forward curve.

See Appendix C for a concrete example.

APPENDIX C TO CHAPTER TWELVE

LPS LATTICE AND THE CANONICAL BASIS OF CAPS AND FLOORS

Figure 12–5 is a linear path space (LPS) lattice of 6-month rates. That part of the lattice representing extremely high and low interest rates has been eliminated.

The following is a list of caps and floors chosen to form a canonical basis for the pathwise value space of path-independent bonds on an empirical level:

FIGURE 12-5

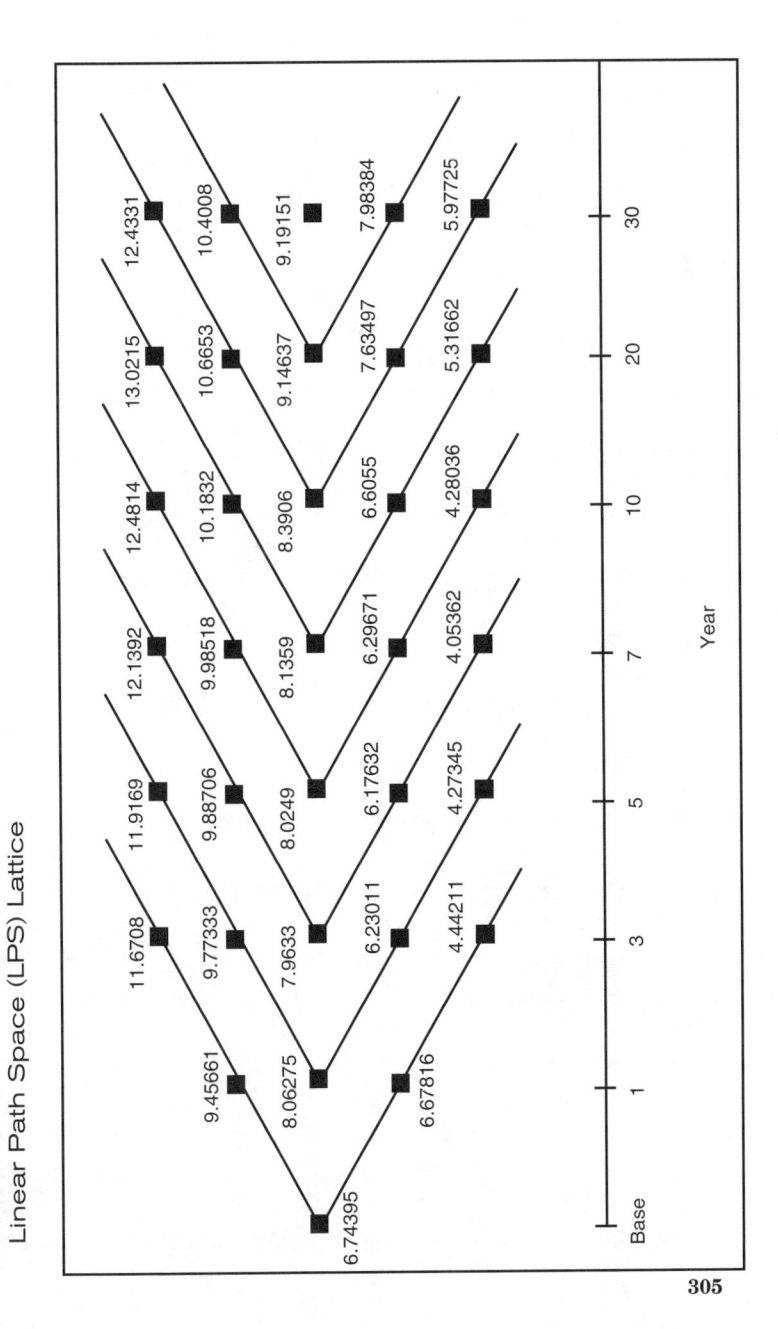

Linear Path Space (LPS) Lattice

		Window (years)	Strike Rate (percent)
1	Cap	1–3	8.5%
2	Floor	1–3	7
3	Cap	3–5	10
4	Cap	3–5	8.5
5	Floor	3–5	7
6	Floor	3–5	5
7	Cap	5–7	10
8	Cap	5–7	8.5
9	Floor	5–7	7
10	Floor	5–7	5
11	Cap	7–10	10
12	Cap	7–10	8.5
13	Floor	7–10	7
14	Floor	7–10	5
15	Cap	10–20	10.5
16	Cap	10–20	8.5
17	Floor	10–20	7
18	Floor	10–20	5
19	Cap	20–30	11
20	Cap	20–30	9.5
21	Floor	20–30	8
22	Floor	20–30	5.5

In accordance with this theory, the set of simple bonds, which has a zero cashflow at all lattice points except one node, forms the basis of the path-independent bond space. Consequently, this basis generates the pathwise value space of all path-independent bonds. The following procedure was adhered to in determining the caps and floors.

The lattice was dissected into 7 segments, namely: 0–1 year, 1–3 years, 3–5 years, 5–7 years, 7–10 years, 10–20 years, and 20–30 years. In every period, different strike rates were used separating every lattice node, choosing strike rates above and below the forward curve for caps and floors respectively. The entire set of caps and floors and zero coupon Treasuries with different maturities (used in the primary decomposition) formed the basis for path-independent bond space. Whenever the basis is fixed, the decomposition of a given bond is unique. In other words, this is the canonical way to decompose any bond.

INDEX

A
Abken, Peter A., 70, 80
Ambarish, Ramasastry, 98
American Council of Life Insurance (ACLI), 166-169
   arbitrage-free bond canonical decomposition (ABCD), 283-307
      advantages of, 285
      basic framework for, 285-287
      caps and, 287, 289, 299-300
      decomposing a CMO, 294-298
      primary canonical decomposition, 289
      secondary canonical decomposition, 290
      tertiary canonical decomposition, 291-292
arbitrage-free conditions, 80
arbitrage-free interest rate models
   and calibration methodology, 84
   combining mean reverting behavior to, 84
   Ho and Lee model, 82-86
   lognormal form, 86
   n-factor model, 86-88, 90
   normal form, 82-86
   and relative valuation, 85
   setting caps with, 85
arbitrage profits, 292
asset allocation
   aligning portfolios, 9
   fixed-income subsector, 1-23
   indexing of, 4-5, 6-8, 21-22
   mean/variance technique for, 2-3, 17
   scenario testing and, 16-18
   standard models for, 2-4
asset cell matrixes, 10-12
asset/liability factors, 13-18
assets
   managing illiquid, 24
   marking, 260-261
   standard asset classes, 2
   synthetic, 12
asset trading set limitations, 30-31
attribution, 46

B
Babbel, D., 91
bailout, 266
Ball, C. A., 77
bankruptcy
   by Barings PLC, 44-45

by Orange County Investment
  Fund, 44
 evaluating, 99-100
 factoring in probabilities for junk
  bonds, 98
 failure of performance
  measurement, 43-45
Barings PLC, bankruptcy by, 44-45
basis risk
 assessing with historical data, 219-227
 conditional expectations of, 228-231
 for floating-rate notes, 212-216, 219-227
binomial lattice, 286-287
binomial pricing models, 105-109
binomial trees, 106-107, 111
Black, F., 71-78, 86
Black-Scholes model
 advantages and disadvantages of, 77-78
 assumptions of, 73-74
 dynamic hedging arguments, 75-76, 79-80
 interest-rate-sensitive securities, 72-75
 and lognormal model of interest rates, 79
 modified for bonds, 75, 77-78
 for stock options, 71-75
Boenawan, K., 83, 86
bond option valuation, 75, 77-78
bond pricing
 bridge process and, 77
 interest rate models and, 78-81
 yield curves for, 79, 80
bonds
 arbitrage profits, 292
 bond option valuation and, 75, 77-78
 cash flow and, 287-288
 decomposing, 284-285, 287-289, 298-301
 fixed-rate bonds, 153-155, 202-204
 with floating-rate coupons, 187-239
 liquidity premiums for, 292

 municipal bonds, 278-280
 underlying, with floaters and inverse floaters, 139-140
 bond structures, 169-171
 bond valuation models, 75, 77-78, 283-307
Brace, A., 91
breakeven analysis, 276-278
Brennan, M. J., 81
bridge process, 77
buffered portfolios, 261-264

C
calculations
 for effective duration and convexity, 270
 yield-to-forward LIBOR, 151-153
calibration methodology
 and arbitrage-free modeling, 84
 standard bivariate normal density function, 108
Campbell, J. Y., 90
canonical decomposition, three steps of, 289-292
caps
 amortizing, 236-238
 arbitrage-free bond canonical decomposition and, 287, 289, 299-300
 canonical basis of, 293-294
 linear path space and, 304-307
 for mortgage derivatives, 156-157
 using arbitrage-free interest rate models, 85
cash flows
 arbitrage-free bond canonical decomposition, 287, 289, 297-298, 300
 inverse floaters and, 156
 option-free bonds, 287-288
 path-independent bonds, 288-289
 perpetual floaters and Eurodollar futures, 205, 209-212, 215-216
 traditional mortgage cash-flow measures, 135-138
catastrophe hedging, 264-265

Index

Chen, Michael Z. H., 283-307
Chen, Si, 117-132
choke point, 249
CMBS; *see* commercial mortgage-backed securities
CMOs; *see* collateralized mortgage obligations
collateralized mortgage obligations (CMOs)
    analyzing relative valuation of, 127-128
    decomposing a, 294-298
    floating rate, 235-237
    option-adjusted spread model and, 122, 127-128
    re-REMIC tranches, 141
commercial mortgage-backed securities (CMBS)
    analyzing credit risks of, 109-113
    default-adjusted credit spreads, 172-176
    default risk-based pricing of, 103-105, 109-112
    equity investments and, 176-181
    outperforming leveraged equities, 182-184
    sample bond structures and, 169-171
    spreads in, 163-164
commercial mortgages, 164-165
conditional expectations, 228-231
conservation of energy and mass, liquidity risk and, 250-251
constrained management, 50-52
constraints, yield curve shifts and, 30-31, 34-38
convexity; *see also* effective duration
    effective, 271-276, 278-280
    fixed-income assets and, 272-273
    mortgages and prepayment assumptions, 124-127
    for mutual bonds, 278-280
    negative, 15-16
Corcoran, Patrick J., 98, 103-105, 163-186
coupling, investment behavior to performance, 251-254, 256, 259

coupon pass-throughs
    convexity and, 125-127
    implied prepayments and, 130-131
    option-adjusted spread of CMOs, 127-128, 129
    prepayments and, 122-124
coupons
    comparisons of FRNs with different indices, 212-216
    current coupons differentials, 216-219
    floating-rate notes, 187-239
Courtadon, G., 70, 79
covariance characteristics, 105-106
Cox, J. C., 79, 80, 90
credit exposure, 12, 15
credit losses
    for commercial mortgages and CMBS, 166-169
    factoring for junk bonds, 98
credit risk
    assessing, 98, 99-100
    commercial mortgage-backed securities as, 109-112
    Zeta credit risk scores, 102
credit spreads, 172-176
current coupons differentials, 216-219
custom liability index, MetLife, 6-8, 21

D
Dattatreya, Ravi E., 88, 241-267
default-losses, 172-176
default risk-based pricing, 97-116
    commercial mortgage-backed securities, 103-105, 109-112
    empirical models and examples of, 100-105
    factoring in default probabilities, 98
    two-asset binomial pricing model, 105-109
default trigger assumption, 100
Derman, E., 86
directional durations, 30
direct property ownership, 164-165
discount bonds, 286

discount margins, 188, 190-195, 200-201
discrete time models, 72
Dothan, L. U., 78
downside risk; *see also* drawdown risk; value at risk
   advantages of, 64-66
   performance measurement and, 63-66
   in real estate, 171-172
   semivariance and, 63-64
drawdown risk, 52-57
Duff & Phelps Rating Company, 169
duration
   assets/liability factors and, 4, 13-14
   directional, 30
   effective, 188, 195-198, 269-282
   key rate, 88
   mortgages and prepayment assumptions, 124-127
   partial, 188, 198-199
   as performance management benchmark, 50-51
   spread, 188, 199-200, 209, 213
   yield curve shifts and, 25-27, 29, 32-38
duration vectors, risk analysis and, 28-29
Dybvig, P. H., 79
dynamic hedging, 75-76, 79-80, 299

E
effective convexity, 271-274
   for municipal bonds, 278-280
   sensitivity to spread changes, 274-276
effective duration, 188, 195-198
   and convexity, 271-274
   defined, 270-271
   for municipal bonds, 278-280
   sensitivity to spread changes, 274-276
efficient frontiers, 38-40
embedded options
   and arbitrage-free bond canonical decomposition, 285

   and breakeven analysis, 277
   in FRNs, 231, 234-235
   managing spread fixed-income assets, 280-281
equity
   leveraged, 179-181
   unleveraged, 177-178
Eurobond market, perpetual floating-rate notes, 207-212
Eurodollar futures, 204-212, 215-216
ex ante/ex post performance, 61
exposure to risk, 45-50, 90

F
fair value, 100-103
federal funds, comparison of changes to prime rate, 229
firm value, 73
fixed-coupon bonds, 255-266
fixed-income assets, 1-23, 272-273
fixed-rate bonds, 150-155, 202-204
fixed-rate mortgage-backed securities, 135-138
floating-rate collateralized mortgage obligations (CMOs), 235-238
floating-rate coupons; *see* floating-rate notes
floating-rate notes (FRN), 187-239
   basis risk for, 212-216, 219-227
   comparing spreads between indices for, 220-227
   discount margins for, 188, 190-195, 200-201
   effective duration, 188, 195-198
   floored corporate, 232-235
   LIB3-indexed, 190-195, 201-203
   mortgage-backed, 188, 235-238
   partial duration, 188, 198-199
   perpetual, 207-212
   pricing and index levels, 193-195
   pricing equations and market conventions, 188-195
   reset margins for, 188, 189-195
   risk and, 213-214
   spread duration, 188, 199-200
   swaps for, 201-203, 209-212

Index

floors
    and arbitrage-free bond canonical decomposition, 287, 289, 299
    canonical basis of, 293-294
    for FRNs, 232-235
    and inverse floaters, 158-161
    and linear path space (LPS), 304-307
    for mortgage derivatives, 156-157
    payments linked to, 159-161
flow simulation, 256
flow temperature, 247-249, 251-255
forward LIBOR, 134
FRN; *see* floating-rate notes

G

general equilibrium, 80-81, 90
Goodman, Laurie S., 19, 133-162
Griffin, M., 91

H

hedging
    and arbitrage-free bond canonical decomposition, 285, 299
    asset cell matrixes and, 12
    catastrophe, 264-265
    dynamic, 75-76, 79-80, 299
    and relative valuation of bonds, 88-89
    on steep yield curves, 85
herd effect, 245
Hiller, Randall S., 27
historical data, assessing basis risk with, 219-227
Ho, Jeffrey, 133-162
Ho, Thomas S. Y., 27, 69-95, 102-103, 105-106, 111, 283-307
Ho and Lee model, 82-86
Hull, J., 70, 82, 84

I

IBM, value of call options, 103
IIOs; *see* inverse interest-only strips

illiquid assets, portfolio management and, 24
immunization, 25-27, 40
implied prepayments
    analyzing IO/PO strips, 129, 130
    assumptions about, 124-128, 131-132
    for mortgage-backed securities, 117-132
    purpose of, 121-122
    risk management for, 131
index bonds, two-tiered, 141-142
index levels, 193-195
indices
    for asset allocation, 4-5, 6-8, 21-22
    comparing FRNs with different, 212-216
    for custom liability, 6-8, 21
    indexing to LIB3, 190-195
    Lehman Index, 21
    MetLife custom liability index, 6-8, 21
    Salomon Index, 21
    two-tiered index bonds, 141-142
infrastructure, providing for portfolio managers, 8
Ingersoll, J. E., 79, 80
institutional investors, relative valuation, 18-21
interest-only strips (IOs), 128-131
interest rate binomial trees, 106-109, 111
interest rate models
    discrete time models, 72
    evolution of, 69-95
    fitting to term structure of volatility, 84-85
    lognormal model for, 79
    one factor models, 78-81, 90
    term structure of volatility, 83-84
    testing, 16-18
    two factor models, 81, 86-87, 90
interest-rate-sensitive securities
    Black-Scholes model and, 72-75
    key rate duration and, 88-89
    term of structure of volatility and, 84

inverse floaters, 133-134
    analyzing payment streams for, 155-156
    floors and, 158-161
    and re-creation analysis, 138-143
    underlying bonds with floaters and inverse floaters, 139-140
    yield table for, 136
inverse interest-only strips (IIOs), 133-134, 156-157
    LIBOR options and, 154
    unbundling options and, 155-161
    yield table for, 137
investment performance, 45
investment return, 45, 48
investment risk, 48-49
investments, developing, 5-9
investor behavior, 251-256
invisible risks, 242-243
IO/PO strips; see interest-only and principal-only strips
Iwanowski, Raymond J., 187-239

J
Jamshidian, F., 82
junk bonds, 97-116

K
Kao, Duen-Li, 97-116, 171
Karasinski, P., 86
key rate duration, 27, 88-89

L
Lally, Robert M., 269-282
Langer, Martha J., 1-23
Lee, S. B., 82, 102-103
Lehman Index, 21
leveraged equity, 179-181
levered securities, 148
liabilities, 3-4, 260-261
LIB3-indexed FRNs, 190-195, 201-203
LIBOR
    LIB3-indexed FRNs, 190-195, 201-203

LIBOR forwards and yield curves, 134
LIBOR swap curve as basis of swap markets, 72
rates correlated to yields, 135-138
yield-to-forward, 150-155, 162
linear path space (LPS)
    and arbitrage-free bond canonical decomposition, 293-294
    and canonical basis of caps and floors, 304-307
    concept of, 111
liquid cash reserve, 261-264
liquidity, 14-15
liquidity premiums, 292
liquidity risk, 241-267
    bailout, 266
    buffered and unbuffered portfolios and, 261-264
    catastrophe hedging, 264-265
    conservation laws and, 250-251
    flow simulation and, 256
    and herd effect, 245
    liquidity crisis, 247-249
    managing, 243-245, 261-264
    physical models for, 246-249
    and quality, 247, 256-259
    returning shares to market value, 265-266
    and risk universe, 242-243
    river model of, 247-249, 251-255
    steps for modeling, 245
Litterman, R., 79
Lo, A. W., 90
loan structures, 181-184
loan-to-value ratios (ltv), 166-169
lognormal model, 79, 86
Longstaff, F. A., 81
long-term interest rates, 81
Lowell, Linda L., 133-162

M
MacKinlay, A. C., 90
market conventions, 188-195
market value, 265-266

Index

marking
  assets and liabilities, 260-261
  managing liquidity risk by correct, 260
  mark-to-market values, 244, 261
  mark-to-model values, 261
  month-end, 139
Markowitz, Harry M., 26-27, 28, 63-64
mark-to-market values, 244, 261
mark-to-model values, 261
mass flow, 247-249, 251-258
maximum drawdown, calculating, 55-57
MCI, value of call options, 103
mean reverting behavior
  and arbitrage-free interest rate models, 84, 86
  of yield curves, 83
mean/variance technique, 108
  for asset allocation, 2-3, 17
  limitations of, 17
measuring investment return, 48
Merton, R. C., 75
MetLife
  asset cell matrix, 10-12
  investment process at, 5-9, 21-23
model error
  analyzing spreads for, 274-276
  and breakeven analysis, 276-278
  detecting, 269
models
  for asset allocation, 2-4
  for arbitrage-free bond canonical decomposition, 285-287
  for bond pricing and interest rates, 78-81
  for default risk-based pricing, 100-105
  for liquidity risk, 245-251
  mean reverting behavior, 84
  option-adjusted spread models, 118-132
month-end marking, 139
mortgage-backed securities
  prepayment behavior, 119-120, 121-122
  prepayment rates for, 117

  unbundling options for, 155-162
mortgage derivatives; *see also* inverse floaters; inverse IOs
  cap/floor/swap parity for, 156-157
  finding value in, 133-162
mortgage duration, and prepayment assumptions, 124-127
mortgages
  mortgage-backed floating-rate notes (FRN), 188, 235-238
  traditional mortgage cash-flow measures, 135-138
  using interest rate models for valuing, 87
  valuation and yield curves, 126-127
  and volatility, 122
municipal bonds, 278-280
Musiela, M., 91

N

National Council of Real Estate Investment Fiduciaries, 176
negative convexity, 15-16
Neilson, Lars T., 105-106
net cash flow, 205, 209-212, 215-216
net credit spread analysis, 112-113
net operating income (NOI), 164, 169, 176
n-factor model, of arbitrage-free interest rate models, 86-88
normal form, for arbitrage-free interest rate models, 82-86
Nye, Jonathan, 43-68

O

OAS models; *see* option-adjusted spread (OAS) analysis
one-factor interest rate models, 78-81, 90
option-adjusted spread (OAS)
  analysis, 118, 143-150, 162
  collateralized mortgage obligations and pass throughs, 127-128, 129
  implied prepayments and, 121-122, 129, 131-132
  misinterpreting, 145-150

for mortgage-backed securities, 117, 121
and prepayment models, 145-147
probability distribution, 144-145
optionality, 15-16
option-free bonds, 287-288
options
Black-Scholes model for, 71-75, 77-78
embedded, 231, 234-235
unbundling, 155-162
Orange County Investment Fund (OCIF), 43-45

P
partial duration, 188, 198-199
pass-throughs; *see* coupon pass-throughs
path-independent bonds, 287-289, 302-304
pathwise values, 291-292, 294-296, 301-302
payment prioritization, 166-169
Pedersen, H., 82, 83, 86
Peng, Scott Y., 88, 241-267
pension funds, 164-165
performance measurement, 43-68
asset/liability factors and, 13-16
for constrained management approaches, 50
desirable qualities of, 47
and downside risk, 63-66
exposure to risk and, 45-50
for junk bonds, 97-116
liquidity risk and, 256-259
maximum drawdown, 52-57
recent failures and, 43-45
Sharpe Ratio and, 61-63
perpetual floating-rate notes, 207-212
physical models, 246-249
pooled loan structures, 181-184
portfolio directional duration values, 40
portfolio management
aligning portfolios, 9
asset cell matrix and, 10-12

effective duration for portfolios, 269-282
at MetLife, 5-9
portfolios
advantages of evaluating downside risk, 63-66
aligning asset allocation of, 9
catastrophe hedging, 264-265
commercial mortgage-backed securities (CMBS) in, 164
efficient frontiers and returns, 40
feedback effect, 253-254
liquidity crisis in, 247-249
liquidity risk management, 243-245, 261-264
managing risk exposure of, 90
performance and investor behavior, 251-256
quantifying loses with VAR, 57
questions for breakeven analysis, 277-278
vicious circle and, 253-254
POs; *see* principal-only strips
predictor yield curves, 28
prepayments
assumptions about implied, 124-129, 131-132
behavior of, 119-120
fears about, 122
linked to floors, 159-161
and option-adjusted spread analysis, 145-147
rates for mortgage-backed securities, 117
pricing, for junk bonds, 97-116
pricing equations, for floating-rate notes, 188-195
prime rate
comparison of changes to federal funds, 229
spreads, 227-228
principal-only strips (POs), 128-131, 157-158
probability distribution, 144-145
publications, relative value, 18-20

Index

Q
quality
  as index for liquidity risk, 247
  and performance measurement, 47
quality limits, as performance management benchmark, 50, 51-52
quality simulation, and liquidity risk, 256-259
quantification, of risk and reward, 46

R
real estate
  calculating default probabilities for, 106
  choosing scenarios for, 171-172
  debt and equity in new markets, 163-186
  equity versus subordinate CMBS, 176-184
  interest rate binomial trees for, 106-109
  and loan-to-value ratios, 167
  risk and, 163-164
  ruthless default rule and, 104-105
  traditional investments in, 164-165
Real Estate Price Tree, 106-109
reasonability checking, 277
re-creation analysis, 138-143
re-creation values, 139, 162
Reitano, Robert R., 27, 28, 88
relative valuation, 18-21, 71
  and arbitrage-free interest rate models, 85
  of collateralized mortgage obligations, 127-128, 129
  hedge ratios and, 88-89
  and option-adjusted spread analysis, 145
  for pricing securities, 72
re-REMIC tranches, 141
reset margins
  for floating-rate notes, 188, 189-195
  FRNs across indices and, 212-213
  for LIB-3 notes, 201-203

return
  expected period, 30
  measuring investment, 48
Richard, S. F., 81
risk; *see also* liquidity risk; credit risk; downside risk
  assessing basis risk, 219-227
  assessing in securities, 49
  basis risk for floating-rate notes, 212-216
  decomposing bonds to assess, 298
  defined for Black-Scholes method, 71
  exposure to, 45-50, 90
  investment, 48-49
  invisible, 242-243
  liquidity risk, 241-267
  matching asset to liability, 244
  performance measurement and, 48-49
  purchasing floaters and, 213-214
  quantification of, 46
  real estate, 163-164
  spread duration, 213
  value at risk, 57-61
  valuing junk bonds and, 98
risk analysis
  duration vectors and, 28-29
  equations in yield curve shifts, 27-29
  ex post measuring of, 46-47
risk management, 131
risk measures, 28-29
risk metrics
  and constrained management, 50-52
  downside risk, 63-66
  drawdown as, 52-57
  Sharpe Ratio and, 61-63
  value at risk as, 57-61
risk minimization
  nonparallel yield curve shift model and, 34-38
  stochastic immunization and, 26-27, 40
  yield curve shift analysis and, 31-33

risk neutrality
  concept of, 99
  valuation of commercial mortgage-backed securities, 109-110
risk premiums
  for arbitrage-free bond canonical decomposition, 291-292
  term premiums, 80
risk universe, 242-243
Ritchken, P., 83, 84, 86
river model
  analogy of liquidity crisis, 247-249
  analysis of fixed-coupon bonds with, 255-266
  feedback effect, 253-254
  liquidity risk and conservation laws, 250-251
  as model for liquidity risk, 246-249, 251-256
  vicious circle, 253-254
Ross, S. A., 79, 80, 90
Rubinstein, M., 90
ruthless default rule, 104-105, 112-113

S
Saa-Requejo, Jesus, 105-106
Salomon Index, 21
Sankarasubramanian, L., 84
Santa-Clara, Pedro, 105-106
scenarios, 16-18, 171-172
Schaak, Christian, 27
Schaefer, S. M., 77
Scheinkman, J., 79
Scheitlin, A. G., 91
Scholes, M., 71-78
Schwartz, E. S., 77, 81
sector delinquency rates, 167
sector limits, 50-51, 52
securities
  assessing risk in, 49
  models for interest-sensitive, 69-95
  and Orange County Investment Fund, 44
  pricing using relative valuation, 72
semivariance, 63-64
Sharpe, William F., 62

Sharpe Ratio, 61-63
Shiu, E., 86
short-term interest rates, 76, 81
Shui, E., 82, 83
significance, 46
spread duration, 188, 199-200, 209, 213
  of perpetual floating-rate notes, 209
  risk and, 213
"spread" fixed-income assets, 280-281
spreads
  analyzing for model error, 274-276
  comparing between indices for FRNs, 220-227
  comparison of prime-Treasury rate, 227-228
  credit, 172-176
  effective convexity and, 274-276
  managing spread fixed-income assets, 280-281
Stabbert, Gerd W., 1-23
standard bivariate normal density function, 108
Stapleton, Richard C., 105-106
static hedging, 299
stochastic immunization, 26-27, 40
stock prices, 73
Stricker, R., 91
subordinate CMBS, 176-184
Subrahmanyam, Martin G., 98, 105-106
swap markets
  and Eurodollar futures, 204-212
  LIBOR (swap) curve and, 72
swaps
  for fixed-rate bonds, 202-204
  for floating-rate notes, 201-203, 232-234
  for mortgage derivatives, 156-157
  for perpetual floating-rate notes, 209-212
synthetic assets, 12

T
Tam, K. O., 91

Index

term premiums, 80
term structure of volatility, 83-85
Thorlacius, A., 82, 83, 86
time horizon, 13-14
Torous, W. N., 77
total rate of return approach, 6, 7, 21
Toy, W., 86
trading set limitations, 30-31
traditional immunization theories, 25
transaction costs, 19
transaction prices, 101-103
Treasury rates
    comparing with municipal bonds, 278-280
    spreads, 227-228
two-asset binomial pricing model, 105-109
    analyzing junk bonds with, 98-116
    splitting a binomial tree, 111
two-factor interest rate models, 81, 86-87, 90
two-tiered index bonds (TTIBs), 141-142

U

unbuffered portfolios, 261-264
unbundling options, 155-162
underlying bonds, 139-140
    determining re-creation values, 141-142
unleveraged equity, 177-178

V

value at risk (VAR), 57-61
Vandell, Kerry D., 104
Vanderhoof, I., 91
VAR; *see* value at risk
variance, 3
Vasicek, O., 78
visible risks, 242-243
volatility
    and Black-Scholes model, 76-77
    mortgage market and, 122
    term structure of, 83-84
volatility hedging, 299

W

White, A., 70, 82, 84

Y

yield curves
    and arbitrage-free interest rate models, 87
    for bond interest rate models, 79, 80
    duration and, 25-27, 29, 32-38
    and forward LIBOR, 134
    hedging on steep, 85
    mean reverting behavior of, 83
    mortgage valuation and, 126-127
    predictor, 28
    yield points, 27
yield curve shifts
    analysis of risk in model, 27-29, 31-33, 34-38
    designing constraints in model, 30-31, 34-38
    duration and, 25-27, 29, 32-38
    example using model, 33-34
    immunization and, 25-27
    nonparallel, 33-34, 38-40
    solving general problem of, 31-33
    testing constraint in models, 34-38
    trading set limitations, 30-31
yield leverage, defined, 137
yield points, 27
yields
    correlated to LIBOR rates, 135-138
    default-adjusted, 172-176
    example using nonparallel yield curve shift model, 33-34
yield tables
    compensating for complex risks, 138
    for inverse floaters, 136
    for inverse interest-only strips, 137
yield-to-current LIBOR, 153
yield-to-forward LIBOR, 150-155, 162

Z

Zeta credit risk scores, 102